Software Design Patterns

Software Design Patterns are reusable solutions to software development difficulties. However, a Software Design Pattern is not code; rather, it is a guide or paradigm that helps software engineers to construct products that follow best practices. A Design Pattern is more of a template to tackle the topic at hand than a library or framework, which can be added and utilized right away. Object-oriented programming (OOP) is supported by Design Patterns, which are based on the ideas of objects (instances of a class; data with unique attributes) and classes (user-defined types of data). Design Patterns are blueprints for resolving typical software engineering issues. They provide reproducible solutions to some of the most prevalent difficulties you'll encounter. That said, Design Patterns aren't a complete solution, nor are they code, classes, or libraries that you may use in your project. They are a type of problem-solving solution. Each job will be approached in a slightly different way.

Why Should You Learn Software Design Patterns?

As a programmer, you can use Software Design Patterns to help you build more reliable structures. Design Patterns give you the skills to create smart and interactive applications or software with simple and easy problem-solving methods; they also allow you to create the greatest user-friendly apps and change them easily to meet the latest requirements. Design Patterns are interesting to deal with since such knowledge enables flexible coding patterns and techniques of structure, reusable codes, loosely written codes, classes, patterns, and so on.

This book contains:

- A step-by-step approach to problem solving and skill development
- A quick run-through of the basic concepts, in the form of a "Crash Course"
- Advanced, hands-on core concepts, with a focus on real-world problems
- Industry level coding paradigm with practice-oriented explanations
- Special emphasis on writing clean and optimized code, with additional chapters focused on coding methodology

Software Design Patterns
The Ultimate Guide

Sufyan bin Uzayr

CRC Press
Taylor & Francis Group
Boca Raton London New York

CRC Press is an imprint of the
Taylor & Francis Group, an **informa** business

First edition published 2023
by CRC Press
6000 Broken Sound Parkway NW, Suite 300, Boca Raton, FL 33487-2742

and by CRC Press
4 Park Square, Milton Park, Abingdon, Oxon, OX14 4RN

CRC Press is an imprint of Taylor & Francis Group, LLC

Library of Congress Cataloging-in-Publication Data

Names: Bin Uzayr, Sufyan, author.
Title: Software Design Patterns : the ultimate guide / Sufyan bin Uzayr.
Description: First edition. | Boca Raton : CRC Press, 2023. | Includes
bibliographical references and index.
Identifiers: LCCN 2022025677 (print) | LCCN 2022025678 (ebook) | ISBN
9781032311777 (hbk) | ISBN 9781032311760 (pbk) | ISBN 9781003308461 (ebk)
Subjects: LCSH: Software patterns.
Classification: LCC QA76.76.P37 B56 2023 (print) | LCC QA76.76.P37 (ebook) |
DDC 005.13/267--dc23/eng/20220804
LC record available at https://lccn.loc.gov/2022025677
LC ebook record available at https://lccn.loc.gov/2022025678

ISBN: 9781032311777 (hbk)
ISBN: 9781032311760 (pbk)
ISBN: 9781003308461 (ebk)

DOI: 10.1201/9781003308461

Typeset in Minion
by KnowledgeWorks Global Ltd.

Contents

Acknowledgments

There are many people who deserve to be on this page, for this book would not have come into existence without their support. That said, some names deserve a special mention, and I am genuinely grateful to:

- My parents, for everything they have done for me.

- My siblings, for helping with things back home.

- The Parakozm team, especially Divya Sachdeva, Jaskiran Kaur, and Vartika, for offering great amounts of help and assistance during the book-writing process.

- The CRC team, especially Sean Connelly and Danielle Zarfati, for ensuring that the book's content, layout, formatting, and everything else remain perfect throughout.

- Reviewers of this book, for going through the manuscript and providing their insight and feedback.

- Typesetters, cover designers, printers, and all related roles, for their part in the development of this book.

- All the folks associated with Zeba Academy, either directly or indirectly, for their help and support.

- The programming community in general, and the web development community in particular, for all their hard work and efforts.

Sufyan bin Uzayr

About the Author

Sufyan bin Uzayr is a writer, coder, and entrepreneur with over a decade of experience in the industry. He has authored several books in the past, pertaining to a diverse range of topics, ranging from History to Computers/IT.

Sufyan is the Director of Parakozm, a multinational IT company specializing in EdTech solutions. He also runs Zeba Academy, an online learning and teaching vertical with a focus on STEM fields.

Sufyan specializes in a wide variety of technologies, such as JavaScript, Dart, WordPress, Drupal, Linux, and Python. He holds multiple degrees, including ones in Management, IT, Literature, and Political Science.

Sufyan is a digital nomad, dividing his time between four countries. He has lived and taught in universities and educational institutions around the globe. Sufyan takes a keen interest in technology, politics, literature, history, and sports, and in his spare time, he enjoys teaching coding and English to young students.

Learn more at sufyanism.com.

## CHAPTER 1

Crash Course in Software Design Patterns

IN THIS CHAPTER

➢ What are Software Design Patterns?

➢ Major concepts

➢ Advantages and disadvantages

➢ Additional info

Design Patterns represent some of the most acceptable practices experienced object-oriented software engineers utilize. In object-oriented systems, a Design Pattern methodically names, motivates, and describes a general design that addresses a recurring design challenge. It explains the problem, the remedy, when to use it, and the repercussions. It also includes tips and examples for implementation.

A Design Pattern is a broad, reusable solution to common software design challenges. Typically, the pattern depicts relationships and interactions between classes or objects. The goal is to accelerate the development process by providing tried-and-true development/design paradigms. Design Patterns are strategies for solving a common problem independent of programming language. A Design Pattern represents an idea rather than

DOI: 10.1201/9781003308461-1

a specific implementation. We can make our code more flexible, reusable, and maintainable by employing Design Patterns.

It is not always necessary to use Design Patterns in our project. Design Patterns are not intended for use in project development. Design Patterns are intended to solve common problems. Whenever there is a need, we must implement a suitable pattern to avoid future problems. To determine which pattern to use, simply try to understand the Design Patterns and their functions. In this manner only will we be able to choose the greatest one.

A Software Design Pattern is a generic, reusable solution to a typically occurring problem in software design within a specific environment.

- It is not a finalized design that can simply translate into source or machine code. It is a description or template for resolving a problem that may use in a variety of circumstances.

- Design Patterns are best practices that have been established that a programmer may apply to overcome common challenges while developing an application or system.

Design Patterns provide answers to common issues, allowing code to be more manageable, extendable, and loosely connected.

Developers have given solutions that handle a specific sort of problem a name. And this is how it all began.

The more one understands them, the easier it is to solve all of our difficulties.

Goal: The goal is to understand the purpose and application of each Design Pattern so that we can select and implement the appropriate pattern as needed.

Example: For example, in many real-world scenarios, we only want to make one instance of a class. For example, a country can only have one active president at any time. A Singleton pattern is the name given to this design. Other software examples include a single database connection shared by several objects, as establishing a separate database connection for each item is expensive. Similarly, instead of developing many managers, an application might have a single configuration manager or error manager that handles all problems.

WHAT IS THE PURPOSE OF DESIGN PATTERNS?

As Software Developers, we frequently assess our code based on criteria such as how clean, expressive, has a small memory footprint and is quick. However, the most critical consideration, which we sometimes overlook, is that we should be able to adjust anything later simply. What we chose now might not be applicable tomorrow. And our code should be adaptable enough that changes are not prohibitively expensive. As a result, Design Patterns are best practices for covering such properties. The essence of Design Patterns, in my opinion, consists of the following six rules:

1. **They are tried-and-true solutions:** Because developers often use Design Patterns, we may be confident that they function. Not only that, but we can also guarantee that they were altered several times and that optimizations were most likely performed.

2. **They are simple to re-use:** Design Patterns describe a reusable solution that may modify to solve various specific situations because they aren't tied to a specific situation.

   Consider the Iterator Design Pattern, reusable across STL despite container and algorithm changes. Iterators act as a glue between the container and the algorithm.

3. **They have a strong personalities:** Design Patterns may elegantly describe a considerable solution. The Visitor pattern, for example, is used to perform a new operation on a range/group of classes. As a result, the standard library adopted this design with a single function, namely the std::visit algorithm. The same is true for boost::flyweight>.

4. **They facilitate communication:** Developers' knowledge about Design Patterns can communicate more readily about potential solutions to a given challenge.

   If we're part of a team of developers, agree on Design Patterns with our colleagues since they can help us solve problems more effectively. We should also follow similar practices for software maintenance, as it makes maintenance operations faster and more efficient.

5. **They eliminate the need for code refactoring:** When an application is created with Design Patterns in mind, we may not need to rewrite the code later since applying the relevant Design Pattern to a specific problem is already an optimum solution.

   If such solutions are later updated, they may be applied effortlessly by any excellent software developer without causing any complications.

6. **They reduce the codebase's size:** Design Patterns use less code than alternative solutions since they are generally beautiful and optimal. This isn't always the case, because many developers add extra code to improve understanding.

WHY SHOULD WE STUDY DESIGN PATTERNS?

Object-Oriented Design is defined as merging data and its operations into a context-bound entity (i.e., class/struct). This is also true while developing a unique thing.

However, when creating an entire program, we must remember that Creational Design Patterns: How will those objects be instantiated/created?

- **Patterns of Structural Design:** How do those items interact with one another to produce a larger entity? This should be scalable in the future.

- **Patterns of Behavioral Design:** We must also consider communication between those things that can quickly foresee future changes and have fewer adverse effects.

Do we see where this is going? Maintainability, scalability, expressiveness, and stability must be considered while thinking about objects. So, in a word, this is a coding mindset. And we're pretty sure we don't have this attitude and thought process if we come from a C background.

DESIGN PATTERN CONFIGURATION

The fundamental structure of the Design Pattern documentation is depicted in the following figure. It focuses on what technology we are employing to address challenges and how we do so.

Design Pattern

Configuration of Design Pattern.

- **Pattern Name:** This is used to define the pattern concisely and effectively.

- **Intent/Motive:** It specifies the pattern's objective or what it does.

- **Applicability:** It specifies all of the conceivable locations the pattern may use.

- **Participants and Repercussions:** It comprises classes and objects utilized in the Design Pattern and a list of the pattern's consequences.

WHAT IS THE SIGNIFICANCE OF THE DESIGN PATTERN?

Design Patterns are used to solve reoccurring design challenges. In a nutshell, Design Patterns do not solve the problem on their own; instead, they assist us in addressing the problem.

Software development Design Patterns began as best practices used repeatedly to similar challenges found in various situations.

Design Patterns have been used to overcome the following frequent problems:

- How to correctly initialize an object.

- How to make two items interact with one other.

TYPES OF DESIGN PATTERNS

Design Patterns are divided into the following three categories.

Creational

Class instantiation or object generation is the focus of these Design Patterns. Class-creational patterns and object-creational patterns are two subsets of these patterns. While class-creation patterns make good use of inheritance in the instantiation process, object-creation patterns use delegation.

Factory Method, Abstract Factory, Builder, Singleton, Object Pool, and Prototype are creational Design Patterns.

Use Case of Creational Design Patterns

1. Assume a programmer wants to create a simple DBConnection class to connect to a database and needs to use the database from code in numerous places. The developer will typically create an instance of the DBConnection class and use it to perform database operations wherever they are needed. As each example of the DBConnection

class has a different connection to the database, numerous connections to the database are created. To deal with it, we make the DBConnection class a singleton class, which means that only one instance of DBConnection is generated, and only one connection is made. We can control load balance, redundant connections, and so on since we can manage DBConnection from a single instance.

2. We can use the Factory design if we wish to create several instances of the same type while maintaining loose coupling. A factory-Design Pattern-implemented class acts as a link between numerous classes – for instance, the use of various database servers such as SQL Server and Oracle. We should use the Factory Design Pattern to achieve loose coupling and create a similar kind of object if we are developing an application with a SQL Server database as the back end. Still, if we need to change the database to Oracle, we will need to modify all of our code. Hence, as Factory Design Patterns maintain loose coupling and easy implementation, we should use the factory layout design to achieve loose coupling and create a similar kind of object.

Structural

These Design Patterns deal with grouping distinct classes and objects together to create larger structures and add new functionality.

Adapter, Bridge, Composite, Decorator, Facade, Flyweight, Private Class Data, and Proxy are structural Design Patterns.

Use Case of Structural Design Patterns

1. An Adapter Design Pattern is used when two interfaces are incompatible and want to establish a relationship between them using an adapter. The adapter pattern transforms a class's interface into another interface or class that the client expects, allowing classes that would otherwise be incompatible with operating together. We can use the adapter pattern in these types of incompatible instances.

Behavioral

Identifying and discovering shared communication patterns between items are all about behavioral patterns.

Chain of Responsibility, Command, Interpreter, Iterator, Mediator, Memento, Null Object, Observer, State, Scheme, Template method, and Visitor are behavioral patterns.

Use Case of Behavioral Design Patterns

1. In an operation, the template pattern defines the skeleton of an algorithm by deferring some stages to subclasses. Subclasses can use the template technique to rewrite specific phases of an algorithm without affecting the algorithm's structure. For example, we might want the module's behavior to be extensible in our project. We can make it act in new and different ways when the application's requirements evolve or satisfy new applications' demands. However, no one is permitted to edit the source code, which means that we can add but not change the structure in circumstances when a developer is permitted to apply the template Design Pattern.

WHAT EXACTLY IS THE GANG OF FOUR (GOF)?

The book *Design Patterns – Elements of Reusable Object-Oriented Software*, written by four writers, Erich Gamma, Richard Helm, Ralph Johnson, and John Vlissides, was published in 1994 and introduced the first concept of Design Patterns in software development.

Gang of Four is the collective name for these four authors (GOF). According to these authors, Design Patterns are essentially based on the following object-oriented design principles:

- Not an implementation, but a program to an interface.

- Object composition should take precedence over the inheritance.

USAGE OF DESIGN PATTERNS

Patterns have two main applications in software development.

Developers' Common Platform

Design Patterns define a common language and are tailored to a given context. A singleton Design Pattern, for example, denotes the use of a single object; thus, all developers who are familiar with single Design Patterns will use single objects, and they will be able to detect whether a program is following a singleton pattern.

Guidelines for Best Practices

Design Patterns have evolved to provide the best answers to specific problems encountered during software development. Learning these patterns makes it easier and faster for inexperienced developers to learn software design.

IMPORTANCE OF LEARNING DESIGN PATTERNS

Many software engineers could work for many years without understanding any single pattern. It can also happen; we can be applying a pattern without even knowing it. So, the question is, why should we examine the Design Pattern? Consider the following arguments, which highlight the importance of Design Patterns in development.

Design Patterns contain the predetermined collection of tried and verified solutions to a common problem faced when designing software. If we know about the Design Pattern, we can implement the solution without wasting time. It also shows us how to tackle the problem using the idea of object-oriented design.

Design Pattern also promotes a common understanding between the developer and their coworkers. Suppose there is an issue in the code, and we may say, "Use Singleton for that," and everyone can understand if they understand the Design Pattern and its name.

Design Patterns are also crucial for the learning purpose since they introduce the common problem we may have neglected. They also allow contemplating that area that may not have received the hands-on experience.

TYPES OF DESIGN PATTERNS

According to the *Design Patterns – Elements of Reusable Object-Oriented Software* reference book, 23 Design Patterns can be grouped into creational, structural, and behavioral patterns. We'll also go over J2EE Design Patterns, which are different.

S. No.	Pattern & Description
1	**Patterns of Creation** Rather of explicitly instantiating objects with the new operator, these Design Patterns provide a way for building things without hiding the creation logic. This gives the software greater flexibility in identifying which items are necessary for a given use case.
2	**Structural Patterns** Structural Patterns are the patterns that make up the structure of a building. These Design Patterns deal with the composition of classes and objects. Inheritance is a concept used to create interfaces and define how to combine items to create new functions.
3	**Patterns of Behavior** These Design Patterns are mostly concerned with object communication.
4	**Patterns for J2EE** These Design Patterns are concerned with the presentation tier in particular. Sun Java Centre has detected these tendencies.

DESIGN PATTERNS AND THEIR APPLICATIONS

By providing tried-and-true development paradigms, Design Patterns can assist to speed the development process. Considering concerns that may not become apparent until later in the implementation process is critical for good software design. Reusing Design Patterns helps to prevent minor issues from becoming significant ones and enhances code readability for experienced coders and architects.

Most people understand how to apply certain software design concepts to specific issues. These methods are challenging to adapt to a wider variety of challenges. Design Patterns give generic answers that are defined in a way that does not necessitate specifics related to a specific situation.

Furthermore, patterns enable developers to talk about software interactions using well-known, well-understood terms. Over time, common Design Patterns may be enhanced, making them more resilient than ad hoc ideas.

PATTERNS OF CREATIONAL DESIGN

Class instantiation is central to several Design Patterns. This pattern is separated into two types: class-creation patterns and object-creation patterns. While class-creation patterns employ inheritance in the instantiation process, object-creation patterns effectively use delegation.

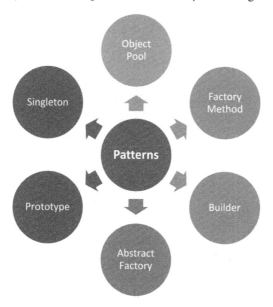

Patterns of creational design.

- **Abstract Factory:** Creates an instance of numerous families of classes using an abstract factory.

- **Builder:** Distinguishes the building of a thing from its representation.

- **Factory Method:** This method creates instances of multiple derived classes.

- **Object Pool:** Recycle objects that are no longer used to save money on resource acquisition and release.

- **Prototype:** An instance that has been fully initialized and is ready to be duplicated or cloned.

- **Singleton:** It is a class that can only have one instance.

PATTERNS OF STRUCTURAL DESIGN

The composition of Classes and Objects is essential to these design principles. Inheritance is used to construct interfaces in structural class-creation patterns. Structural object-patterns outline how objects may combine to provide new functionality.

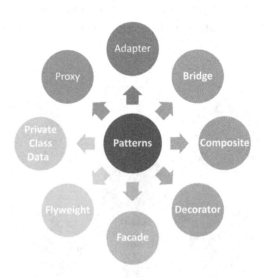

Patterns of creational design.

- **Adapter:** Interfaces from several classes must match.

- **Bridge:** Separates the interface of an object from its implementation.

- **Composite:** A basic and composite object tree structure.

- **Decorator:** Dynamically assign responsibilities to objects

- **Facade:** A single class represents a whole subsystem.

- **Flyweight:** A fine-grained instance for distributing.

- **Private Class Data:** Restricts accessor/mutator access.

- **Proxy:** An object that is a representation of another item.

PATTERNS OF BEHAVIORAL DESIGN

These Design Patterns are mostly about Class object communication. Behavioral patterns are concerned largely with the transfer of objects.

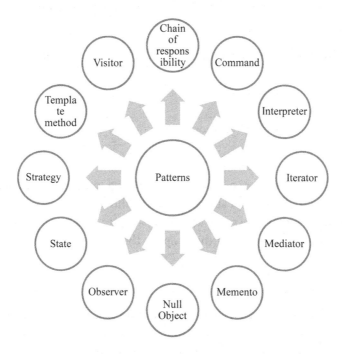

Patterns of creational design.

- **Chain of responsibility:** A chain of responsibility is transmitting a request between objects in a chain.

- **Command:** As an object, encapsulate a command request.

- **Interpreter:** A method of incorporating linguistic features into a program.

- **Iterator:** A method for accessing the items of a collection in a sequential manner.

- **Mediator:** A class that facilitates communication between classes.

- **Memento:** Capture and restore the internal state of an item.

- **Null object:** Intended to serve as an object's default value.

- **Observer:** A method of informing a group of classes of a change.

- **State:** When an object's state changes, it affects its behavior.

- **Strategy:** A class that encapsulates an algorithm.

- **Defer:** Defer the particular stages of an algorithm to a subclass using the Template method.

- **Visitor:** Adds a new action to a class without modifying it.

CRITICISM

Some programmers have questioned the concept of Design Patterns.

Focusing on the Incorrect Issue

Patterns are required as a result of employing computer languages or approaches with insufficient abstraction capabilities. A notion should not be duplicated, but rather referred to according to optimal factoring. However, if something is referred to rather than copied, there is no "pattern" to identify and categorize.[1]

No Official Foundations

The study of Design Patterns has been overly ad hoc, and some suggest that the subject urgently needs to be formalized. One of the GOF was exposed to a show trial at OOPSLA 1999, in which they were "charged" with several crimes against computer science. Twenty-three of the "jurors" present at the trial "convicted" them.

---

[1] https://sourcemaking.com/design_patterns

May Result in Inefficient Solutions

A Design Pattern is an initiative to standardize well-known best practices. In theory, this appears to be advantageous, but it frequently leads to unneeded code duplication. Using a well-factored implementation rather than a "barely good enough" design style is nearly always a more efficient approach.

It is Not Notably Different from Other Abstractions

Some writers argue that Design Patterns are not fundamentally different from other types of abstraction and that using new vocabulary (taken from the architectural industry) to explain existing occurrences in the field of programming is superfluous. The Model-View-Controller (MVC) paradigm is often used as an example of a "pattern," even though the notion of "Design Patterns" precedes it by several years. Some claim that the most important contribution of the Design Patterns community was the use of Alexander's pattern language as form of documentation, a technique that is largely ignored in the literature.

WHAT IS THE PURPOSE OF USING DESIGN PATTERNS?

Design Patterns provide a best practice approach to object-oriented software development, making it easier to design, build, alter, test, and reuse. These Design Patterns provide best practices and frameworks.

1. **Tested Solution:** Design Patterns give a tried-and-true solution to a frequent problem, removing the need for the software developer to "reinvent the wheel" whenever that problem arises.

2. **Recyclable:** Design Patterns may use to handle a wide range of issues; they are not limited to a specific issue.

3. **Expressive:** Expressive Design Patterns provide a sophisticated solution.

4. **Avoid the Need for Code Refactoring:** Because the Design Pattern is already the best solution to the problem, reworking is unnecessary.

5. **Reduce the Codebase Size:** Each pattern assists software engineers in changing how the system functions without requiring a complete rebuild. Furthermore, being the "best" option, the Design Pattern frequently necessitates less code.

DESIGN PATTERNS' ADVANTAGES IN SOFTWARE ENGINEERING

As stated above in "Why do we need Design Patterns?," the finest Software Design Patterns will use a common language, making it simpler for engineers to communicate about difficulties and improve code readability and architecture in the early planning phases. When implemented correctly, Design Patterns may speed up the development process and lessen the likelihood of mistakes.

Design Patterns are also language-neutral (for object-oriented languages); however, some are more beneficial with some languages than others.

SOFTWARE DESIGN PATTERN CRITIQUES

Overuse of Software Design Patterns has been criticized as a crutch for programmers to rely on when a more straightforward solution would suffice. Furthermore, there is not always a simple way to apply each pattern, with the possibility of developing an anti-pattern (an inefficient or counterproductive solution) if the wrong approach is used.

Furthermore, a Design Pattern can be used as a bridge for flaws or missing features in the programming language, frequently resulting in more bloat than is required to get the program to perform appropriately. Ensure that the language offers the characteristics required to avoid an over-reliance on Design Patterns throughout the critical phase of selecting the correct tech stack. Alternatively, our tech stack selection may bring us to a framework that already has these Design Patterns implemented directly in the framework in the best way possible.

BEST SOFTWARE DESIGN PATTERNS

Although *Design Patterns – Elements of Reusable Object-Oriented Software* lists 23 Design Patterns, seven are the most influential or important. This section discusses the top seven Software Design Patterns, their significance, and when to utilize them.

1. **Singleton Pattern Method Design:** The singleton Design Pattern belongs to the "creational" category since it limits object creation for a class to only one instance and provides global access to a global variable. Many web developers, for example, limit the "sitemap" to a single version with global reach. Singletons may also use in other

patterns such as factory method, builder, and prototype. Singletons are also common in the facade and state objects.

While we may only have or require one instance of a class, this does not always imply that we should use the singleton pattern to lock that object down or put it into a global state. Singletons are a contentious Design Pattern, with some even saying that they should avoid since locking up objects limit future flexibility.

2. **Factory Pattern Design:** The factory pattern is a "creation" Design Pattern in which developers generate objects with a standard interface but enable a class to postpone instantiation to subclasses. The factory function encourages loose coupling and code reuse by acting as a "virtual constructor" that works with any class that implements the interface and gives subclasses more latitude in selecting the objects to be constructed. New classes can be added to the factory as needed.

The factory approach is not ideal for basic applications, as developers run the danger of overcomplicating operations to utilize a Design Pattern.

3. **Facade Pattern Design:** A "structural" Design Pattern that aids in providing a single interface (class) for access to a massive body of code/different objects. With a simple interface, a facade hides the intricacies of multiple sub-systems (typically arranged into a class). For example, an eCommerce client prefers to connect with a brand through a single point rather than communicating (interfacing) with each system that supports the sale, such as product inventories, authentication, security, payment processing, and order fulfillment, and so on. In this scenario, the Facade has isolated all "order" operations and systems into a single interface, leaving the client entirely oblivious of what's going on behind the scenes. The facade is a critical notion in supporting the loosely linked microservices architecture.

4. **Strategy Pattern Design:** A strategy Design Pattern is a type of "behavioral" Software Design Pattern that is sometimes referred to as a policy pattern. The strategy pattern encapsulates replaceable algorithms into a "family," with one of the algorithms being picked at runtime as needed. A family of algorithms, for example, may connect to "sorting" things in an eCommerce website – by size, color, reward, and so on. The plan is adopted in response to the customer's behaviors.

The strategy Design Pattern is highly effective in customization marketing techniques, responding to the client location, inputs, or actions to give a unique experience to each user.

5. **Observer Pattern Design:** The observer Design Pattern is "behavioral," with a one-to-many relationship relating an item (subject) to dependents (observers). The subject is told when any of the observers' changes. The observer Design Pattern is helpful in event-driven programs, such as informing a user of a new Facebook remark, sending an email when an item delivers, etc.

6. **Builder Pattern Design:** The builder Design Pattern is "creative," as it separates object building from representation. This Design Pattern gives us more control over the design process (it's more step-by-step). Still, it also decouples the representation so that we may support alternative representations of an item with the same basic construction code (the ConcreteBuilder step).

   As the object is being created, the builder pattern executes in sequential phases, invoking just those required steps for each iteration of the object.

7. **Adapter Pattern Design:** An adapter Design Pattern is a "wrapper" that turns one type into another type of interface that already exists. The adapter Design Pattern allows incompatible classes to operate together, allowing programs to function together. Adapter patterns are essential for transforming heterogeneous interfaces into a uniform API.

PATTERNS OF POPULAR SOFTWARE ARCHITECTURE

It is vital to note that architectural patterns may use in the software's overall design. What exactly is a Design Pattern in architecture? A generic, reusable solution to common architectural challenges (see how the concept is nearly identical to that of software design?). These three Design Patterns are related, although they have different sets of dependencies and levels of coupling.

1. **The MVC Design Pattern:** The MVC Design Pattern was the first architectural pattern, and it consists of the following three parts:

   • **Model:** The model consists of the backend business logic and data.

- **View:** The data-display interface components. It makes the Observer Pattern to update with Model and shows the updated model when needed.

- **Controller:** Managing Director Input is initially routed here, where the model processes it and returns it to view.

The MVC Design Pattern is crucial because it enables the separation of concern. It divides the front and backend code into discrete areas to allow updating and scaling the program simpler without interference or interruption. The MVC paradigm also enables many developers to concurrently work on various aspects of the program. The downside, however, is that exposing the model to public scrutiny may raise security and performance problems.

MVC is commonly used for online applications, libraries, and user interfaces.

2. **Model-View-Presenter (MVP) Design Pattern:** The MVP Design Pattern is developed on MVC but replaces the controller with the presenter and focuses solely on modeling the presentation layer.

   - **Model:** The model consists of the backend business logic and data.

   - **View:** Input starts here, and the required action is displayed here.

   - **Presenter:** Listens to the views and models one-on-one, processes the request through the model, and returns it to the view.

The presenter in this architecture functions as a bridge between the view and the model, allowing for a more loosely linked model. MVP is suitable for reusing views and supporting unit testing.

MVP is often used for websites, online applications, and mobile applications (mainly Android).

3. **Model View View-Model (MVVM) Design Pattern:** In the MVVM Design Pattern, there is two-way data binding between view and view-model (replacing presenter in the MVP Design Pattern), which more clearly separates the user interface and application logic:

   - **Model:** The model consists of the backend business logic and data.

- **View:** Input starts here, and the required action is displayed here.

- **View-Model:** It has no reference to view; its sole function is to keep the state of view and adjust the model when view actions change.

MVVM enables the creation of view-specific portions of a model with the state and logic connected to the view, needing less logic in the code to run the view. MVVM is good for improving speed and allowing for more customization and customization of the display.

MVVM is also widely utilized in mobile apps (particularly in Android), where bidirectional data binding is essential.

LIMITATIONS OF DESIGN PATTERNS

- It might be challenging to decide whether or not to use a Design Pattern.

- Due to their generic character, Design Patterns may not be able to handle specific difficulties. We will need to adjust and modify their implementation to meet our specific requirements in such circumstances.

- To successfully implement Design Patterns, a certain level of skill is necessary.

- Unexperienced teams may fail to implement them, resulting in defects and unanticipated delays effectively.

PROS OF DESIGN PATTERNS

- It is simple to predict and correct future issues.

- Assists in preserving binary compatibility with future versions.

- Simply adhering to SOLID Principles aids immensely in agile or adaptive software development.

- The method makes it easier to create highly coherent modules with the minimum connection. As a result, extensibility and reusability are increased.

- Some designs, such as Facade and Proxy, encapsulate the complexity to give the client a simple and understandable interface. As a result, the total system is easier to grasp, and the learning curve is reduced.

- Design Patterns improve the clarity and precision of communication between designers and developers. When discussing software design, a developer may quickly visualize the high-level design in their thoughts when they mention the name of the pattern employed to tackle a particular issue.

DESIGN PATTERN CLASSIFICATION

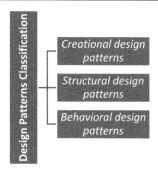

Classification of Design Patterns.

Creational Design Patterns

A creational pattern gives critical information about the instantiation of a class or an object. The creational Design Patterns have been divided into Class-Creational Patterns and Object-Creational Patterns. While class-creation patterns employ inheritance in the instantiation process, object-creation patterns effectively use delegation.

Classification of Creational Design Patterns

- Factory Pattern

- Abstract Factory Pattern

- Builder Pattern

- Prototype Pattern

- Singleton Pattern

Structural Design Patterns

Structural design patterns organize different classes and objects to form larger structures and provide new functionality while keeping these structures flexible and efficient. Mostly they use inheritance to compose all the interfaces. It also identifies the relationships which led to the simplification of the structure.

Classification of Structural Design Patterns

- Adapter Pattern
- Bridge Pattern
- Composite Pattern
- Decorator Pattern
- Facade Pattern
- Proxy Pattern
- Flyweight Pattern

Behavioral Design Patterns

Behavioral Design Patterns are all about identifying the common communication patterns between objects and realizing these patterns. These patterns are concerned with algorithms and the assignment of responsibilities between objects.

Classification of Behavioral Design Patterns

- Chain of Responsibility Pattern
- Command Pattern
- Iterator Pattern
- Mediator Pattern
- Memento Pattern
- Observer Pattern
- State Pattern
- Strategy Pattern

- Template Pattern

- Visitor Pattern

Creational Design Patterns

Creational Design Patterns are focused with the creation of items. These Design Patterns are used when a decision must be made during the instantiation of a class (i.e., creating an object of a class).

This pattern is separated into two types: class-creation patterns and object-creation patterns. In the instantiation process, class-creation patterns leverage inheritance, whereas object-creation patterns effectively use delegation.

Structural Design Patterns

Structural Design Patterns are concerned with the composition of classes and objects to construct more significant structures. By recognizing linkages, structural Design Patterns simplify the structure.

These theories are associated with how classes inherit from one another and are constructed by other classes.

Inheritance is used to construct interfaces in structural class-creation patterns. Structural object-patterns outline how objects may be combined to provide new functionality.

Behavioral Design Patterns

Behavioral Design Patterns are associated with the interaction and responsibility of things. The interaction between the items in these Design Patterns should be such that they may readily communicate with one other while being loosely connected.

The implementation and client should be loosely connected to prevent hard coding and dependencies.

DESIGN PATTERNS IN JAVA

Design Patterns are recommended practices for solving well-known challenges. This article will provide an overview of best practices in object-oriented programming and links to several design-pattern lessons.

Design Patterns in Software Development

Design Patterns are tried-and-true techniques to solve specific challenges. A Design Pattern is not a framework and cannot be deployed directly via code.

There are two primary applications for Design Patterns:

- **Developers' common language:** They give a common language for developers to solve specific challenges. For example, if one developer informs another that he is using a Singleton, the other developer (should) understand precisely what this entails.

- Design Patterns are used to record solutions that have been effectively applied to issues. An inexperienced developer learns a lot about software design by studying these patterns and the corresponding challenge.

Design Patterns are founded on the fundamental concepts of object-oriented design:

- Not an implementation, but a program to an interface

- Prefer object composition over inheritance.

Design Patterns are classified as follows:

- Creational Patterns

- Structural Patterns

- Behavioral Patterns

Object Orientated Programming

According to good programming practice, the following principles should be followed while designing software. The following are not design principles but rather examples of excellent software design.

Encapsulation

To guarantee data encapsulation, widespread manipulation of an object's variables by other objects or classes is often discouraged. A class should provide methods that allow other objects to access variables. Objects that are no longer in use are deleted by Java (garbage collection).

Abstraction

Java supports the abstraction of data specification and its concrete application.

The idea is separated from the concrete, which means that we define a class first, which contains the variables and the behavior (methods), and then we construct the actual objects, which all behave how the class described it.

A class is the behavior and data specification. A class cannot use directly.

A genuine object that may be dealt with is an object is an instance of this class.

Polymorphisms

The capacity of object variables to hold objects of various kinds. If class X1 is a subclass of class X, then a method specified with a parameter for an object X may be invoked on an object X1.

If we establish a supertype for a collection of classes, any subclass of that supertype may use in place of the supertype.

Any object that implements the interface may be used as an argument when an interface is utilized as a polymorphic type.

Inheritance

Classes may be based on each other because of inheritance. When class A inherits another class B, this is referred to as "class A extends class B."

For example, we may design a basic class that offers logging capability and is extended by another class that adds email notification to the functionality.

Delegation

Delegation occurs when we transfer responsibility for a certain job to another class or method.

If we need to access functionality from another class but do not want to alter it, use delegation instead of inheritance.

Composition

When referring to a group of behaviors, you use composition. We program against an interface, and any class that implements that interface may be created. The composition class is still declared in the caller class in composition.

When you use composition, the composing object owns the behaviors that it employs, and they cease to exist when the composing object disappears.

Aggregation

Aggregation enables us to utilize functionality from another class without restricting its lifespan.

Aggregation occurs when one class is utilized as a part of another class yet exists independently of that class.

Contract Design

Contract programming requires that both parties in a transaction understand what actions cause what behavior and will abide by that contract.

When failures occur in the programming by contract environment, methods often produce null or unchecked exceptions.

Throw an unchecked runtime exception if you feel a method should not be invoked in a certain manner. This has the potential to be really effective. Instead of checking for exceptions in your calling code, you just throw an exception in the called function. As a result, you may more easily pinpoint the location in the code where an issue occurred. This adheres to the "crash-early" philosophy, which states that if an error happens in your software, you should crash promptly rather than later in the program since this makes it challenging to discover the issue.

Cohesion

A system's cohesiveness should be high.

Cohesion is how closely connected and concentrated a particular class's obligations are. It is advantageous in object-oriented programming to allocate responsibilities to classes to maintain good cohesion.

In a highly coherent system, code readability and the chance of reuse are raised while complexity is maintained reasonably.

As a result, avoid classes with many responsibilities; for example, a Logger class should solely be responsible for logging.

Principle of Least Knowledge

Only talk to our closest buddies.

Also known as Demeter's Law.

The Open-Closed Principle

Software elements like classes, modules, and functions should be extensible but not adjustable.

This approach encourages developers to build readily extensible code with minimum or no modifications to current code.

An example of good use of these ideas would be when a specific class invokes an abstract class inside to perform a specific action. This class is given with a concrete implementation of this abstract class during runtime.

This enables the developer to subsequently create more concrete calls to this abstract class without modifying the class code that utilizes it.

The Eclipse Extension Point method is another outstanding example. Eclipse plugins or Eclipse-based applications may establish extension points to which other plug-ins might add functionality afterward.

Composition vs. Inheritance in Object-Oriented Design Patterns

Now, let us compare Composition with Inheritance.

Inheritance

An element that inherits from a parent element is said to have a "is a" connection in terms of class relationships. Because a square is a shape, it makes it logical for the square to inherit from form.

When we realize that we're specifying the same behavior across several instances, inheritance might be a useful pattern. In the case of software that works with numerous sorts of shapes, we may have a method drawBorder that is replicated across several distinct types of forms. So, what's the big deal, we may wonder? The problems occur when we wish to adjust drawBorder, or worse when we uncover a fault in the method. Refactoring involves crawling through our project and updating each and every occurrence of the method. A faulty drawBorder method implies we've now strewn the same flaw across our source, resulting in extensive vulnerabilities.

Inheritance attempts to address this issue by abstracting the commonly used method into a parent class that offers a generic enough implementation of drawBorder that it can be used to draw the border of any shape regardless of type (this "genericness" is critical, as having an overly specialized base can lead to a slew of downstream issues).

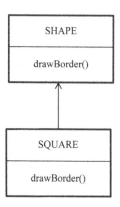

Every new class that "is a" shape may now inherit from the parent shape class and utilize its drawBorder specification. One of the primary advantages is efficient code reuse and easy message delegation across classes. We also gain from following the open-closed concept, which specifies that components should be open to expansion but closed to alteration. Assume we wanted to add additional shapes to our software, each with its own distinct properties. We may utilize inheritance to enhance the current drawBorder method to add additional features without changing any code in the parent class.

While open-closed is ideal, we will sometimes need to alter the parent class – maybe because we uncovered a problem or a new technique to increase performance. Before inheritance, we had to track down every instance of drawBorder, but now if we want to alter anything, all we have to do is update the implementation of the parent class, and the change will cascade down every subclass. That's quite cool.

The disadvantage of this strategy is that altering the implementation of the parent class would have cascade consequences on all subclasses. Isn't that an advantage? We've arrived at the double-edged sword of inheritance, where enormous power comes with immense responsibility. Because inheritance makes it easy to modify the behavior of a wide portion of our codebase with simple changes in one place, it has established tightly coupled dependencies in our application. Every subclass is directly dependent on its parent, and modifications in one may require changes in the other.

Another disadvantage of inheritance is that we must normally make broad assumptions about how the program will use in the future. Maybe we as a programmer can't envision our drawBorder method ever being given a form it doesn't recognize, but we also never imagined that the mind-bending Mobius strip would attempt to inherit from shape, and your software would crumble.

This is why the refrain of favoring composition over inheritance is so popular. It's not that inheritance isn't beneficial; nevertheless, when used carelessly or as a solution to the incorrect issue, it may cause considerable problems down the line, perhaps to the point where adding new functionality without breaking current features is almost difficult.

Composition

Composition defines a "has-a" connection, while inheritance defines a "is-a" relationship. A project that employs composition to orchestrate component interaction focuses on merging several little pieces that combine forces to form something that is greater than the sum of their parts.

If we put composition over our previous shape metaphor, we may conceive of the distinct pieces merged to form a shape. We may end up with things like straightLine, curvedLine, and so on that, we can mix and rearrange in various ways to get the forms we want to utilize. Then we might write a class that implements drawBorder with an interface that takes an object made of lines, and drawBorder would be able to carry out its obligations as long as it has lines. Separating the roles in this way provides for more freedom and flexibility in the separate sections.

Composition, unlike inheritance, does not provide automatic message delegation. We must clearly define the public interface of each unit so that it understands how to communicate with other portions of the program. There may be some duplication in these interfaces, but unlike inheritance, there is no built-in method to reuse that code via composition. The flip side of the coin is that since they are not directly inheriting behavior, each unit is immune to possible side-effects of other components.

Another concern with composition is that, although each unit is simple and (hopefully) easy to grasp, the combination of all the pieces might result in a complicated and difficult-to-understand whole.

Is it really better to choose composition over inheritance?

In simple terms, Yes, but not in the way we always imagined. If we don't have a compelling need to use inheritance, we should aim toward composition. When inheritance is handled incorrectly or carelessly, it might provide serious issues for the future or any developer to whom we will pass over the project.

The composition creates fewer dependencies than inheritance and assumes less about how the program will use in the future. Having stated that, inheritance has significant characteristics that, when utilized appropriately, may deliver tremendous advantages.

Favoring Composition over Inheritance in Java (with Examples)

Composition over inheritance is an object-oriented programming paradigm (OOP). Polymorphic behavior and code reuse should be achieved using class composition rather than inheritance from a base or parent class. The design concept states that composition should prefer over inheritance to provide more design flexibility.

Inheritance should be utilized only when a subclass is a superclass. Use inheritance to avoid code repetition. If there is no "is a" connection, utilize composition to reuse code.

Arguments for Choosing Composition over Inheritance in Java and OOP: One rationale for selecting composition over inheritance in Java because Java does not enable multiple inheritances. Because Java only allows us to extend one class, we'll need Reader and Writer functionality if we require various functionalities, such as reading and writing character data into a file. Having them as private members simplifies our task, known as composition.

Composition allows for more testing of a class than Inheritance. If one class comprises another, we can simply create a Mock Object simulating the combined class for testing purposes. This privilege is not passed down via families.

Although both Composition and Inheritance enable us to reuse code, Inheritance has the downside of breaking encapsulation. If the function of the subclass is dependent on the activity of the superclass, it becomes unstable. When the behavior of the superclass changes, the functionality of the subclass might be broken without any adjustment on its side.

Several object-oriented Design Patterns outlined by GOF: Elements of Reusable Object-Oriented Software support composition over inheritance in the timeless classic Design Patterns. A famous example of this is the strategy Design Pattern, in which composition and delegation are used to alter the behavior of the context without affecting the context code. Because context employs composition to carry strategy, it is straightforward to have a new implementation of strategy at run-time rather than inheriting it.

Another advantage of composition over inheritance is flexibility. If you utilize Composition, you have the flexibility to substitute a better and more recent version of the Composed class implementation. The usage of the comparator class, which gives properties for comparison, is one example.

Inheritance

In object-oriented programming, inheritance is the design method used to establish a connection between objects. In Java, extends keyword is used to implement inheritance.

```
class People {
    String titles;
    String names;
    int ages;
}
```

```
class Employee extends People {
    int salary;
    String titles;
}
```

In the above example, The Employee "is" or "descends from" People. All "is-a" connections are inheritance ties. The employee also shadows the titles property from People, thus title will return the Employee's titles rather than the People's.

Composition

The composition architecture technique in object-oriented programming is used to execute a connection between objects. In Java, the composition is accomplished by using instance variables from other objects.

```
class People {
    String titles;
    String names;
    int ages;

    public Person(String titles, String names, String
ages) {
        this.titles = titles;
        this.names = names;
        this.ages = ages;
    }

}

class Employee {
    int salary;
    private Pople people;

    public Employee(People p, int salary) {
        this.people = p;
        this.salary = salary;
    }
}

People p = new People ("Mrs.", "Kashish", 23);
Employee kapil = new Employee (p, 110000);
```

The connection is often expressed as "has a" or "uses a." A People are present in the Employee class. It does not inherit from People, but rather receives the People object as a parameter, which is why it "has" a People.

Composition over Inheritance

Assume we wish to build a Manager type, which results in the following syntax, which is not permitted in Java (multiple inheritance is not permitted in Java):

```
//Multiple inheritance is not permitted
```

```
class Manager extends People, Employee {
}
```

Now, using the syntax below, we must prioritize composition above inheritance:

```
Class Manager {
    public string title;
    public Manager(Pople p, Employee e)
    {
        this.titles = e.titles;
    }
}
```

IS INHERITANCE EXTINCT? A CLOSER LOOK AT THE DECORATOR PATTERN

Inheritance was the primary technique used to enhance object capabilities when object-oriented programming was introduced. Today, inheritance is often seen as a design odor. Indeed, it has been shown that expanding objects via inheritance often leads to an inflating class hierarchy. Furthermore, multiple inheritance is not supported in some prominent programming languages, like Java and C#, limiting the advantages of this method.

The decorator pattern is a versatile alternative to inheritance for expanding the functionality of objects. Multiple decorators may be piled on top of one other in this style, each providing additional functionality.

A decorator, unlike inheritance, may function on any implementation of a given interface, eliminating the need to subclass a whole class hierarchy. Furthermore, using the decorator approach results in clean, testable code.

Unfortunately, many of today's software engineers are unfamiliar with the decorator pattern. This is due in part to a lack of knowledge, but it is also related to the fact that programming languages have not kept up with the advancement of object-oriented design principles in a manner that encourages developers to understand and utilize those patterns.

In this part, we will examine the advantages of utilizing the decorator pattern over inheritance and argue that it should support natively in object-oriented programming languages. In fact, we believe that the decorator pattern should use more frequently than inheritance in clean and tested programs.

Exploding Class Hierarchy

When the number of classes required to add additional functionality to a given class hierarchy rises exponentially, the class hierarchy explodes. Consider the following interface as an example:

```
public interface IEmailService
{
    void send(Email email);
    Collection<EmailInfo> listsEmail(int indexBegin, int
indexEnd);
    Email downloadEmail(EmailInfo emailInfo);
}
```

If an email server request fails, the default implementation of EmailService raises an exception. We'd want to improve the EmailService implementation such that unsuccessful queries are retried a few times before failing. We'd also want to specify whether or not the implementation is thread-safe.

We can add optional retries and thread-safety capabilities to the EmailService class itself. The class's constructor would take arguments that activate or disable each functionality. This method, however, violates both the Single Responsibility Principle (since the EmailService would have additional jobs) and the Open-Closed Principle (because the class itself would have to be modified for extension). Furthermore, the EmailService class may be included in a third-party package that we are unable to modify.

Inheritance is a frequent way to expand a class without altering it. A derived class inherits the attributes and behavior of its parent and may possibly expand or override parts of its functionality. In the EmailService example, we may develop three subclasses: one that adds retries, one that adds thread-safety, and one that incorporates both features. The class structure would be as follows:

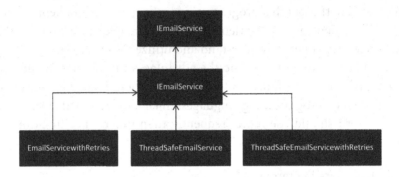

Structure of class.

It should be noted that the ThreadSafeEmailServiceWithRetries might also derive from EmailServiceWithRetries or ThreadSafeEmailService (or both if multiple inheritance is supported). The number of classes, though, and the consequent functionality, would be comparable.

In addition to retries and thread safety, we'd like to add logging to our email service API as an option. We utilize inheritance once more to increase the class hierarchy, which becomes as follows:

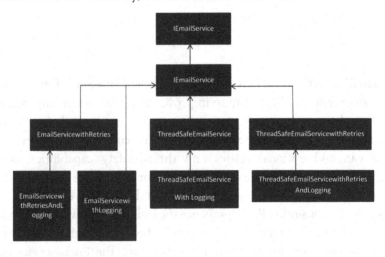

Extended structure of class.

It is worth mentioning that number of extra classes required for adding logging functionality is equal to the entire number of classes in the current hierarchy.

To the Rescue Comes the Decorator Pattern

Instead of inheritance, the decorator approach enhances object capabilities through composition. It solves the problem of ballooning class hierarchy by requiring only one decorator for each new feature. As an example, let's make a decorator for the retries functionality. A basic for loop with three retries is employed for simplicity. The EmailServiceRetryDecorator looks like this:

```
public class EmailServiceRetryDecorator implements
IEmailService
{
    private final IEmailService emailService;

    public EmailServiceRetryDecorator(IEmailService
emailService) {
        this.emailService = emailService;
    }

    @Override
    public void send(Email email) {
        executeWithRetries(() -> emailService.send(email));
    }

    @Override
    public Collection<EmailInfo> listsEmail(int indexBegin,
int indexEnd) {
        final List<EmailInfo> emailInfos = new
ArrayList<>();
        executeWithRetries(() -> emailInfos.
addAll(emailService.listsEmail(indexBegin, indexEnd)));
        return emailInfos;
    }

    @Override
```

It is worth noting that the constructor of EmailServiceRetryDecorator accepts a reference to IEmailService, which can any implementation of IEmailService (including the decorator itself). This totally decouples the decorator from individual IEmailService implementations, increasing its reusability and reliability. Likewise, decorators for thread safety, logging, and caching can be created.

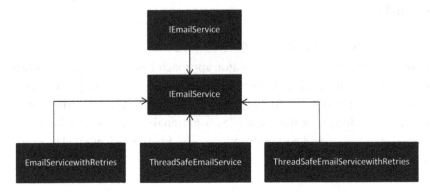

Decorator structure of class.

Decorators Queue

At first look, it may appear that the decorator pattern can only add one functionality to a particular implementation. The options are unlimited, though, because decorators may be piled on top of one other. For example, we can develop a dynamic equivalent to the EmailServiceWithRetriesAndCaching that we established through inheritance as follows:

```
IEmailService emailServiceWithRetriesAndCaching = new
EmailServiceCacheDecorator(
```

Furthermore, by rearranging decorators or utilizing the same decorator at various levels, we may design novel implementations that would be impossible to develop using inheritance. For example, we may log before and after retries as follows:

```
IEmailService emailService = new EmailServiceLoggingDecorat
or(new EmailServiceRetryDecorator(
```

The status of the request before and after retries will note with this combination. This enables verbose logging, which may be utilized for troubleshooting or creating complex dashboards.

Testability

Another significant advantage of the decorator over inheritance is testability. Consider building a unit test for the retries functionality as an example.

Because there is no means for replacing a parent class with a stub, we cannot test EmailServiceWithRetries in isolation from its parent class (EmailService) (also known as mocking). Furthermore, since EmailService makes network connections to a backend server, unit testing all of its subclasses becomes tough (because network calls are often slow and unreliable). In such instances, integration tests are often used instead of unit tests.

However, since the EmailServiceRetryDecorator constructor requires a reference to IEmailService, the decorated object may be simply substituted with a stub implementation (i.e., mock). This allows you to test the retry functionality in isolation, which inheritance does not allow. As an example, consider writing a unit test that confirms that at least one retry is completed.

```
// Create mock that fails first time and then succeed
IEmailService mock = mock(IEmailService.class);
when(mock.downloadEmail(emailInfo))
    . thenThrow(new EmailServiceTransientError())
    . thenReturn(email);

EmailServiceRetryDecorator decorator = new
EmailServiceRetryDeco
```

In contrast to an integration test, which would rely on the development of EmailService and remote service calls, this test is simple, rapid, and consistent.

Other Advantages

The decorator pattern helps developers to produce code that conforms to the SOLID design principles in addition to reducing the class hierarchy and enhancing testability. Indeed, the decorator technique is used to provide new functionality to new focused objects (Single Responsibility Principle) without altering old classes (Open-Closed Principle). Furthermore, since decorators rely on abstractions rather than concretions, the decorator pattern supports the usage of dependency inversion (which has several advantages such as loose coupling and durability).

Drawbacks

Despite the fact that the decorator pattern has several benefits over the alternatives (inheritance or changing existing classes), it has a few limitations that are preventing its widespread adoption.

The decorator class must implement all methods in the decorated interface, which is a recognized disadvantage of this style. Methods that do not provide any new behavior must, in reality, be implemented as forwarding methods in order to preserve current behavior. In contrast, inheritance only requires subclasses to provide methods that alter or extend the parent class's functionality.

Consider the following IProcess interface and develop a decorator for it to demonstrate the difficulty of forwarding methods.

```
public interface IProcess
{
    void start(String args);
    void kills();
    ProcessInfo getInfo();
    ProcessStatus getStatus();
    ProcessStatistics getStatistics();
}
```

If the process fails to start, the default implementation of the start method throws a FailedToStartProcessException. We'd want to modify the default implementation such that launching the process is attempted three times before failing. The decorator pattern would use in the following implementation:

```
public class RetryStartProcess implements IProcess
{
    private IProcess process;

    public RetryStartProcess(IProcess process) {
        this.process = process;
    }

    @Override
    public void start(String args) {
        for(int c=0; c<3; ++c) {
            try {
```

```
            process.start(args);
        } catch (FailedToStartProcessException e) {
            continue;
        }
        break;
    }
```

It's worth noting that this approach has a lot of boilerplate code. In fact, the only significant element of the code is the implementation of the start method. Such boiler-plate might be viewed as a productivity and maintenance burden for interfaces with multiple methods.

Another disadvantage of the decorator pattern is its low popularity, particularly among junior developers. In reality, being less popular frequently implies more difficulty to grasp, which might result in a longer development period.

Decorator Pattern Has Native Support

Both of the disadvantages highlighted in the preceding section may be solved if the decorator pattern has native support in object-oriented programming languages (similar to what is provided today for inheritance). Indeed, with such native support, forwarding methods would be unnecessary, and the decorator pattern would be simpler to implement. Furthermore, native support for the decorator pattern would undoubtedly expand its popularity and use.

The addition of native support for the Observer pattern in C# is a nice illustration of how computer languages may influence the adoption of Design Patterns (also known as events). To transmit events across loosely connected classes, today's C# developers (including junior ones) readily employ the Observer design. Many developers would build direct dependencies between classes to transmit events if events did not exist in C#, resulting in code that is less reusable and more difficult to verify. Likewise, native support for the decorator pattern would encourage developers to design decorators rather to modifying existing classes or erroneously using inheritance, leading in higher code quality.

The following implementation shows what native decorator support in Java might look like:

```
public class RetryStartProcess decorates IProcess
{
    @Override
    public void start(String args) {
        for(int c=0; c<3; ++c) {
            try {
                decorated.start(args);
            } catch (FailedToStartProcessException e) {
                continue;
            }
            break;
        }
    }
}
```

The decorated keyword is used instead of implements, and the decorated field is used to access the decorated object. To make this work, the decorator's default constructor would need to accept an IProcess argument (which will handle at the language level much like parameter-less default constructors are handled today). As we can see, such native support will eliminate boiler-plate and make the decorator pattern as simple to implement as inheritance (if not easier).

Abstract Decorator

If, like us, we frequently utilize the decorator pattern and end up with several decorators for each interface, there is a way we can use to reduce the boilerplate of forwarding procedures (in the meantime until native support for decorator pattern becomes available). The solution is to create an abstract decorator that implements all methods as forwarding methods and derive (inherit) all decorators from it. Only decorated methods will need to reimplement since forwarding methods are inherited from the abstract decorator. This solution makes use of the native inheritance capabilities to implement the decorator pattern. The code below exemplifies this method.

```
public abstract class AbstractProcessDecorator implements
IProcess
{
    protected final IProcess process;
```

```
    protected AbstractProcessDecorator(IProcess process) {
        this.process = process;
    }

    public void start(String args) {
        process.start(args);
    }

    public void kill() {
        process.kill();
    }

    public ProcessInfo getInfo() {
        return process.getInfo();
    }

    public ProcessStatus getStatus() {
        return process.getStatus();
    }

    public ProcessStatistics getStatistics() {
        return process.getStatistics();
    }


public class RetryStartProcess extends AbstractProcessDecorator
{
    public RetryStartProcess(IProcess process) {
        super(process);
    }

    @Override
    public void start(String args) {
        for(int c=0; c<3; ++c) {
            try {
                process.start(args);
            } catch (FailedToStartProcessException e) {
                continue;
            }
            break;
```

One disadvantage of this technique is that decorators cannot inherit from other classes (for languages that do not enable multiple inheritance).

When Should We Use Inheritance?

Although we feel that the decorator pattern should prefer over inheritance where feasible, inheritance is more appropriate in certain instances.

A decorator would be tough to build when derived classes need to access nonpublic fields or methods in the parent class. Decorators do not have access to attributes or methods that are exclusive to one implementation or another since they are only aware of the public interface.

As a general rule, if our subclass exclusively relies on its parent's public interface, it's a sign that we should use a decorator instead. It would be fantastic if static analysis tools proposed that inheritance be replaced with a decorator in such circumstances.

KEY POINTS

- When feasible, the decorator pattern is preferred over inheritance.

- The decorator approach solves the issue of inheritance's expanding class hierarchy. The resultant class hierarchy is straightforward and scales linearly when the decorator pattern is used.

- Decorators may be tested separately from decorated objects; however, subclasses cannot be tested apart from their parents. If the parent class is difficult to unit test (e.g., because it makes remote calls), its descendant classes inherit this problem. On the other hand, Decorators may be unit tested independently since they only rely on the interface of decorated objects (injected through the decorator class's constructor).

- The decorator pattern helps developers to produce code that follows SOLID design principles.

- The decorator pattern would be more straightforward and more widely adopted if it were supported natively in object-oriented programming languages.

In this chapter, we discussed Software Design Patterns, major concepts, benefits, and drawbacks of these methods.

## CHAPTER 2

Factory Pattern

IN THIS CHAPTER

> ➤ What is Factory Pattern?

> ➤ Real-world examples

> ➤ Why is Factory Pattern useful?

> ➤ Advantages/disadvantages

> ➤ Implementation in Python

> ➤ UML diagram

We discussed software design and its ideas in the previous chapter. This chapter will explain the Factory Pattern and provide an example of how one might use it.

FACTORY METHOD

The Factory Pattern is a Creational Design Pattern, which means it is concerned with the creation of objects. In the Factory design, we generate objects without disclosing the creation mechanism to the client, and the client creates new types of objects using the same standard interface.

The goal is to employ a static member-function (static Factory Pattern) that builds and returns instances while keeping class module information hidden from the user.

DOI: 10.1201/9781003308461-2

A Factory Pattern is one of the key design ideas for creating an object, allowing clients to generate library objects in a way that isn't tightly coupled with the library's class hierarchy.

What exactly do we mean when saying "library" and "clients"?

A library is given by a third party and exposes some public APIs to which clients make calls to perform their jobs. Different types of views supplied by Android OS are a simple illustration.

UML FOR FACTORY METHOD

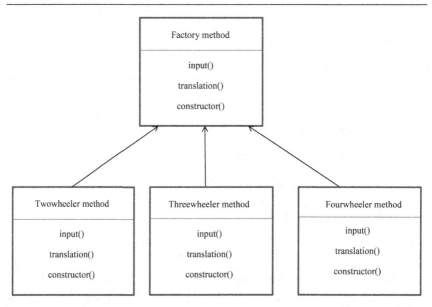

UML for Factory Pattern Method.

PATTERNS FOR FACTORY PATTERN DESIGN

A Factory Design Pattern is a form of Creational Design Pattern that allows us to build an object to instantiate by using an interface or a class. The factory is the most efficient approach to constructing an object. Objects are produced in this method without providing the reasoning to the client. The client utilizes the same standard interface to construct a new object type.

Problem

Assume we intend to build a website that sells books in various parts of the country. The website's first edition only accepts book orders, but as time passes and our website grows in popularity, we will not add additional things to sales, such as clothing and footwear. It's an excellent concept, but what about the software developers? Now they must update the entire codebase because most of the code is involved with the book's class, and they must alter the entire codebase. It may result in a messy code.

Let's look at another example to comprehend this concept further:

```python
# Python Code for the Object
# Oriented Concepts without
# using the Factory method

class FrenchLocalizer:

    """ it simply returns the french version """

    def __init__(self):

        self.translations = {"Scooter": "voiture", "car":
"bicyclette",
                             "bike":"cyclette"}

    def localize(self, message):

        """change message using translations"""
        return self.translations.get(msg, msg)

class SpanishLocalizer:
    """it simply returns the spanish version"""

    def __init__(self):

        self.translations = {"scooter": "coche", "car":
"bicicleta",
                             "bike":"ciclo"}

    def localize(self, msg):

        """change message using translations"""
        return self.translations.get(msg, msg)

class EnglishLocalizer:
    """Simply return same message"""

    def localize(self, msg):
        return msg
```

```
if __name__ == "__main__":

    # the main method to call others
    f = FrenchLocalizer()
    e = EnglishLocalizer()
    s = SpanishLocalizer()

    # list of the strings
    message = ["Scooter", "car", "bike"]

    for msg in message:
        print(f.localize(msg))
        print(e.localize(msg))
        print(s.localize(msg))
```

Let's look at how we can address challenges like these.

Solution

Instead of utilizing straightforward object building, we utilize the specific Factory Pattern in the solution to invoke the construction object. Both methods of producing objects are pretty similar, yet they are referred to within the Factory function.

For example, our selling products, such as Books, Mobiles, Clothes, and Accessories, should have a purchasing interface that declares a method buy. These methods will implement differently in each class.

Let's look at the diagram below to get a better understanding of it.

```
# Solution using the factory design pattern

class French_Language:

    #it'll return the french version

    def __init__(self):

        self.translations = {"books": "voiture", "phoneno":
"biclothtte",
                    "cloths":"clothtte"}
```

```
    def localize(self, message):

        """change message using translations"""
        return self.translations.get(msg, msg)

class Spanish_Language:
    #it will return the spanish version

    def __init__(self):
        self.translations = {"books": "libro", "phoneno":
"teléfono",
                             "cloths":"paño"}

    def localize(self, msg):

        #change message using translations
        return self.translations.get(msg, msg)

class English_Language:
    """Simply return the same message"""

    def localize(self, msg):
        return msg

def Factory(language ="English"):

    """Factory-Method"""
    localizers = {
        "German": German_Language,
        "English": English_Language,
        "French": French_Language,
    }

    return localizers[language]()

if __name__ == "__main__":

    fr = Factory("German")
    en = Factory("English")
    sp = Factory("French")

    message = ["books", "phoneno", "cloths"]

    for ml in message:
        print(fr.localize(ml))
        print(en.localize(ml))
        print(sp.localize(ml))
```

ADVANTAGES OF USING THE FACTORY PATTERN

The benefits of the factory technique are listed below:

- Factory methods are convenient for introducing new sorts of products without redistributing the current client code.

- It prevents close coupling between the products and creator classes and objects.

DRAWBACKS OF USING THE FACTORY PATTERN METHOD

The drawbacks of employing Factory techniques are listed below:

- It will create a massive number of tiny files or the cluttering of the files.

- The client may use the subclass to construct a specific real product object.

APPLICABILITY

Its principle is similar to polymorphism in that no modifications to the client code are required. Assume we wish to draw various forms such as rectangles, squares, circles, etc. The Factory Pattern Method may use to build the instance based on the user's input.

We can book a 1-wheeler, 2-wheeler, 3-wheeler, and 4-wheeler in a taxi application. The customer may book any of the rides he wishes from this page. We may construct a class called Booking with the aid of the Factory function, which will allow us to generate an instance that accepts the user's input. As a result, the developer does not need to alter the complete code to implement the new feature.

The Factory method removes the difficult-to-preserve complex logical code. It also inhibits us from making changes to the codebase since altering existing code might produce subtle flaws and cause behavior to change.

USES OF THE FACTORY DESIGN PATTERN

- When a class does not know what subclasses it must generate.

- When a class wants its subclasses to indicate the objects that will produce.

- When the parent classes opt to create objects for their subclasses.

WHEN SHOULD WE UTILIZE FACTORY PATTERN METHODS?

First, we must determine the instances in which the Factory technique may be used. It may be utilized when an application relies on an interface (product) to perform a job and there are several actual implementations of that stated interface.

The Factory technique may be used to tackle a wide range of issues. We describe a few examples that fulfill this definition.

Complex Logical Code Is Being Replaced

In general, the code contains logic such as if/else/elif that is difficult to maintain owing to the addition of new routes when certain needs change.

Using the Factory technique, we can insert the body of each logical route into the many declared functions or classes that have a common interface. The developer may offer the modification's concrete implementation.

Bringing Together Related Functions under a Single Interface

Assume we want to apply a certain filter on a picture. The Factory Pattern Method will discover the specific filter according to the user input. The real implementation may be used via the Factory Pattern Method.

Multiple Implementations of the Same Functionality Are Supported

A group of scientists requires conversions of the satellite photos from one coordinate system to another. A system, on the other hand, contains several algorithms to execute the various levels of change. The program may enable the user to pick an optimum algorithm. Factory method may implement firmly algorithm depending on this option.

Integrating External Series That Are Linked

A video streaming application aims to integrate the many external providers. The tool gives the users to identify where their video originates from. The Factory method provides the proper integration depending on a user's choice.

PROBLEMS WE CONFRONT IN THE ABSENCE OF THE FACTORY METHOD

Assume we have our own business that offers ridesharing in various regions of the nation. The app's original version only offers two-wheeler ridesharing, but as time passes, our service grows in popularity, and we now want to include three and four-wheeler ridesharing as well.

That's fantastic news, but what about our startup's software developers? They must alter the whole codebase since the majority of the code is now connected with the two-wheeler class, and developers must make modifications to the entire codebase.

After completing all of these adjustments, the developers are left with either a jumbled code or a resignation letter.

DISCUSSION

The Factory Method is used to create things, while the Template Method is used to implement an algorithm. A superclass describes all standard and general behavior (using pure virtual "placeholders" for creation stages) and then delegated the creation details to client-supplied subclasses.

The Factory Pattern Method makes a design more adaptable while also making it somewhat more difficult. Other Design Patterns need the creation of new classes, while the Factory Pattern Method just necessitates the creation of a new action.

People often use the Factory Method to generate objects; however, it isn't required if: the class that's instantiated never changes, or instantiation occurs in an action that subclasses may readily override (such as an initialization operation).

The Factory Pattern Method is comparable to the Abstract Factory, except it does not place as much focus on families.

Factory Methods are often described by an architectural framework and then implemented by the framework's user.

GENERAL GUIDELINES

Abstract Factory classes are often created with Factory Methods, although they may also be done using Prototype.

Factory Methods are often invoked from inside Template Methods.

Inheritance is used to create objects in the Factory Method. Delegation is used to create prototypes.

Typically, designs begin with the Factory Method (less difficult, more adaptable, subclasses proliferate) and progress to the Abstract Factory, Prototype, or Builder (more flexible, more complex) when the designer realizes where more flexibility is required.

Although prototyping does not need subclassing, it does require an initialize action. Factory Method necessitates subclassing but does not need to initialize.

A Factory Method offers the advantage of repeatedly returning the same instance or of returning a subclass instead of an object of the same type.

Some Factory Method proponents argue that all constructors should be private or protected as a matter of language design (or, failing that, as a matter of style). It is none of your concern whether a class creates a new object or recycles an old one.

The new operator is seen as hazardous. There is a distinction between requesting and generating an item. The new operator always returns an object and does not contain object creation. A Factory Method ensures such encapsulation, allowing an object to be requested without being inextricably linked to the process of production.

Examples of Real-World Applications of the Factory Pattern Method Design in Java

This Design Pattern is extensively used in JDK, for example, the java.util. getInstance() function.

The Factory Pattern Method Design is used by Calendar, NumberFormat, and ResourceBundle.

Calculate An Electricity Bill: A Real-World Application of the Factory Method in Java

- **Step 1:** Create an abstract class called Plan.

```
import java.io.*;
abstract class Plan{
        protected double rate;
        abstract void getRate();

        public void calculateBills(int units){
            System.out.println(units*rate);
        }
}//end of the Plan class
```

- **Step 2:** Create concrete classes that extend the abstract Plan class.

```
class  DomesticPlan extends Plan{
    //@override
     public void getRate(){
         rate=4.50;
    }
}//end of the DomesticPlan class.
```

```
class  CommercialPlan extends Plan{
//@override
public void getRate(){
   rate=7.50;
}
/end of the CommercialPlan class.
```

```
class  InstitutionalPlan extends Plan{
//@override
public void getRate(){
   rate=4.50;
}
/end of the InstitutionalPlan class.
```

- **Step 3:** Create a GetPlanFactory to produce concrete class objects depending on the information provided.

```
class GetPlanFactory{

    //use the getPlan method to get object of the type
Plan
        public Plan getPlan(String planType){
            if(planType == null){
            return null;
            }
        if(planType.equalsIgnoreCase("DOMESTIC-PLAN")) {
               return new DomesticPlan();
            }
        else if(planType.
equalsIgnoreCase("COMMERCIAL-PLAN")){
               return new CommercialPlan();
            }
        else if(planType.
equalsIgnoreCase("INSTITUTIONAL-PLAN")) {
               return new InstitutionalPlan();
            }
        return null;
        }
}//end of the GetPlanFactory class
```

- **Step 4:** Create a bill by calling GetPlanFactory and giving information such as the kind of plan (DOMESTICPLAN, COMMERCIALPLAN, or INSTITUTIONALPLAN) to it.

```
import java.io.*;
class GenerateBill{
    public static void main(String args[])throws
IOException{
        GetPlanFactory planFactory = new GetPlanFactory();

        System.out.print("Enter name of plan for which bill
will generate: ");
BufferedReader br=new BufferedReader(new
InputStreamReader(System.in));

        String planName=br.readLine();
        System.out.print("Enter number of units for bill will
calculate: ");
        int units=Integer.parseInt(br.readLine());

        Plan p1 = planFactory.getPlan(planName);
        //call getRate() method and calculateBill()method of
the DomesticPaln.

        System.out.print("Bill amount for "+p1lanName+"
of  "+units+" units is: ");
            p1.getRate();
            p1.calculateBill(units);
            }
    }//end of the GenerateBill class
```

A Real-World Example of the Factory Design Pattern in C#

Assume we have three distinct cards, MoneyBack, Titanium, and Platinum, all of which implement the abstract class CreditCard. We must instantiate one of these classes, but we do not know which one; this is determined by the user.

The following classes and objects are represented in the above class diagram:

- **Product:** CreditCard

- **ConcreteProduct:** MoneyBackCreditCard, TitaniumCreditCard, PlatinumCreditCard

- **Creator:** CardFactory

- **ConcreteCreator:** MoneyBackCardFactory, TitaniumCardFactory, PlatinumCardFactory

The code blocks for each participant are listed below:

1. **Product**

```
namespace FactoryMethodDesignPatternInCSharp
{
    /// <summary>
    /// 'Product' Abstract Class
    /// </summary>
    abstract class CreditCard
    {
        public abstract string CardType { get; }
        public abstract int CreditLimit { get; set; }
        public abstract int AnnualCharge { get; set; }
    }
}
```

2. **ConcreteProduct**
   MoneyBackCreditCard:

```
using System;

namespace FactoryMethodDesignPatternInCSharp
{
    /// <summary> 'ConcreteProduct' class </summary>
    class MoneyBackCreditCard : CreditCard
    {
        private readonly string _cardType;
        private int _creditLimit;
        private int _annualCharge;

        public MoneyBackCreditCard(int creditLimit,
int annualCharge)
        {
            _cardType = "MoneyBack";
            _creditLimit = creditLimit;
            _annualCharge = annualCharge;
        }

        public override string CardType
        {
            get { return _cardType; }
        }

        public override int CreditLimit
        {
```

```
                get { return _creditLimit; }
                set { _creditLimit = value; }
            }

        public override int AnnualCharge
        {
                get { return _annualCharge; }
                set { _annualCharge = value; }
        }
    }
}
```

TitaniumCreditCard:

```
using System;

namespace FactoryMethodDesignPatternInCSharp
{
    /// <summary>
    /// 'ConcreteProduct' class </summary>
    class TitaniumCreditCard : CreditCard
    {
        private readonly string _cardType;
        private int _creditLimit;
        private int _annualCharge;

        public TitaniumCreditCard(int creditLimit, int
annualCharge)
            {
                _cardType = "Titanium";
                _creditLimit = creditLimit;
                _annualCharge = annualCharge;
            }

        public override string CardType
        {
                get { return _cardType; }
        }

        public override int CreditLimit
        {
                get { return _creditLimit; }
                set { _creditLimit = value; }
        }

        public override int AnnualCharge
```

```
            {
                get { return _annualCharge; }
                set { _annualCharge = value; }
            }
        }
    }
```

PlatinumCreditCard:

```csharp
using System;

namespace FactoryMethodDesignPatternInCSharp
{
    /// <summary> A 'ConcreteProduct' class </summary>
    class PlatinumCreditCard : CreditCard
    {
        private readonly string _cardType;
        private int _creditLimit;
        private int _annualCharge;

        public PlatinumCreditCard(int creditLimit, int
annualCharge)
        {
            _cardType = "Platinum";
            _creditLimit = creditLimit;
            _annualCharge = annualCharge;
        }

        public override string CardType
        {
            get { return _cardType; }
        }

        public override int CreditLimit
        {
            get { return _creditLimit; }
            set { _creditLimit = value; }
        }

        public override int AnnualCharge
        {
            get { return _annualCharge; }
            set { _annualCharge = value; }
        }

    }
}
```

3. Creator

```
namespace FactoryMethodDesignPatternInCSharp
{
    /// <summary> 'Creator' Abstract Class </summary>
    abstract class CardFactory
    {
        public abstract CreditCard GetCreditCard();
    }
}
```

4. ConcreteCreator
MoneyBackFactory:

```
namespace FactoryMethodDesignPatternInCSharp
{
    /// <summary> 'ConcreteCreator' class </summary>
    class MoneyBackFactory : CardFactory
    {
        private int _creditLimit;
        private int _annualCharge;

        public MoneyBackFactory(int creditLimit, int
annualCharge)
        {
            _creditLimit = creditLimit;
            _annualCharge = annualCharge;
        }

        public override CreditCard GetCreditCard()
        {
            return new MoneyBackCreditCard(_
creditLimit, _annualCharge);
        }
    }
}
```

TitaniumFactory:

```
namespace FactoryMethodDesignPatternInCSharp
{
    class TitaniumFactory: CardFactory
```

```
        {
            private int _creditLimit;
            private int _annualCharge;

            public TitaniumFactory(int creditLimit, int
annualCharge)
            {
                _creditLimit = creditLimit;
                _annualCharge = annualCharge;
            }

            public override CreditCard GetCreditCard()
            {
                return new TitaniumCreditCard(_
creditLimit, _annualCharge);
            }
        }
    }
```

PlatinumFactory:

```
namespace FactoryMethodDesignPatternInCSharp
{
    class PlatinumFactory: CardFactory
    {
        private int _creditLimit;
        private int _annualCharge;

        public PlatinumFactory(int creditLimit, int
annualCharge)
        {
            _creditLimit = creditLimit;
            _annualCharge = annualCharge;
        }

        public override CreditCard GetCreditCard()
        {
            return new PlatinumCreditCard(_
creditLimit, _annualCharge);
        }
    }
}
```

Client Factory Pattern Example

```csharp
using System;

namespace FactoryMethodDesignPatternInCSharp
{
    /// <summary> Factory Pattern Demo </summary>
    public class ClientApplication
    {
        static void Main()
        {
            CardFactory factory = null;
            Console.Write("Enter card type we would
like to visit: ");
            string car = Console.ReadLine();

            switch (car.ToLower())
            {
                case "moneyback":
                    factory = new
MoneyBackFactory(50000, 0);
                    break;
                case "titanium":
                    factory = new
TitaniumFactory(100000, 500);
                    break;
                case "platinum":
                    factory = new
PlatinumFactory(500000, 1000);
                    break;
                default:
                    break;
            }

            CreditCard creditCard = factory.
GetCreditCard();
            Console.WriteLine("\nYour card details are
below : \n");
            Console.WriteLine("Card Type: {0}\nCredit
Limit: {1}\nAnnual Charge: {2}",
                creditCard.CardType, creditCard.
CreditLimit, creditCard.AnnualCharge);
            Console.ReadKey();
        }
    }
}
```

This chapter covered Factory Method, where we discussed Factory Design, problems, advantages, and disadvantages. We also discussed the UML diagram, general guidelines, and applicability.

## CHAPTER 3

Observer Pattern

IN THIS CHAPTER

> ➢ What is Observer Pattern?

> ➢ Real-world examples

> ➢ Why is Observer Pattern useful?

> ➢ Advantages/disadvantages

> ➢ Implementation in Python

> ➢ UML diagram

In the previous chapter, we covered Factory Method Pattern in Software Design Pattern. In this chapter, we will discuss Observer Pattern, discussing real-life examples, advantages, and disadvantages. We will also cover implementation and UML.

The Observer Pattern is a Behavioral Design Pattern that lets us establish or create a subscription mechanism to notify numerous objects of each new event that occurs to the object they are viewing. Multiple objects are essentially watching the topic. The topic must observe, and the observers are alerted anytime there is a change in the subject. This pattern provides one-to-many dependencies between items, such that when one object changes state, all of its dependents are immediately alerted and changed.

DOI: 10.1201/9781003308461-3

PARTICIPANTS IN DESIGN

Four people are involved in the Observer Pattern.

- **Subject:** Subject is an interface or abstract class that defines the procedures for attaching and detaching observers from the subject.

- **ConcreteSubject:** It is a class that represents a concrete subject. It keeps track of the object's status and tells the linked Observers when it changes.

- **Observer:** An interface or abstract class that defines the methods utilized to notify this object.

- **ConcreteObserver:** Concrete implementations of the Observer.

A PROBLEM

Assume we want to design a calculator application with many capabilities such as addition, subtraction, changing the basis of the numbers to hexadecimal or decimal, and many more. However, one of our pals is interested in altering the basis of his favorite number to Octal, and we are still working on the program. So, what may be the solution? Should our buddy check the application every day to see what the status is? But don't we think that would result in many extra trips to the application that wasn't really necessary? Alternatively, we might consider it each time we introduce a new feature and send a reminder to each user. Is it all right? Yes, but not all of the time. Some consumers may be upset by a large number of needless alerts that they do not want.

SOLUTION BASED ON THE OBSERVER PATTERN

Let's talk about how to solve the situation indicated above. Here comes the subject into the spotlight. However, it also informs the other objects, which is why it is often referred to as the Publisher. Subscribers are all objects that desire to follow changes in the publisher's state.

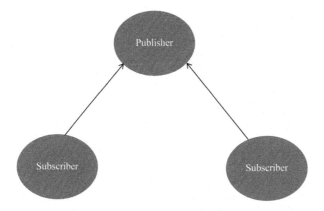

Solution of Observer Pattern.

```
class Subject:

    """ Describes what is being seen"""

    def __init__(self):

        """"create empty observer list"""

        self._observers = []

    def notify(self, modifier = None):

        """"Alert observers"""

        for observer in self._observers:
            if modifier != observer:
                observer.update(self)

    def attach(self, observer):

        """"If observer is not in list,
        append it into the list"""

        if observer not in self._observers:
            self._observers.append(observer)

    def detach(self, observer):

        """"Remove observer from observer list"""
```

```
        try:
            self._observers.remove(observer)
        except ValueError:
            pass


class Data(Subject):

    """monitor object"""

    def __init__(self, name =''):
        Subject.__init__(self)
        self.name = name
        self._data = 0

    @property
    def data(self):
        return self._data

    @data.setter
    def data(self, value):
        self._data = value
        self.notify()


class HexViewer:

    """updates Hewviewer"""

    def update(self, subject):
        print('HexViewer: Subject {} has data 0x{:x}'.
format(subject.name, subject.data))

class OctalViewer:

    """updates Octal viewer"""

    def update(self, subject):
        print('OctalViewer: Subject' + str(subject.name) +
'has data '+str(oct(subject.data)))


class DecimalViewer:

    """updates Decimal viewer"""

    def update(self, subject):
```

```
        print('DecimalViewer: Subject % s has data % d' %
(subject.name, subject.data))

"""main function"""

if __name__ == "__main__":

    """provide data"""

    obj1 = Data('Data 1')
    obj2 = Data('Data 2')

    view1 = DecimalViewer()
    view2 = HexViewer()
    view3 = OctalViewer()

    obj1.attach(view1)
    obj1.attach(view2)
    obj1.attach(view3)

    obj2.attach(view1)
    obj2.attach(view2)
    obj2.attach(view3)

    obj1.data = 20
    obj2.data = 25
```

CLASS DIAGRAM

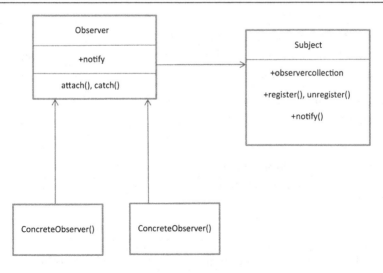

Class Diagram of Observer Pattern.

ADVANTAGES

- **Open/Closed Principle:** Providing subscriber classes in the Observer Pattern is simpler than in others since no changes to the client's code are required.

- **Establishes Relationships:** Building relationships between objects at runtime is quite simple.

- It thoroughly specifies the connection that exists between the objects and the observer. As a result, there is no need to edit the Subject to add or delete observers.

DISADVANTAGES

- **Memory Leakage:** Memory leaks are produced by the Lapsed Listener Problem due to explicit observer registration and unregistration.

- **Random Notifications:** Notifications are provided to all subscribers in a random sequence.

- **Risky Implementations:** If the pattern is not implemented correctly, there is a good risk that we will wind up with a high-complexity code.

APPLICABILITY

- **Multi-Dependency:** This pattern should be used when numerous objects are dependent on the state of one object since it gives a tidy and well-tested design for the same.

- **Receiving Notifications:** It is utilized in social media, RSS feeds, and email subscriptions where we may follow or subscribe and get the most recent notice.

- **Object Reflections:** When we do not closely link the objects, each change in state in one object must reflect in another.

USAGE

- When the status of one item must be mirrored in another without the objects remaining tightly connected.

- When we build a framework that has to be updated in the future with new observers with minimal changes.

OBSERVER PATTERN'S PURPOSE

- The Observer pattern is used to alert interested observers of a change. We can add and delete observers at any point throughout the execution.

- As an example, we have a color selection form. We must update the complete application for each color change. There will be observers listening to the color change event to keep themselves updated.

INTENT

Define a one-to-many dependence between objects such that when one object changes state, all of its dependents are immediately alerted and changed.

In a Subject abstraction, encapsulate the core (or standard or engine) components, and in an Observer hierarchy, the variable (or optional or user interface) components.

Model-View-"View" Controller's component.

PROBLEM

A vast monolithic architecture does not scale effectively because additional graphing or monitoring needs are imposed.

DISCUSSION

Create an object that serves as the "keeper" of the data model and business logic (the Subject). Delegate all "view" behavior to be discrete and decoupled Observer objects. As they are generated, Observers register with the Subject. When the Subject changes, it broadcasts the change to all registered Observers, and each Observer requests the Subject for the subset of the Subject's state that it is responsible for monitoring.

This enables the number and "type" of "view" objects to be dynamically defined rather than statically provided at compilation time.

The protocol as mentioned above defines a "pull" interaction paradigm. Rather than the Subject "pushing" what has changed to all Observers, each Observer is in charge of "drawing" its own "window of interest" from the Subject. The "push" paradigm reduces reuse, but the "pull" model is inefficient.

Implementing event compression (only sending a single change broadcast after a series of consecutive changes has occurred), having a single Observer monitor multiple Subjects, and ensuring that a Subject notifies its Observers when it is about to leave are all discussed left to the designer's discretion.

The Observer Pattern dominates the Model-View-Controller architecture, which has been popular in the Smalltalk community for many years.

EXAMPLE

The Observer creates a one-to-many connection such that when one object changes state, the others are alerted and updated automatically. Some auctions show this trend. Each bidder carries a numbered paddle that is used to signal a bid. The auctioneer begins the bidding and "observes" when a paddle is raised to accept the bid. The acceptance of the bid modifies the bid price, which is communicated to all bidders in the form of a new bid.

CHECKLIST

- Differentiate between the core functionality and the optional functionality.

- Model the separate functionality using a "subject" abstraction.

- Model the dependent functionality via an "observer" structure.

- The Subject is connected exclusively to the Observer base class.

- The client configures the number and kind of Observers.

- Observers register themselves with the Subject.

- The Subject communicates events to all registered Observers.

- The Subject may "push" information toward the Observers; alternatively, the Observers may "pull" the information they need from the Subject.

RULES OF THUMB

- Chain of Responsibility, Command, Mediator, and Observer address how we may decouple senders and receivers, but with various trade-offs. Chain of Responsibility sends a sender request down a chain of possible recipients. Command generally defines a sender-receiver relationship with a subclass. The mediator has senders and receivers reference each other indirectly. Observer presents a highly decoupled interface that enables various receivers to be set up at run-time.

- Mediator and Observer are competing patterns. The distinction between both is that Observer spreads communication by introducing "observer" and "subject" objects, while a Mediator object wraps the communication between other things. We've found it simpler to build reusable Observers and Subjects than to make reusable Mediators.

- On the other side, Mediator may employ an Observer to enroll colleagues and converse with them dynamically.

Here's A Real-World Example of an Observer Pattern in Java

Any social media network, such as Facebook or Twitter, may serve as a real-world illustration of the Observer Pattern. When someone changes his status, all of his followers are notified.

A follower can follow or unfollow another individual at any moment. If a person unfollows a topic, they will no longer get alerts from that subject in the future.

Observer Patterns are the foundation of message-oriented applications in programming. When an application's status is modified, the subscribers are notified. This paradigm is used by frameworks such as HornetQ and JMS.

Similarly, all keyboard and mouse events in Java UI programming are handled by listeners' objects and assigned functions. When the user clicks the mouse, the function registered to the mouse click event is called, and all context data is sent to it as a method parameter.

IMPLEMENT THE OBSERVER PATTERN

- **Step 1:** Create a class called ResponseHandler1 that implements the java.util.Observer interface.

```
//This is class.

import java.util.Observable;
import java.util.Observer;

public class ResponseHandler1 implements Observer {
    private String resp1;
```

```
    public void update(Observable obj, Object arg) {
        if (arg instanceof String) {
            resp1 = (String) arg;
            System.out.println("\nReceived-Response:
" + resp1 );
        }
    }
}// End of ResponseHandler1 interface
```

- **Step 2**: Make a new ResponseHandler2 class that implements the java.util.Observer interface.

```
//This is a class.

import java.util.Observable;
import java.util.Observer;

public class ResponseHandler2 implements Observer {
    private String resp1;
    public void update(Observable obj, Object arg) {
        if (arg instanceof String) {
            resp1 = (String) arg;
            System.out.println("\nReceived Response:
" + resp1 );
        }
    }
}// End of ResponseHandler2 interface
```

- **Step 3**: Make an EventSource class by extending the java.util. Observable class.

```
//This is class.

import java.io.BufferedReader;
import java.io.IOException;
import java.io.InputStreamReader;
import java.util.Observable;

public class EventSource extends Observable implements
Runnable {
    @Override
```

```
    public void run() {
        try {
            final InputStreamReader isr1 = new
InputStreamReader(System.in);
            final BufferedReader br1 = new
BufferedReader(isr);
            while (true) {
                String response = br1.readLine();
                setChanged();
                notifyObservers(response);
            }
        }
        catch (IOException e) {
            e.printStackTrace();
        }
    }
}// End of Eventsource class
```

Another Example

The observer design allows class users to subscribe to events while this class processes data, for example, and be alerted when these events occur. In the following example, we develop a processing class and an observer class that will inform if it identifies words that are longer than 5 letters when processing a phrase.

The LongWordsObserver interface defines the observer. Implement this interface to add an observer to an event.

```
// observe that can register and receive the notifications
public interface LongWordsObserver {
    void notify(WordEvent event);
}
```

When specified events occur, the WordEvent class will send an event to the observer classes (in this case, long words were found).

```
// Event class which contains long word that was found
public class WordEvent {
private String word;
```

```
public WordEvent(String word) {
this.word = word;
}

public String getWord() {
return word;
}
}
```

The PhraseProcessor class is responsible for processing the provided phrase. The addObserver method is used to register observers. When long words are discovered, these observers will notify through an instance of the WordEvent class.

```
import java.util.ArrayList; import java.util.List;

public class PhraseProcessor {

// list of observers
private List<LongWordsObserver> observers = new
ArrayList<>();

// register observer
public void addObserver(LongWordsObserver observer) {
observers.add(observer);
}

// inform all observers that long word was found private
void informObservers(String word) {
observers.forEach(o -> o.notify(new WordEvent(word)));
}

// the main method - process phrase and look for the long
words. If such are found,
// notify all observers
public void process(String phrase) {
for (String word : phrase.split(" ")) {
if (word.length() > 6)
{
informObservers(word);
}
}
}
}
```

The LongWordsExample class demonstrates how to register observers, use the process function, and get notifications when lengthy words are discovered.

```java
import java.util.ArrayList; import java.util.List;

public class LongWordsExample {

public static void main(String[] args) {

// create list of words to fill when long words were found
List<String> longWords = new ArrayList<>();
// create PhraseProcessor
class PhraseProcessor
processor = new PhraseProcessor();

// register observer and specify what it should do when it
receives the events,
// namely to append long words in the longwords list
processor.addObserver(event -> longWords.add(event.
getWord()));

// call process method
processor.process("Lorem ipsum dolor sit amet, consectetuer
adipiscing elit");

// show list of long words after processing is done System.
out.println(String.join(", ", longWords));
// consectetuer, adipiscing
}
}
```

IObservable and IObserver (C#) Observer

In.NET, the IObserver<T> and IObservable<T> interfaces can use to implement the Observer Pattern.

- The IObservable<T> interface represents the class that sends notifications.

- The IObserver<T> interface

- It represents the class that receives them.

```
public class Stocks {
   private string Symbol { get; set; } private decimal
Price { get; set; }
   }

   public class Investor : IObserver<Stocks> { public
IDisposable unsubscriber;
   public virtual void Subscribe(IObservable<Stocks>
provider) { if(provider != null) {
   unsubscriber = provider.Subscribe(this);
   }
   }
   public virtual void OnCompleted() { unsubscriber.
Dispose();
   }
   public virtual void OnError(Exception e) {
   }
   public virtual void OnNext(Stocks stocks) {
   }
   }

   public class StocksTrader : IObservable<Stocks> { public
StocksTrader() {
   observers = new List<IObserver<Stocks>>();
   }
   private IList<IObserver<Stocks>> observers;
   public IDisposable Subscribe(IObserver<Stocks> observer) {
if(!observers.Contains(observer)) {
   observers.Add(observer);
   }
   return new Unsubscriber(observers, observer);
   }
   public class Unsubscriber : IDisposable { private
IList<IObserver<Stocks>> _observers; private
IObserver<Stocks> _observer;
      public Unsubscriber(IList<IObserver<Stock>>
observers, IObserver<Stocks> observer) {
         _observers = observers;
         _observer = observer;
         }

      public void Dispose() { Dispose(true);
         }
      private bool _disposed = false;
      protected virtual void Dispose(bool disposing) {
if(_disposed) {
      return;
      }
      if(disposing) {
```

```
        if(_observer != null && _observers.Contains
(_observer)) {
        _observers.Remove(_observer);
        }
        }
        _disposed = true;
        }
        }
        public void Trade(Stocks stocks) { foreach(var
observer in observers) {
        if(stocks== null) {
        observer.OnError(new ArgumentNullException());
        }
        observer.OnNext(stocks);
        }
        }
        public void End() {
        foreach(var observer in observers.ToArray()) {
observer.OnCompleted();
        }
        observers.Clear();
        }
        }
```

USAGE

```
...
var provider = new StocksTrader(); var x1 = new Investor();
x1.Subscribe(provider);
var x2 = new Investor(); x2.Subscribe(provider);

provider.Trade(new Stocks()); provider.Trade(new Stocks());
provider.Trade(null); provider.End();
...
```

This chapter covered Observer Pattern, along with its implementation, as well as UML diagram.

## CHAPTER 4

Template Method Pattern

IN THIS CHAPTER

➤ What is Template Method Pattern?

➤ Real-world examples

➤ Why is Template Method Pattern useful?

➤ Advantages/disadvantages

➤ Implementation in Python

➤ UML diagram

In the previous chapter, we covered the Observer Method, and in this chapter, we will cover Template Pattern Method with its relevant examples.

The Template Method Design Pattern specifies the skeleton of an algorithm in an operation while delegating some phases to subclasses. This pattern allows subclasses to redefine specific phases of an algorithm without affecting the algorithm's structure. We may use the Template Method Design Pattern to develop a base class with a certain number of steps required to finish a procedure. When these stages are defined using a template, building one or more concrete classes and overriding the template steps is possible. This allows you to implement part or all of the phases, depending on the specific class, without rewriting the whole process.

DOI: 10.1201/9781003308461-4

We need an abstract class to utilize the Template Method. The abstract class is one extensive process that has been split into smaller phases or subsidiary processes. Put another way, the abstract class will call the Template Method (the main process), and inside the template will call the smaller steps that finish the significant process. These smaller procedures will be implemented as methods/functions that the actual classes may call.

We don't have to instantiate the whole base class to access the steps provided by the Template function since we're using an abstract class. Instead, we may build abstract class subclasses and replace just the steps we require in the specific subclasses.

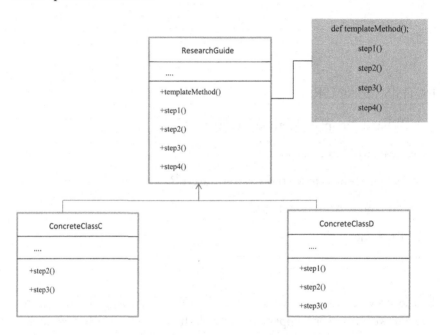

Class Diagram of Template Method Design Pattern.

After defining the abstract class, we can develop the concrete classes that will replace the required steps. To do this, we'll employ an inheritance connection. Depending on the context of the particular class, we will override all or parts of the stages.

THE FACTORY METHOD VS. THE TEMPLATE METHOD

There is considerable misunderstanding about the distinctions between the Template Method Pattern and the Factory Method Pattern. Their structures are similar, even though they are not the same entity. A Creational

Pattern used to construct objects from a superclass is the Factory Method. On the other hand, the Template Method is a Behavioral Pattern that is used to construct a generic method made of steps that may be customized by subclasses of the abstract class that contains the Template Method.

In other words, the Factory Method generates objects, while the Template Method replaces the functionality of a significant/base process.

Now that we've established the distinction between these patterns, let's look at using the Template Method Design Pattern in Python.

It should note that without using a special library, Python does not allow abstract classes. We must import the ABC library to utilize abstract class associations.

THE ABC LIBRARY

The ABC package in Python offers an infrastructure for maintaining abstract base classes. This implies we may build class connections such as inheritance or implementations for abstract classes, which is essential for implementing most Design Patterns and is especially significant in the case of the Template Method.

WHEN SHOULD THE TEMPLATE METHOD PATTERN BE USED?

When you need to utilize or alter any or all of the stages of an algorithm, you should use the Template Method. In these circumstances, you will need to separate the phases of your algorithm or process and make them independently available via inheritance or implementation.

Let's look at a real-world example: We have two research groups, one from University A and one from University B. These two organizations are researching the impacts of quarantine, which was adopted by nations in response to the SARS-CoV-2 epidemic. The basic research procedure is the same for both groups. The basic research procedure serves as a pattern for the two research groups to follow while conducting their examination. However, research organizations may tailor the research process in terms of:

- Which measures are taken throughout the research.

- How each phase of the research process is carried out.

Before writing Python code, let's draw a class diagram to illustrate this study.

The research protocol consists of four steps:

- University A chooses to implement two of the four steps (2 and 3).

- The three stages are used by University B (1, 3, and 4).

- Both groups altered all of the selected stages.

- Finally, both groups must do step 3 since it is required.

We already have our class diagram; we just need to modify it to fit our problem.

After modifying the diagram to fit the conditions we specified, we arrive at the following model:

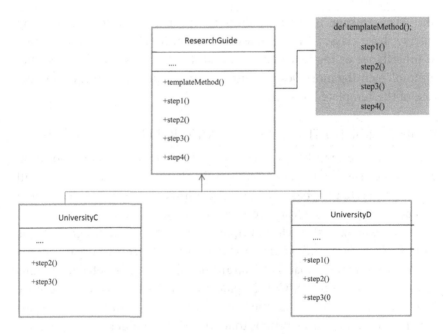

Modify Class Diagram of Template Method Design Pattern.

USING PYTHON TO IMPLEMENT THE TEMPLATE METHOD DESIGN PATTERN

Now that we've sketched out our abstract and concrete classes let's put them into action in Python.

Let's begin with our abstract class, researchGuideline.py, which will contain our Template Methods for the four significant research steps.

We'll start by importing the ABC library. This library includes a class called ABC, which we'll use as a superclass for our research template, transforming it into an abstract base class.

Following that, we'll define our steps as class methods. These methods will be empty for the time being, but when the subclasses are defined, they will overwrite the steps:

```python
# Importing ABC library
from abc import ABC, abstractmethod

# Creation of our abstract class:
class ResearchGuideline(ABC):

    # Template Method definition:
    def templateMethod(self):
        # Calling all the steps
        self.step1()
        self.step2()
        self.step3()
        self.step4()

    # Defining Template Method Steps
    def step1(self):
        pass

    def step2(self):
        pass

    @abstractmethod
    def step3(self):
        pass

    def step4(self):
        pass
```

Step 3 now includes the @abstractmethod decorator. This demonstrates that subclasses of an abstract class must always overwrite that method. This decorator must include in the imports because it is also part of the ABC library.

Let us now define our concrete classes. We're talking about Universities A and B, each with its own steps. Using the ResearchGuideline template, we will create a subclass for each university.

We must import the ResearchGuideline class into both classes and establish inheritance between the superclass and the subclass. This enables us to overwrite the steps defined in the guideline/template. In this case, the steps will apply through a simple log/print.

Let's begin with the most basic subclass:

```python
from researchGuideline import ResearchGuideline

class UniversityA(ResearchGuideline):
    def step2(self):
        print("Step 2 - Applied by University C")

    def step3(self):
        print("Step 3 - Applied by University D")
```

This will save in a Python file named universityC. Let us now create the second subclass:

```python
from researchGuideline import ResearchGuideline

class UniversityB(ResearchGuideline):
    def step1(self):
        print("Step 1- Applied by University D")

    def step3(self):
        print("Step 3- Applied by University D")

    def step4(self):
        print("Step 4- Applied by University D")
```

This will be saved in a Python file named universityD.

It's worth noting that we've mentioned which university is taking various actions. This allows us to appreciate the differences between the two concrete groups.

Our Template Method Model, including the abstract and concrete classes, is complete! Now, let's write our client script to use the model.

Let's start by importing our classes. Importing the abstract class as well as the two concrete classes is required. Then, as our template/abstract class, we'll write a function that takes a ResearchGuideline object as a parameter.

The beauty of the inheritance relationship is that the university classes share the same object type because they are subclasses of ResearchGuideline.

We can pass either the UniversityC or UniversityD object as an argument to our function that calls the Template Method (client_call()), and the steps overwritten by the concrete class will change how the Template Method executes.

We use both classes here so that we can compare the results:

```python
# Imports
from researchGuideline import *
from universityA import UniversityC
from universityB import UniversityD

# Auxiliary function
def client_call(research_guideline: ResearchGuideline):
    research_guideline.templateMethod();

# Entry point
if __name__ == '__main__':
    # Calling Template Method using the University A class
as parameter
    print("University C:")
    client_call(UniversityC())

    # Calling Template Method using the University A class
as parameter
    print("University D:")
    client_call(UniversityD())
```

ADVANTAGES

- **Equivalent Content:** It's simple to think about the duplicate code in the superclass by dragging it there where you wish to utilize it.

- **Flexibility:** It gives a great deal of flexibility, allowing subclasses to choose how to implement the stages of the algorithms.

- **Inheritance:** We can reuse our code since the Template Method leverages inheritance, allowing code reusability.

DISADVANTAGES

- **Complex Code:** When employing the Template approach, the code might grow so complex that it is difficult to comprehend even for developers developing it.

- **Limitations:** Clients may request an enhanced version if they see a lack of algorithms in the offered skeleton.

- **Violation:** By utilizing the Template approach, you may wind up breaking the Liskov Substitution Principle, which is not a good thing to do.

APPLICABILITY

- **Client Extension:** This strategy is always chosen when you wish to allow customers to extend the algorithm using certain stages but not the whole structure of the algorithm.

- **Similar Algorithms:** When you have several similar algorithms with slight differences, it's always preferable to utilize the Template Design Pattern since if any changes occur in the algorithm, you won't have to alter each one.

- **Framework Development:** It is strongly advised to adopt the Template Design Pattern while constructing a framework since it will assist us in avoiding duplicate code as well as reusing the piece of code again and again by making minor modifications.

USAGE

- It is used when similar behavior among subclasses should relocate to a single standard class to reduce duplication.

- In this chapter, we will cover Template Pattern, where we covered real-life examples, advantages, disadvantages, and applicability.

IMPORTANT POINTS

1. The Template Method Pattern employs inheritance.

2. The Template Method of the base class should no overridden. In this manner, the superclass controls the framework of the algorithm, while the specifics are handled in the subclasses.

TEMPLATE METHOD PATTERN IMPLEMENTATION IN JAVA

- **Step 1:** Create an abstract class called Game.

```java
//This is abstract class.
public abstract class Game {

    abstract void initialize();
    abstract void start();
    abstract void end();

    public final void play(){

        //initialize-game
        initialize();

        //start-game
        start();

        //end-game
        end();
    }
}// End of Game abstract class
```

- **Step 2:** Create a Chess class that extends the Game abstract class to define its function.

```java
//This is class.

public class Chess extends Game {
    @Override
      void initialize() {
         System.out.println("Chess Game Initialized!
Start playing.");
      }
    @Override
      void start() {
         System.out.println("Game Started and Welcome
to the chess game");
      }
    @Override
      void end() {
         System.out.println("Game Finished!");
      }
}// End of Chess class.
```

- **Step 3:** Create a Soccer class that extends the Game abstract class to define its function.

```java
//This is class.


public class Soccer extends Game {

   @Override
     void initialize() {
        System.out.println("Soccer Game Initialized
and Start playing.");
        }

   @Override
     void start() {
        System.out.println("Game Started and Welcome
to the Soccer game!");
        }

   @Override
     void end() {
        System.out.println("Game Ended!");
        }
}// End of Soccer class.
```

- **Step 4:** Make a class called TemplatePatternDemo.

```java
//This is class.
public class TemplatePatternDemo {

   public static void main(String[] args) throws
InstantiationException, IllegalAccessException,
ClassNotFoundException {

            Class cl=Class.forName(args[0]);
            Game game=(Game) cl.newInstance();
            game.play();
        }
    }// End of Soccer class.
```

Code Example

```
import java.util.List; class GameRule{
}
class GameInfo{ String gameName;
List<String> players;
List<GameRule> rules;
}

abstract class Game{ protected GameInfo info;
   public Game(GameInfo info){ this.info = info;
   }
   public abstract void createGame();
public abstract void makeMoves();
public abstract void applyRules();

   /* playGame is the template method. This algorithm
skeleton cannot change by sub-classes. sub-class can
change behaviour only of steps like createGame() etc.
*/

   public void playGame(){
createGame();
makeMoves();
applyRules();
closeGame();
   }
   protected void closeGame(){
   System.out.println("Close-game:"+this.getClass().
getName()); System.out.println("   ");
   }
   }
   class Chess extends Game{
   public Chess(GameInfo info){ super(info);
   }
   public void createGame(){
   // Use GameInfo and create Game System.out.
println("Creating Chess game");
   }
   public void makeMoves(){
System.out.println("Make the Chess moves");
   }
   public void applyRules(){
System.out.println("Apply the Chess rules");
   }
   }
```

```java
class Checkers extends Game{
public Checkers(GameInfo info){ super(info);
}
public void createGame(){
// Use GameInfo and create the Game System.out.
println("Creating Checkers game");
}
public void makeMoves(){
System.out.println("Make the Checkers moves");
}
public void applyRules(){
System.out.println("Apply the Checkers rules");
}


}
class Ludo extends Game{
public Ludo(GameInfo info){ super(info);
}
public void createGame(){
// Use GameInfo and create Game System.out.
println("Creating the Ludo game");
}
public void makeMoves(){ System.out.println("Make
the Ludo moves");
}
public void applyRules(){ System.out.println("Apply
the Ludo rules");
}
}

public class TemplateMethodPattern{
public static void main(String args[]){
System.out.println("   ");

Game game = new Chess(new GameInfo()); game.playGame();

game = new Ludo(new GameInfo()); game.playGame();

game = new Checkers(new GameInfo()); game.playGame();
}
}
```

Explanation:

1. Game is an abstract superclass with a template function called playGame().

2. The playGame() skeleton is defined in the base class: Game.

3. Subclasses, such as Chess, Ludo, and Checkers, cannot modify the skeleton of playGame (). They can, however, change the behavior of some processes.

TEMPLATE METHOD IN C#

Participants

This pattern's classes and objects are as follows:

- AbstractClass (DataObject) contains abstract primitive operations that concrete subclasses specify to accomplish algorithm stages. It also implements a template function that defines the skeleton of an algorithm. The template method invokes primitive operations and AbstractClass operations, and those of additional objects.

- ConcreteClass (CustomerDataObject) implements the primitive operations required to carry out the algorithm's subclass-specific phases.

C# Structural Code

This structure code showcases the Template Method, which offers a skeleton method call sequence. One or more stages can delegate to subclasses that implement them without altering the overall calling sequence.

```
using System;
namespace Template.Structural
{
    /// <summary> Template Design Pattern </summary>
    public class Program
    {
        public static void Main(string[] args)
        {
            AbstractClass aX = new ConcreteClassX();
            aX.TemplateMethod();
            AbstractClass aY = new ConcreteClassY();
            aY.TemplateMethod();
            // Wait for the user
            Console.ReadKey();
        }
    }
    /// <summary> 'AbstractClass' abstract class </summary>
    public abstract class AbstractClass
    {
```

```csharp
        public abstract void PrimitiveOperation1();
        public abstract void PrimitiveOperation2();
        //"Template-method"
        public void TemplateMethod()
        {
            PrimitiveOperation1();
            PrimitiveOperation2();
            Console.WriteLine("");
        }
    }
    /// <summary> 'ConcreteClass' class </summary>
    public class ConcreteClassX : AbstractClass
    {
        public override void PrimitiveOperation1()
        {
            Console.WriteLine("ConcreteClassX.
PrimitiveOperation1()");
        }
        public override void PrimitiveOperation2()
        {
            Console.WriteLine("ConcreteClassX.
PrimitiveOperation2()");
        }
    }
    /// <summary> 'ConcreteClass' class </summary>
    public class ConcreteClassB : AbstractClass
    {
        public override void PrimitiveOperation1()
        {
            Console.WriteLine("ConcreteClassY.
PrimitiveOperation1()");
        }
        public override void PrimitiveOperation2()
        {
            Console.WriteLine("ConcreteClassY.
PrimitiveOperation2()");
        }
    }
}
```

Real-World C# Code

This real-world code shows a Template function called Run(), which gives a Skeleton Pattern calling sequence. The CustomerDataObject subclass, which implements the Connect, Select, Process, and Disconnect methods, is responsible for carrying out these tasks.

```csharp
using System;
using System.Collections.Generic;

namespace Template.RealWorld
{
    /// <summary> Template Design Pattern </summary>

    public class Program
    {
        public static void Main(string[] args)
        {
            DataAccessor categories = new Categories();
            categories.Run(5);

            DataAccessor products = new Products();
            products.Run(3);

            // Wait for the user

            Console.ReadKey();
        }
    }

    /// <summary> The 'AbstractClass' abstract class
</summary>

    public abstract class DataAccessor
    {
        public abstract void Connect();
        public abstract void Select();
        public abstract void Process(int top);
        public abstract void Disconnect();

        //'Template-Method'

        public void Run(int top)
        {
            Connect();
            Select();
            Process(top);
            Disconnect();
        }
    }

    /// <summary> 'ConcreteClass' class </summary>

    public class Categories : DataAccessor
    {
        private List<string> categories;
```

```csharp
    public override void Connect()
    {
        categories = new List<string>();
    }

    public override void Select()
    {
        categories.Add("Black");
        categories.Add("Grey");
        categories.Add("Blue");
        categories.Add("Green");
        categories.Add("Yellow");
        categories.Add("Pink");
        categories.Add("Orange");
    }

    public override void Process(int top)
    {
        Console.WriteLine("Categories.. ");

        for(int x = 0; x < top; x++)
        {
            Console.WriteLine(categories[x]);
        }

        Console.WriteLine();
    }

    public override void Disconnect()
    {
        categories.Clear();
    }
}

/// <summary> A 'ConcreteClass' class </summary>

public class Products : DataAccessor
{
    private List<string> products;

    public override void Connect()
    {
        products = new List<string>();
    }

    public override void Select()
    {
        products.Add("Bike");
```

```
        products.Add("Boat");
        products.Add("Car ");
        products.Add("Moped ");
        products.Add("Truck");
        products.Add("Stroller ");
        products.Add("Rollerskate");
    }

    public override void Process(int top)
    {
        Console.WriteLine("Products.. ");

        for (int x = 0; x < top; x++)
        {
            Console.WriteLine(products[i]);
        }

        Console.WriteLine();
    }

    public override void Disconnect()
    {
        products.Clear();
    }
    }
}
```

This chapter discussed the Template Method Pattern, including its representation and examples in Java, C# and Python.

## CHAPTER 5

Singleton Pattern

IN THIS CHAPTER

➢ What is Singleton Pattern?

➢ Real-world examples of Singleton Pattern

➢ Why is Singleton Pattern useful?

➢ Advantages/disadvantages

➢ Implementation in Python

➢ UML diagram

In the previous chapter, we covered the Template Method Pattern, and in this chapter, we will cover Singleton Pattern with its relevant examples.

The Singleton Pattern is a Creational Design Pattern and among the most fundamental Design Patterns we may use. It is a method of providing one and only one object of a particular type. It simply takes one class to define methods and identify objects.

According to the Singleton Pattern, "create a class that has only one instance and gives a global point of access."

In other words, a class must insure that only one instance is created and that all other classes may access only one object.

The Singleton Design Pattern comes in two varieties.

- **Early Instantiation:** The construction of an instance at the time of load.

- **Lazy instantiation:** Creating instances only when needed.

DOI: 10.1201/9781003308461-5

A basic example of a database connection will help you understand the Singleton Design Pattern. When each item makes a unique Database Connection to the Database, it significantly impacts the project's cost. As a result, it is always better to construct a single connection rather than numerous unrelated connections, as enabled by the Singleton Design Pattern.

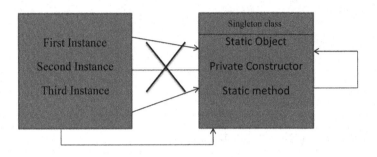

Pattern of Singleton.

MOTIVATION

This pattern is frequently used in features that require control over a shared resource, such as a database connection or a file. Access to the shared resource may be regulated and integrity preserved by guaranteeing that a class can only use to construct a single instance and giving a single global access point.

The use of single instances also ensures that some features of our programs are not rewritten by other classes, which may result in dangerous or inefficient code. This also allows us to access the same object from many places in our applications without the danger of it being overwritten at some time.

For example, database connections are once made in our applications, and the same object is utilized to conduct database actions. If distinct portions of our program could make their database connections, integrity concerns may occur when each part tries to access the database independently.

REAL-WORLD EXAMPLE

Consider this: a program on a server contains numerous sections, each of which creates its connection to a database and performs distinct actions on the database. Sounds crazy, doesn't it?

A Singleton lets us construct just one instance of the database connection, and that same object is used to do additional database actions in other portions of the program.

IMPLEMENTATION

The Singleton Pattern stipulates that a class can only be instantiated by one object. Implementing a creation method that saves the produced object in a static field gives you control over object creation.

All calls to this creation method either return the original Singleton object or an error indicating that an instantiated object already exists. This keeps the Singleton property and avoids generating multiple objects for our class.

A country can have a single government that controls access and operations, which is an excellent example of a Singleton Design. Any attempt to establish a new government is prohibited.

Let's have a look at the many Singleton Design Pattern implementations.

Method 1: Design Pattern of Monostate/Borg Singleton

Borg's pattern may be used to design Singleton behavior, but numerous instances share the same state instead of having just one instance of the class. We don't focus on sharing the instance identification here but rather on the sharing state.

```
# Singleton Borg pattern
class Borg:

    # Each instance shares a state
    __shared_state = dict()

    # constructor-method
    def __init__(self):

        self.__dict__ = self.__shared_state
        self.state = 'PeeksforPeeks'

    def __str__(self):

        return self.state

# main method
if __name__ == "__main__":
```

```
people1 = Borg()     # object of the class Borg
people2 = Borg()     # object of the class Borg
people3 = Borg()     # object of the class Borg

people1.state = 'DataStructure' # people1 changed state
people2.state = 'Algorithm'     # people2 changed state

print(people1)     # output --> Algorithms
print(people2)     # output --> Algorithms

people3.state = 'Peeks'  # people3 changed
                         # the shared state

print(people1)     # output --> Peeks
print(people2)     # output --> Peeks
print(people3)     # output --> Peeks
```

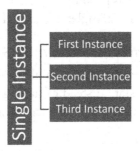

Design Pattern of Singleton.

It is simple to see that thread synchronization is no longer relevant after an object is formed because the object will never be equal to None, and any sequence of actions will provide consistent results.

So, when the object is equal to None, we will only obtain the Lock on the getInstance function.

```
# Double Checked Locking singleton-pattern
import threading
class SingletonDoubleChecked(object):

    # resources shared by every instance

    __singleton_lock = threading.Lock()
    __singleton_instance = None
```

```
# define classmethod
@classmethod
def instance(cls):

    # check for singleton instance
    if not cls.__singleton_instance:
        with cls.__singleton_lock:
            if not cls.__singleton_instance:
                cls.__singleton_instance = cls()

    # return singleton instance
    return cls.__singleton_instance

# main method
if __name__ == '__main__':

    # create class C
    class C(SingletonDoubleChecked):
        pass

    # create class D
    class D(SingletonDoubleChecked):
        pass

    A1, A2 = C.instance(), C.instance()
    B1, B2 = D.instance(), D.instance()

    assert A1 is not B1
    assert A1 is A2
    assert B1 is B2

    print('A1 : ', A1)
    print('A2 : ', A2)
    print('B1 : ', B1)
    print('B2 : ', B2)
```

CLASSIC IMPLEMENTATION OF SINGLETON DESIGN PATTERN

In the implementation of the Singleton Design Pattern, we utilize the static method to create the getInstance method, which can return the shared resource. We also utilize the so-called Virtual Private Constructor to raise an exception against it, though this is not strictly necessary.

```
# classic implementation of the Singleton Design pattern
class Singleton:

    __shared_instance = 'PeeksforPeeks'
```

```
        @staticmethod
        def getInstance():

            """Static Access Method"""
            if Singleton.__shared_instance == 'PeeksforPeeks':
                Singleton()
            return Singleton.__shared_instance

        def __init__(self):

            """virtual private constructor"""
            if Singleton.__shared_instance != 'PeeksforPeeks':
                raise Exception ("This class is singleton
class !")
            else:
                Singleton.__shared_instance = self

# main-method
if __name__ == "__main__":

    # create object of the Singleton Class
    obj = Singleton()
    print(obj)

    # pick instance of the class
    obj = Singleton.getInstance()
    print(obj)
```

CLASS DIAGRAM

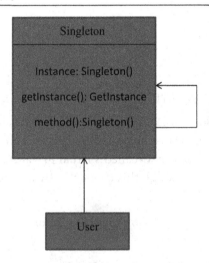

Class Diagram of Singleton.

BENEFITS OF USING THE SINGLETON PATTERN

- **Initializations:** An object generated by the Singleton Pattern is only initialized the first time it is requested.

- **Obtaining access to the object:** We gained global access to the object's instance.

- **Count of occurrences:** Classes that use the Singleton Method can only have one instance.

DISADVANTAGES OF EMPLOYING THE SINGLETON PATTERN

- **An environment with Multiple Threads:** It is challenging to utilize the Singleton Pattern in a multithread environment because we must ensure that the multithread does not build the Singleton object multiple times.

- **Principle of exclusive responsibility:** Because the Singleton technique solves two issues at once, it violates the idea of single responsibility.

- **Procedure for unit testing:** Because they add a global state into the program, unit testing becomes very difficult.

APPLICABILITY

- **Controlling global variables:** In projects where we explicitly require tight control over global variables, it is highly suggested to adopt the Singleton Pattern.

- Singleton Patterns are often combined with the Factory Design Pattern to provide logging, caching, thread pools, and configuration settings.

USAGE OF SINGLETON DESIGN PATTERN

The Singleton pattern is commonly used in multithreaded and database applications. It is utilized in logging, caching, thread pools, and configuration settings, among other things.

How to Implement the Singleton Design Pattern in Java

We require a static member of the class, a private constructor, and a static factory function to build a Singleton class.

- **Static member:** It only uses memory once since it is static, and it includes an instance of the Singleton class.

- **Private constructor:** This prevents the Singleton class from instantiating from outside the class.

- **Static factory method:** This method gives the Singleton object's global point of access and returns the instance to the caller.

UNDERSTANDING EARLY SINGLETON PATTERN INSTANTIATION

In this scenario, we construct the class instance when we declare the static data member; therefore, the class instance is formed during classloading.

Let's look at an example of a Singleton Design Pattern that uses early instantiation.

```
class X{
   private static X obj=new X();//Early, instance will
create at load time
   private A(){}

   public static X getX(){
     return obj;
   }

   public void doSomething(){
   //write our code
   }
}
```

UNDERSTANDING THE LAZY SINGLETON INSTANTIATION PATTERN

In such cases, we build the class instance in a synchronized method or synchronized block, so that the class instance is produced only when needed.

Let's look at a basic Singleton Design Pattern utilizing lazy instantiation.

```
class X{
    private static X obj;
    private X(){}

    public static X getX(){
        if (obj == null){
            synchronized(Singleton.class){
                if (obj == null){
                    obj = new Singleton();//instance will create
at request time
                }
            }
        }
        return obj;
    }

    public void doSomething(){
    //write our code
    }
}
```

IMPORTANCE OF SERIALIZATION IN THE SINGLETON PATTERN

If the Singleton class is Serializable, the Singleton instance can serialize. We can deserialize it once it has been serialized, but it will not return the Singleton object.

We must override the readResolve() function to fix this problem, which enforces the Singleton. It is invoked immediately after the object has been deserialized. It gives back the Singleton object.

```
public class X implements Serializable {
    //your code of singleton
    protected Object readResolve() {
        return getX();
    }
}
```

UNDERSTANDING A REAL-WORLD EXAMPLE OF THE SINGLETON PATTERN

- We will construct a JDBCSingleton class. This JDBCSingleton class has a private constructor and a private static instance jdbc of itself.

- The JDBCSingleton class has a static method for exposing its static instance to the outside world. JDBCSingletonDemo will now use the JDBCSingleton class to obtain the JDBCSingleton object.

ASSUMPTION

In our MySQL database, you have built a table called userdata with three fields: uid, uname, and upassword. The database's name is kashikakaur, the username is the root, and the password is root1234.

File: JDBCSingleton.java

```java
import java.io.BufferedReader;
import java.io.IOException;
import java.io.InputStreamReader;
import java.sql.Connection;
import java.sql.DriverManager;
import java.sql.PreparedStatement;
import java.sql.ResultSet;
import java.sql.SQLException;

class JDBCSingleton {
    //Step1
    // create JDBCSingleton class.
    //static member holds only one instance of JDBCSingleton
class

        private static JDBCSingleton jdbc;

    //JDBCSingleton prevents instantiation from any other
class
        private JDBCSingleton() {  }

    //we are providing gloabal point of the access
        public static JDBCSingleton getInstance() {
                                if (jdbc==null)
                                {
                                        jdbc=new
JDBCSingleton();
                                }
                        return jdbc;
        }
```

```
    // to get connection from the methods like insert,
view, etc.
        private static Connection getConnection()throws
ClassNotFoundException, SQLException
        {

            Connection con=null;
            Class.forName("com.mysql.jdbc.Driver");
            con= DriverManager.
getConnection("jdbc:mysql://localhost:3306/kashikakaur",
"root", "root1234");
            return con;


        }

 //to insert record into a database
        public int insert(String name, String pass)
throws SQLException
        {
            Connection c=null;

            PreparedStatement ps=null;

            int recordCounter=0;

            try {

                c1=this.getConnection();
                ps=c1.prepareStatement("insert into
userdata(uname,upassword)values(?,?)");
                ps.setString(1, name);
                ps.setString(2, pass);
                recordCounter=ps.executeUpdate();

            } catch (Exception e) { e.printStackTrace();
} finally{
                if (ps!=null){
                ps.close();
                }if(c1!=null){
                C1.close();
                }
            }
            return recordCounter;
        }
//to view data from the database
    public  void view(String name) throws SQLException
        {
            Connection con = null;
```

```java
        PreparedStatement ps = null;
        ResultSet rs = null;

            try {

                    con=this.getConnection();
                    ps=con.prepareStatement("select *
from userdata where uname=?");
                    ps.setString(1, name);
                    rs=ps.executeQuery();
                    while (rs.next()) {
                            System.out.println("Name=
"+rs.getString(2)+"\t"+"Paasword= "+rs.getString(3));

                    }

            } catch (Exception e) { System.out.println(e);}
            finally{
                    if(rs!=null){
                        rs.close();
                    }if (ps!=null){
                      ps.close();
                    }if(con!=null){
                      con.close();
                    }
                }
        }

    // to update password for given username
    public int update(String name, String password)
throws SQLException  {
            Connection c=null;
            PreparedStatement ps=null;

            int recordCounter=0;
            try {
                    c1=this.getConnection();
                    ps=c.prepareStatement(" update
userdata set upassword=? where uname='"+name+"' ");
                    ps.setString(1, password);
                    recordCounter=ps.executeUpdate();
            } catch (Exception e) {  e.printStackTrace();
} finally{

                if (ps!=null){
                    ps.close();
                }if(c1!=null){
                    c1.close();
```

```
                    }
                }
            return recordCounter;
        }

// to delete the data from database
        public int delete(int userid) throws SQLException{
            Connection c=null;
            PreparedStatement ps=null;
            int recordCounter=0;
            try {
                    c1=this.getConnection();
                    ps=c1.prepareStatement(" delete from
userdata where uid='"+userid+"' ");
                    recordCounter=ps.executeUpdate();
            } catch (Exception e) { e.printStackTrace(); }
            finally{
            if (ps!=null){
                    ps.close();
            }if(c1!=null){
                    c1.close();
            }
        }
            return recordCounter;
        }
    }// End of JDBCSingleton class
```

File: JDBCSingletonDemo.java

```
import java.io.BufferedReader;
import java.io.IOException;
import java.io.InputStreamReader;
import java.sql.Connection;
import java.sql.DriverManager;
import java.sql.PreparedStatement;
import java.sql.ResultSet;
import java.sql.SQLException;
class JDBCSingletonDemo{
    static int count=1;
    static int  choice;
    public static void main(String[] args) throws
IOException {

        JDBCSingleton jdbc= JDBCSingleton.getInstance();
```

```
        BufferedReader br=new BufferedReader
(new InputStreamReader(System.in));
   do{
        System.out.println("DATABASE-OPERATIONS");
        System.out.println(" --------------------- ");
        System.out.println(" 1. Insert ");
        System.out.println(" 2. View       ");
        System.out.println(" 3. Delete     ");
        System.out.println(" 4. Update     ");
        System.out.println(" 5. Exit       ");

        System.out.print("\n");
        System.out.print("Enter the choice of what we want
to perform in database: ");

        choice=Integer.parseInt(br.readLine());
        switch(choice) {

        case 1:{
                System.out.print("Enter username we
want to insert data into database: ");
                String username=br.readLine();
                System.out.print("Enter password we
want to insert data into database: ");
                String password=br.readLine();

                try {
                        int x= jdbc.insert(username,
password);
                        if (x>0) {
                        System.out.println((count++) +
" Data has insert successfully");
                        }else{
                                System.out.println("Data
has not inserted ");
                        }

                } catch (Exception e) {
                  System.out.println(e);
                }

                System.out.println("Enter key to
continue");
                System.in.read();

        }//End of the case 1
        break;
     case 2:{
```

```
                    System.out.print("Enter username : ");
                    String username=br.readLine();

                    try {
                            jdbc.view(username);
                         } catch (Exception e) {
                          System.out.println(e);
                         }
                    System.out.println("Enter key to
continue");
                    System.in.read();

                 }//End of the case 2
                break;
            case 3:{
                    System.out.print("Enter the
userid,  we want to delete: ");
                    int userid=Integer.parseInt
(br.readLine());

                    try {
                            int x= jdbc.delete(userid);
                            if (x>0) {
                            System.out.println((count++)
+ " Data has delete successfully");
                            }else{
                                System.out.println("Data
has not delete");
                            }

                        } catch (Exception e) {
                          System.out.println(e);
                         }
                    System.out.println("Enter key to
continue");
                    System.in.read();

                 }//End of the case 3
                break;
            case 4:{
                    System.out.print("Enter username,  we
want to update: ");
                    String username=br.readLine();
                    System.out.print("Enter new
password ");
                    String password=br.readLine();

                    try {
```

```
                      int x= jdbc.update(username,
password);

                      if (x>0) {
                      System.out.println((count++)
+ " Data has update successfully");
                      }

                } catch (Exception e) {
                   System.out.println(e);
                }
                System.out.println("Enter key to
continue");

                System.in.read();

                }// end of the case 4
             break;

          default:
                return;
      }

      } while (choice!=4);
   }
}
```

C# Singleton Pattern

Participants

This pattern's classes and objects are as follows:

Solitary (LoadBalancer)

- It provides an Instance operation that allows customers to access its one-of-a-kind instance. Instance is a type of class operation.

- It is in charge of generating and maintaining its distinct instance.

C# Structural Code

This structured code exhibits the Singleton pattern, which ensures that just one instance of the class (the Singleton) may be produced.

```
using System;

namespace Singleton.Structural
{
```

```csharp
/// <summary> Singleton Design Pattern </summary>

public class Program
{
    public static void Main(string[] args)
    {
        // Constructor is protected - can't use new

        Singleton ss1 = Singleton.Instance();
        Singleton ss2 = Singleton.Instance();

        // Test for same instance

        if (ss1 == ss2)
        {
            Console.WriteLine("Objects are same instance");
        }

        // Wait for the user

        Console.ReadKey();
    }
}

/// <summary> The 'Singleton' class </summary>

public class Singleton
{
    static Singleton instance;

    // Constructor : 'protected'

    protected Singleton()
    {
    }

    public static Singleton Instance()
    {
        // Uses the lazy initialization.
        // Note: this is not thread safe.
        if (instance == null)
        {
            instance = new Singleton();
        }

        return instance;
    }
}
```

Real-World C# Code

As a LoadBalancing object, this real-world code shows the Singleton Design. Because servers may come on- or off-line dynamically, only a single instance (the Singleton) of the class may be constructed, and every request must go via the one object that knows the state of the (web) farm.

```csharp
using System;
using System.Collections.Generic;

namespace Singleton.RealWorld
{
    /// <summary> Singleton Design Pattern </summary>

    public class Program
    {
        public static void Main(string[] args)
        {
            LoadBalancer bb1 = LoadBalancer
.GetLoadBalancer();
            LoadBalancer bb2 = LoadBalancer
.GetLoadBalancer();
            LoadBalancer bb3 = LoadBalancer
.GetLoadBalancer();
            LoadBalancer bb4 = LoadBalancer
.GetLoadBalancer();

            // Same instance?

            if (bb1 == bb2 && bb2 == bb3 && bb3 == bb4)
            {
                Console.WriteLine("Same-instance\n");
            }

            // Load-balance 15 server requests

            LoadBalancer balancer = LoadBalancer.
GetLoadBalancer();
            for (int x = 0; x < 15; x++)
            {
                string server = balancer.Server;
                Console.WriteLine("Dispatch the Request to: "
+ server);
            }

            // Wait for the user
```

```
            Console.ReadKey();
        }
    }

    /// <summary> The 'Singleton' class </summary>

    public class LoadBalancer
    {
        static LoadBalancer instance;
        List<string> servers = new List<string>();
        Random random = new Random();

        // Lock the synchronization object

        private static object locker = new object();

        // Constructor-(protected)

        protected LoadBalancer()
        {
            // List of the available servers
            servers.Add("ServerI");
            servers.Add("ServerII");
            servers.Add("ServerIII");
            servers.Add("ServerIV");
            servers.Add("ServerV");
        }

        public static LoadBalancer GetLoadBalancer()
        {
            // Support the multithreaded applications
through
            // 'Double checked locking' pattern which
            // (once instance exists) avoids the locking
each
            // time the method is invoked

            if (instance == null)
            {
                lock (locker)
                {
                    if (instance == null)
                    {
                        instance = new LoadBalancer();
                    }
                }
            }

            return instance;
        }
```

```
        // Random load balancer that is simple but
effective

        public string Server
        {
            get
            {
                int r1 = random.Next(servers.Count);
                return servers[r1].ToString();
            }
        }
    }
}
```

This chapter covered Singleton Design Pattern, along with its implementation, benefits, and drawbacks.

## CHAPTER 6

Strategy Pattern

IN THIS CHAPTER

> ➤ What is Strategy Pattern?

> ➤ Real-world examples

> ➤ Why is Strategy Pattern useful?

> ➤ Advantages/disadvantages

> ➤ Implementation in Python

> ➤ UML diagram

In the previous chapter, we covered Singleton Design Pattern, and in this chapter, we will discuss Strategy Pattern.

We may have difficulties implementing the functionality we want while designing software applications. Software Design Patterns are standard solutions to some of these issues that arise when utilizing object-oriented design to construct software applications. In this piece, we'll look at one of the most common Design Patterns, the Strategy Pattern, and how it's implemented in Python.

INTRODUCTION

Before delving into the Strategy Pattern, we need be familiar with some of the core concepts of Object-Oriented Programming (OOP). Classes and objects are at the heart of the Design Pattern notion. The Design Patterns are higher-level solutions to problems that arise frequently. They serve as

DOI: 10.1201/9781003308461-6

a roadmap for resolving a specific issue. They aren't restricted to just one programming language. Design Patterns may be used in any programming language that supports OOP; the same approach, but the terminology varies.

Types of Design Pattern.

Design Patterns are divided into creational, structural, and behavioral categories. Different approaches to constructing things that boost the flexibility of our programs are referred to as creational patterns. Structural Patterns are about object relationships and using objects and classes to make bigger structures more flexible. Effective communications and interactions between objects are the focus of Behavioral Patterns.

STRATEGY

The Strategy Pattern is a Design Pattern that allows our program to choose algorithms during runtime, making it more adaptable. "Strategy Pattern attempts to describe a family of algorithms, encapsulates each one, and makes them interchangeable." More precisely, it allows us to specify a collection of algorithms that may swap out at runtime based on specific variables. The Strategy Pattern belongs to the behavioral Design Patterns category since it allows an algorithm's behavior to be changed during runtime.

USAGE

We may have a few options for doing anything in our code while designing software applications. We may wish to do something different without modifying the code depending on our client's preferences, data sources, or other considerations. In the main class of the code, we frequently use conditional statements to construct algorithms for various scenarios.

However, it is not an elegant method of improving code. It lengthens the primary class of our code, making it difficult to maintain the program.

The Strategy Pattern is an excellent choice in these circumstances. The Strategy Pattern advises that we create classes for our algorithms, referred to as strategies. The context variable refers to the strategy in the main class, and the code reacts to that scenario. The case's context does not choose a suitable approach. Instead, the customer informs the context of the intended strategy.

For example, if we have a chess app, we may choose between easy, medium, and high difficulty levels. The computer selects an algorithm based on the level we select. It's one of the most effective instances of the Strategy Pattern in action.

The Open/Close concept governs the Strategy Pattern; a software program is open for extension but closed for alteration. It implies we may add as many new tactics as we like without changing the primary class. It makes our code more adaptable and maintainable.

UML DIAGRAMS

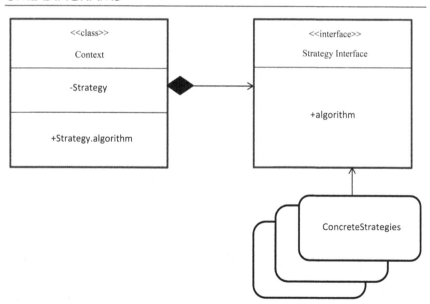

UML diagram of Strategy Pattern.

- **Context:** It is the most important class in our application. It keeps a reference to one of the concrete strategies.

- **Strategy:** All supported strategies use a single strategy interface. Only the strategy interface allows Context to communicate with other strategies.

- **ConcreteStrategies:** The classes use the Strategy interface to implement the algorithm.

IMPLEMENTATION

Let's look at how to implement a Strategy Pattern step by step.

1. In the primary class, we should first identify the algorithms we want to use as concrete strategies.

2. Add a reference to the strategy, a method to set the strategy, and another method to execute the strategy to the context (main class). We may also set a default strategy so that users only switch between strategies if they don't like the default.

```
## context - primary class
class Context:
    strategy: Strategy  ## strategy interface

    def setStrategy(self, strategy: Strategy = None)
-> None:
        if strategy is not None:
            self.strategy = strategy
        else:
            self.strategy = Default()

    def executeStrategy(self) -> str:
        print(self.strategy.execute())
```

We begin by defining the strategy field, which stores a reference to a strategy object and the setStrategy and executeStrategy functions. If a user selects an option, setStrategy sets the selected strategy; otherwise, it sets the default strategy.

3. Create a Strategy Interface that is shared by all concrete strategies. The abstract technique in the Strategy interface can change in concrete strategies.

```
from abc import ABC, abstractmethod

## Strategy-interface
class Strategy(ABC):
    @abstractmethod
    def execute(self) -> str:
        pass
```

4. Define the specific strategies that will use to implement the Strategy interface. These concrete strategies must share a method that overrides the Strategy interface's execute function.

```
## Concrete-strategies
class ConcreteStrategyC(Strategy):
    def execute(self) -> str:
        return "ConcreteStrategy C"

class ConcreteStrategyD(Strategy):
    def execute(self) -> str:
        return "ConcreteStrategy D"

class Default(Strategy):
    def execute(self) -> str:
        return "Default"
```

5. Users may now specify the approach they wish at runtime. Create a context object and give a concrete strategy.

```
## Example-application
appC = Context()
appD = Context()
appE = Context()

## selecting stratigies
appC.setStrategy(ConcreteStrategyC())
appD.setStrategy(ConcreteStrategyD())
appE.setStrategy()      ## sets to default strategy

## each object below execute different strategy with
the same method
appC.executeStrategy()
appD.executeStrategy()
appE.executeStrategy()
```

If we wish to utilize a different strategy, replace the ConcreteStrategy instance with the one we want. We can introduce a new concrete strategy without altering the context.

EXAMPLE

Let's use the Strategy Pattern to create a rock, paper, scissors game. To play against the computer, we can choose any strategy from rock, paper, scissors, or random. The Strategy Pattern is used in the example code below to implement multiple tactics.

```
## Changing strategy among Rock, Paper, Scissors, and
Random

import random
from abc import ABC, abstractmethod

## Strategy-interface
class Strategy(ABC):
    @abstractmethod
    def selection(self) -> None:
        pass

## Concrete-strategies
class Rock(Strategy):
    ## actual application will have the algorithm instead
this method
    def selection(self) -> str:
        return "Rock"

class Paper(Strategy):
    def selection(self) -> str:
        return "Paper"

class Scissors(Strategy):
    def selection(self) -> str:
        return "Scissors"

class Random(Strategy):
    def selection(self) -> str:
        options = ["Rock", "Paper", "Scissors"]
        return random.choice(options)

## Context-class
class Game:
    strategy: Strategy
```

```
    def __init__(self, strategy: Strategy = None) -> None:
        if strategy is not None:
            self.strategy = strategy
        else:
            self.strategy = Random()

    def play(self, sec) -> None:
        s1 = self.strategy.selection()
        s2 = sec.strategy.selection()
        if s1 == s2:
            print("It's tie")
        elif s1 == "Rock":
            if s2 == "Scissors":
                print("Player-1 wins!")
            else:
                print("Player-2 wins!")
        elif s1 == "Scissors":
            if s2 == "Paper":
                print("Player-1 wins!")
            else:
                print("Player-2 wins!")
        elif s1 == "Paper":
            if s2 == "Rock":
                print("Player-1 wins!")
            else:
                print("Player-2 wins!")

## Example-application
## Player-1 can select his strategy
player1 = Game(Paper())

# Player-2 gets to select
player2 = Game(Rock())

# After second player choice, we call play method
player1.play(player2)
```

BENEFITS

The open/closed concept states that it is always simple to implement new strategies without affecting the client's code.

- **Isolation:** We can separate the algorithms' unique implementation details from the client's code.

- **Encapsulation:** Strategy classes entirely encapsulate the data structures necessary to implement the algorithm. As a result, an algorithm's implementation may be altered without impacting the Context class.

- **Run-time Switching:** The program may be able to switch strategies while running.

DOWNSIDES

In most circumstances, the application configures the Context with the needed Strategy object. As a result, the program must generate and manage two instead of one object.

- **Client awareness:** Clients should be aware of the differences between the techniques to choose the best one for them.

- **Increases complexity:** When there are only a few algorithms to implement, the Strategy approach is a waste of time and resources.

APPLICABILITY

When we have many similar classes but differ in how they execute, this strategy is highly recommended.

Conquering Isolation is a technique for isolating a class's business logic from its algorithmic implementation.

Example of a Real-Time Strategy Pattern – Payment in Java

Let's look at a real-world example of the Strategy Design Pattern. Stella visits a shopping center and spends roughly Rs 80,000 on an LED television and a washing machine. After acquiring the LED TV and washing machines, Stella walks to the bill counter, and he wants to pay the money. There are three methods for paying the money. Credit card, debit card, and cash are the available alternatives. So, he must select one of these three alternatives and pay the money at the bill counter.

STRATEGY PATTERN IMPLEMENTATION IN JAVA

- **Step 1:** Create an interface for Strategy.

```java
//This is interface.

public interface Strategy {
```

```
    public float calculation(float x, float y);

}// End of Strategy interface.
```

- **Step 2:** Make an Addition class that implements the Startegy interface.

```
//This is class.
public class Addition implements Strategy{

    @Override
    public float calculation(float x, float y) {
        return x+y;
    }

}// End of Addition class.
```

- **Step 3:** Make a Subtraction class that implements the Startegy interface.

```
//This is class.
public class Subtraction  implements Strategy{

    @Override
    public float calculation(float x, float y) {
        return x-y;
    }

}// End of Subtraction class.
```

- **Step 4:** Make a Multiplication class that implements the Startegy interface.

```
//This is class.

public class Multiplication implements Strategy{

    @Override
```

```
    public float calculation(float x, float y){
        return x*y;
    }
}// End of Multiplication class.
```

- **Step 5:** Create Context class that will query the Startegy interface for the type of strategy to execute.

```
//This is class.


public class Context {

    private Strategy strategy;

    public Context(Strategy strategy){
        this.strategy = strategy;
    }

    public float executeStrategy(float numb1, float
numb2){
        return strategy.calculation(numb1, numb2);
    }
}// End of Context class.
```

- **Step 6:** Make a class called StartegyPatternDemo.

```
//This is a class.
import java.io.BufferedReader;
import java.io.IOException;
import java.io.InputStreamReader;

public class StrategyPatternDemo {

    public static void main(String[] args) throws
NumberFormatException, IOException {

        BufferedReader br=new BufferedReader(new
InputStreamReader(System.in));
        System.out.print("Enter first value: ");
        float value1=Float.parseFloat(br.
readLine());
```

```
            System.out.print("Enter second value: ");
            float value2=Float.parseFloat(br.
readLine());
            Context context = new Context(new
Addition());
            System.out.println("The Addition is = " +
context.executeStrategy(value1, value2));

            context = new Context(new Subtraction());
            System.out.println("Subtraction = " +
context.executeStrategy(value1, value2));

            context = new Context(new Multiplication());
            System.out.println("The Multiplication is =
" + context.executeStrategy(value1, value2));
        }

}// End of StrategyPatternDemo class.
```

C# Strategy Pattern

Participants

This pattern's classes and objects are as follows:

1. Strategy (SortStrategy)

   - It specifies an interface that is shared by all supported algorithms. Context calls the algorithm provided by a ConcreteStrategy using this interface.

2. ConcreteStrategy (QuickSort, ShellSort, MergeSort)

   - The Strategy interface is used to implement the algorithm.

3. Context (SortedList)

   - It contains a ConcreteStrategy object.

   - It keeps a reference to a Strategy object.

   - It may specify an interface via which Strategy can access its data.

C# Structural Code

This structural code exemplifies the Strategy Pattern, which encapsulates functionality in an object. This enables clients to modify algorithmic strategies.

```csharp
using System;

namespace Strategy.Structural
{
    /// <summary> Strategy Design Pattern </summary>

    public class Program
    {
        public static void Main(string[] args)
        {
            Context context;

            // Three contexts following the different
strategies

            context = new Context(new ConcreteStrategyA());
            context.ContextInterface();

            context = new Context(new ConcreteStrategyB());
            context.ContextInterface();

            context = new Context(new ConcreteStrategyC());
            context.ContextInterface();

            // Wait for the user

            Console.ReadKey();
        }
    }

    /// <summary> The 'Strategy' abstract class </summary>

    public abstract class Strategy
    {
        public abstract void AlgorithmInterface();
    }

    /// <summary> A 'ConcreteStrategy' class </summary>

    public class ConcreteStrategyA : Strategy
    {
        public override void AlgorithmInterface()
        {
            Console.WriteLine(
                "Called ConcreteStrategyA.
AlgorithmInterface()");
        }
    }
```

```csharp
    /// <summary> A 'ConcreteStrategy' class </summary>

    public class ConcreteStrategyB : Strategy
    {
        public override void AlgorithmInterface()
        {
            Console.WriteLine(
                "Called ConcreteStrategyB.
AlgorithmInterface()");
        }
    }

    /// <summary> A 'ConcreteStrategy' class </summary>

    public class ConcreteStrategyC : Strategy
    {
        public override void AlgorithmInterface()
        {
            Console.WriteLine(
                "Called ConcreteStrategyC.
AlgorithmInterface()");
        }
    }

    /// <summary> The 'Context' class </summary>

    public class Context
    {
        Strategy strategy;
        // Constructor

        public Context(Strategy strategy)
        {
            this.strategy = strategy;
        }

        public void ContextInterface()
        {
            strategy.AlgorithmInterface();
        }
    }
}
```

Real-World C# Code

The Strategy Pattern, which encapsulates sorting algorithms in the form of sorting objects, is demonstrated in this real-world code. This enables clients to change sorting techniques such as Quicksort, Shellsort, and Mergesort.

```csharp
using System;
using System.Collections.Generic;

namespace Strategy.RealWorld
{
    /// <summary> Strategy Design Pattern </summary>

    public class Program
    {
        public static void Main(string[] args)
        {
            // Two contexts following the different strategies

            SortedList studentRecords = new SortedList();

            studentRecords.Add("Simran");
            studentRecords.Add("Rimmy");
            studentRecords.Add("Sarita");
            studentRecords.Add("Vicky");
            studentRecords.Add("Annaya");

            studentRecords.SetSortStrategy(new QuickSort());
            studentRecords.Sort();
            studentRecords.SetSortStrategy(new ShellSort());
            studentRecords.Sort();

            studentRecords.SetSortStrategy(new MergeSort());
            studentRecords.Sort();

            // Wait for the user

            Console.ReadKey();
        }
    }

    /// <summary> The 'Strategy' abstract class </summary>

    public abstract class SortStrategy
    {
        public abstract void Sort(List<string> list);
    }

    /// <summary> A 'ConcreteStrategy' class </summary>

    public class QuickSort : SortStrategy
    {
        public override void Sort(List<string> list)
        {
```

```csharp
            list.Sort();  // Default is Quicksort
            Console.WriteLine("QuickSorted list ");
        }
    }

    /// <summary> A 'ConcreteStrategy' class </summary>

    public class ShellSort : SortStrategy
    {
        public override void Sort(List<string> list)
        {
            //list.ShellSort();  not-implemented
            Console.WriteLine("ShellSorted list is");
        }
    }

    /// <summary> A 'ConcreteStrategy' class </summary>

    public class MergeSort : SortStrategy
    {
        public override void Sort(List<string> list)
        {
            //list.MergeSort(); not-implemented
            Console.WriteLine("MergeSorted list ");
        }
    }

    /// <summary> The 'Context' class </summary>

    public class SortedList
    {
        private List<string> list = new List<string>();
        private SortStrategy sortstrategy;

        public void SetSortStrategy(SortStrategy
sortstrategy)
        {
            this.sortstrategy = sortstrategy;
        }

        public void Add(string name)
        {
            list.Add(name);
        }

        public void Sort()
        {
            sortstrategy.Sort(list);
```

```
        // Iterate over list and display results

        foreach (string name in the list)
        {
            Console.WriteLine(" " + name);
        }
        Console.WriteLine();
    }
  }
}
```

In this chapter, we covered Strategy Pattern with relevant examples.

## CHAPTER 7

Proxy Pattern

IN THIS CHAPTER

➤ What is Proxy Pattern?

➤ Real-world examples

➤ Why is Proxy Pattern useful?

➤ Advantages/disadvantages

➤ Implementation in Python

➤ UML diagram

In the previous chapter, we covered Strategy Pattern, and in this chapter, we will discuss Proxy Pattern with advantages, disadvantages, UML, and its implementation.

Proxy Design Patterns are classified as Structural Design Patterns. It essentially provides an interface to real objects of various types, such as networking, large memory, files, etc. The Proxy class sits between the requester and the supplier. The Proxy server is the greatest illustration of this pattern when serving web requests. When a new request arrives at the Proxy server, it is evaluated before being forwarded to the proper server and receiving a response to return to the requester. This Proxy server also offers enhanced security and other features.

DOI: 10.1201/9781003308461-7

The Proxy Pattern can apply in the following situations:

- When constructing a complicated system, it is beneficial to provide a proxy interface for the benefit of the client.

- When we want more protection before approaching genuine items.

- When we require secure access to numerous servers from a single server.

- To prevent having to load heavy memory actual objects before they were required.

Let's look at an example of the Proxy Pattern before getting into the academic description.

Have you ever gone through a door with an access card? There are other ways to unlock that door, including using an access card or hitting a button that bypasses the security system. The door's primary role is to open, however, a proxy has been put on top of it to provide other functions. Let me demonstrate this using the code sample below.

```
class Door:
    def open_method(self) -> None:
        pass

class SecuredDoor:
    def __init__(self) -> None:
        self._klass = Door()

    def open_method(self) -> None:
        print(f"Adding the security measure to method of
{self._klass}")

secured_door = SecuredDoor()
secured_door.open_method()
```

The code line above illustrates the previous example. The Door class has only one method, the open method, which represents the operation of opening the Door object. This function is expanded in the SecuredDoor class, and we've simply added a print statement to the latter class's method in this example.

Take note of how SecuredDoor invoked the class Door via composition. With the Proxy Pattern, we may replace the primary object with the proxy object without making any further code modifications. The Liskov Substitution Principle is followed here. It reads as follows:

- A superclass's objects must be interchangeable with objects from its subclasses without causing the application to break. This necessitates that the objects of our subclasses behave similarly to the objects of our superclass.

- The SecuredDoor class can replace the Door object, and it does not provide any new methods; instead, it extends the functionality of the Door class's open method.

In simple terms, a class that uses the Proxy Pattern represents the functionality of another class.

WHY WOULD WE USE IT?

The Loose Coupling Proxy style allows us to easily detach our main logic from any additional functionality that may be required. The modular design of the code makes it much easier to maintain and enhance the functionality of our primary logic.

Assume we're creating a division function that accepts two integers as parameters and returns the result of dividing them. It also handles and logs edge situations such as ZeroDivisionError and TypeError.

```python
import logging
from typing import Union

logging.basicConfig(level=logging.INFO)

def division(a: Union[int, float], b: Union[int, float]) ->
float:
    try:
        result = c / d
        return result

    except ZeroDivisionError:
        logging.error(f"Argument d can't be {d}")

    except TypeError:
        logging.error(f"Arguments must integers/floats")

print(division(2.9, 2))
```

This function is already executing three things at once, which is a violation of the Single Responsibility Principle (SRP). According to SRP, a function or class should only change for one reason. A change in any of the three duties in this scenario might compel the function to alter. This also implies that modifying or extending the function might be difficult to track.

We can instead create two classes. The main class Division will simply implement the essential logic, while the ProxyDivision class will enhance Division's capabilities by adding exception handlers and logs.

```python
import logging
from typing import Union

logging.basicConfig(level=logging.INFO)

class Division:
    def div(self, c: Union[int, float], d: Union[int,
float]) -> float:
        return c / d

class ProxyDivision:
    def __init__(self) -> None:
        self._klass = Division()

    def div(self, c: Union[int, float], d: Union
[int, float]) -> float:
        try:
            result = self._klass.div(c, d)
            return result

        except ZeroDivisionError:
            logging.error(f"Argument d cannot be {d}")

        except TypeError:
            logging.error(f"Arguments must integers/floats")

klass = ProxyDivision()
print(klass.div(12, 0))
```

Because the Division and ProxyDivision classes implement the same interface in the example above, we may replace Division with ProxyDivision and vice versa. The second class does not directly inherit from the first class and does not add any new methods to it. This means you can simply enhance the functionality of the Division or DivisionProxy classes without having to modify their underlying logic.

BETTER TESTABILITY

Another significant benefit of the proxy design is increased testability. Because our core logic and extra features are loosely connected, you may test them individually. This simplifies and modularizes the test. With our previously stated Division and ProxyDivision classes, demonstrating the benefits is simple. The primary class's logic is simple to understand, and because it only contains the basic logic, it's critical to create unit tests for it before testing the other functions. It's far easier to test the Division class than it is to test the previously described division function, which tries to accomplish several things at once. After we've finished testing the main class, we may go on to the other features. Unit tests are usually more reliable and rigorous as a result of isolating key functionality from the cruft and encapsulation of extra features.

INTERFACE USING PROXY PATTERN

Our class won't look like the basic Division class with only one method in the real world. Typically, our major class will have several methods and perform multiple complex tasks. We've probably figured out that the proxy classes must implement all of the primary class's methods by now. When creating a proxy class for a complex primary class, the author may neglect to implement all of the original class's methods. This will result in a Proxy Pattern violation. In addition, if the primary class is huge and intricate, it may be difficult to follow all of its methods.

The solution is an interface that notifies the proxy class's author of all the methods that must implement. An interface is a generic class that specifies all of the methods that a concrete class must implement. Interfaces, on the other hand, cannot be started individually. We'll need to create an interface subclass and implement all of the functions there. If our subclass fails to implement any of the interface's methods, an error will raise. Let's look at a simple example of how to use Python's xyz.XYZ and xyz.abstractmethod to create an interface and achieve the Proxy Pattern.

```
from xyz import XYZ, abstractmethod

class Interface(XYZ):
    """Interfaces of Interface, Concrete & Proxy should
    be same, because client should be able to use
    Concrete or Proxy without any change in their internals.
    """
```

```python
    @abstractmethod
    def job_x(self, user: str) -> None:
        pass

    @abstractmethod
    def job_y(self, user: str) -> None:
        pass

class Concrete(Interface):
    """This is the main job doer. External services like
    payment gateways can good example.
    """

    def job_x(self, user: str) -> None:
        print(f"We are doing the job_x for {user}")

    def job_y(self, user: str) -> None:
        print(f"We are doing the job_y for {user}")

class Proxy(Interface):
    def __init__(self) -> None:
        self._concrete = Concrete()

    def job_a(self, user: str) -> None:
        print(f"We're extending job_x for user {user}")

    def job_b(self, user: str) -> None:
        print(f"We're extending job_y for user {user}")

if __name__ == "__main__":
    klass = Proxy()
    print(klass.job_x("red"))
    print(klass.job_y("nafi"))
```

As we can see from the sequence above, we'll need to create an Interface class first. The ABC module in Python offers abstract foundation classes. Interface is an abstract class that inherits from ABC and defines all of the methods that the concrete class must implement afterward. The concrete class inherited the interface, which implements all of the methods defined in it. The @abstractmethod decorator is used to adorn each method in the Interface class. If we're not sure what a decorator is, check out this page on Python decorators. The @abstractmethod decorator converts a regular method into an abstract method, which implies it's only a blueprint for the needed methods that the concrete subclass will have to implement later.

We can't utilize any of the abstract methods or instantiate Interface without first creating subclasses and implementing the methods.

Concrete is the real class that inherits from the abstract base class (interface) Interface and implements all of the abstract methods described. This is a genuine class that we can instantiate and utilize the methods. We'll get TypeError if we neglect to implement any of the abstract methods specified in the Interface.

The base concrete class Concrete functionality is extended by the third class Proxy. It uses the composition pattern to call the Concrete class and implements all of the methods. In this case, though, we took the outputs of the concrete methods and increased their functionality without duplicating code.

ANOTHER USEFUL EXAMPLE

Let's experiment with one last real-world example to solidify the notion further. Assume you wish to get information from an external API endpoint. Use our http client to send GET queries to the endpoint and gather the results in json format. Then assume we want to look at the response header and the arguments given during the request.

Public APIs frequently impose rate restrictions in the real world, and our client will most certainly throw an http connection-timeout error if you exceed the limit with multiple get requests. For example, suppose we wish to manage errors outside of the main logic that sends http GET queries.

Let's imagine we want to cache the answers if the client has already seen the arguments in the requests. This implies that instead of hitting the APIs with repetitive queries, the client will display the replies from the cache when we submit requests with the same parameters several times. Caching significantly reduces API response time.

We'll be utilizing Postman's publicly available GET API for this example.

```
https://postman-echo.com/get?foo1=bar_1&foo2=bar_2
```

Because it contains a rate limitation that kicks in at random and causes the client to raise ConnectTimeOut and ReadTimeOutError, this API is ideal for the example. Take a look at how this routine will work:

- Define the IFetchUrl interface, which will implement three abstract methods. The first method, get data, retrieves data from a URL, and serialize it in json format. The second function, get headers, will probe the data and return a dictionary with the header. The third function, get args, will explore the data in the same way as the second method, but will return the query arguments as a dictionary this time. However, we will not be implementing anything inside the methods of the interface.

- Make a concrete class called FetchUrl that inherits from the IFetchUrl interface. This time, we'll implement all three of the abstract class's methods. However, no edge situations should handle here. The method should have only a logic flow and no other information.

- Create an ExcFetchUrl proxy class. It will inherit from the interface as well, but we will add our exception handling mechanism here this time. All of the methods in this class now include logging capabilities. We use the methods that have already been implemented in the concrete class to call the concrete class FetchUrl in a composition format, avoiding code repetition. You must implement all of the methods in the abstract class, just as we must in the FetchUrl class.

- The fourth and final class extends ExcFetchUrl and adds caching to the get data method. It will behave similarly to the ExcFetchUrl class.

Since you're already aware of the Proxy Pattern's approach, we'll dump the complete 110-line solution at once.

```python
import logging
import sys
from xyz import XYZ, abstractmethod
from datetime import datetime
from pprint import pprint

import httpx
from httpx._exceptions import ConnectTimeout, ReadTimeout
from functools import lru_cache

logging.basicConfig(level=logging.INFO)

class IFetchUrl(XYZ):
    """Abstract base class. We can't instantiate this
independently"""
```

```python
    @abstractmethod
    def get_data(self, url: str) -> dict:
        pass

    @abstractmethod
    def get_headers(self, data: dict) -> dict:
        pass

    @abstractmethod
    def get_args(self, data: dict) -> dict:
        pass

class FetchUrl(IFetchUrl):
    """Concrete class that does not handle exceptions and
loggings"""

    def get_data(self, url: str) -> dict:
        with httpx.Client() as client:
            response = client.get(url)
            data = response.json()
            return data

    def get_headers(self, data: dict) -> dict:
        return data["headers"]

    def get_args(self, data: dict) -> dict:
        return data["args"]

class ExcFetchUrl(IFetchUrl):
    """This class can swap out with the FetchUrl class.
    It provides additional exception handling and logging."""

    def __init__(self) -> None:
        self._fetch_url = FetchUrl()

    def get_data(self, url: str) -> dict:
        try:
            data = self._fetch_url.get_data(url)
            return data

        except ConnectTimeout:
            logging.error("Connection time-out. Try again
later.")
            sys.exit(1)

        except ReadTimeout:
            logging.error("Read timed-out. Try again later.")
            sys.exit(1)
```

```python
    def get_headers(self, data: dict) -> dict:
        headers = self._fetch_url.get_headers(data)
        logging.info(f"Getting the headers at {datetime.
now()}")
        return headers

    def get_args(self, data: dict) -> dict:
        args = self._fetch_url.get_args(data)
        logging.info(f"Getting the args at {datetime.now()}")
        return args

class CacheFetchUrl(IFetchUrl):
    def __init__(self) -> None:
        self._fetch_url = ExcFetchUrl()

    @lru_cache(maxsize=32)
    def get_data(self, url: str) -> dict:
        data = self._fetch_url.get_data(url)
        return data

    def get_headers(self, data: dict) -> dict:
        headers = self._fetch_url.get_headers(data)
        return headers

    def get_args(self, data: dict) -> dict:
        args = self._fetch_url.get_args(data)
        return args

if __name__ == "__main__":

    # url = "https://postman-echo.com/
get?foo1=bar_1&foo2=bar_2"

    fetch = CacheFetchUrl()
    for arg1, arg2 in zip([11, 12, 13, 11, 12, 13], [11,
12, 13, 11, 12, 13]):
        url = f"https://postman-echo.com/
get?foo1=bar_{arg1}&foo2=bar_{arg2}"
        print(f"\n {'-'*75}\n")
        data = fetch.get_data(url)
        print(f"Cache Info: {fetch.get_data.cache_info()}")
        pprint(fetch.get_headers(data))
        pprint(fetch.get_args(data))
```

We used the excellent httpx client to get data from the URL in the FetchUrl class's get data function. Keep in mind that we've mostly neglected all of the additional logic of error handling and reporting in this example.

The ExcFetchUrl proxy class was used to provide exception handling and logging logic. CacheFetchUrl is a class that extends the proxy class ExcFetchUrl by adding cache capabilities to the get_data method.

In the main part, we can utilize any of the FetchUrl, ExcFetchUrl, or CacheFetchUrl classes without modifying their functionality. The FetchUrl is the barebone class that will fail in case of any exceptions. Later classes offer extra functionality while keeping the same interface.

The output just outputs the results of the get headers and get args functions. Take note of how we choose the endpoint arguments to mimic caching. On the third line of the report, the Cache Info: displays when data is served from the cache. Here, hits=0 indicates that the data is supplied straight from the external API. However, if we look at the later results, we can see that when the query inputs are repeated ([11, 12, 13, 11, 12, 13]), Cache Info: displays larger hit counts. This indicates that the information is being provided from the cache.

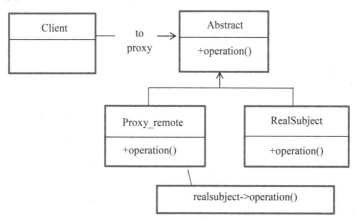

UML of Proxy Pattern

HOW SHOULD THE PROXY PATTERN BE IMPLEMENTED?

Let's have a look at how to use the Proxy Pattern.

```
class Image:
    def __init__( self, filename ):
        self._filename = filename
    def load_image_from_disk( self ):
        print("Loading " + self._filename )
    def display_image( self ):
        print("display " + self._filename)
```

```
class Proxy:
   def __init__( self, subject ):
      self._subject = subject
      self._proxystate = None
class ProxyImage( Proxy ):
   def display_image( self ):
      if self._proxystate == None:
         self._subject.load_image_from_disk()
         self._proxystate = 1
      print("display " + self._subject._filename )
proxy_image1 = ProxyImage ( Image("HiRes_10Mb_Photo1") )
proxy_image2 = ProxyImage ( Image("HiRes_10Mb_Photo2") )
proxy_image1.display_image() # loading-necessary
proxy_image1.display_image() # loading-unnecessary
proxy_image2.display_image() # loading-necessary
proxy_image2.display_image() # loading-unnecessary
proxy_image1.display_image() # loading-unnecessary
```

ADVANTAGES

- **Open/Closed Principle:** We can simply incorporate new proxies into our application without modifying the client code.

- **Smooth Service:** The Proxy we establish works even if the service object is not ready or is not available in the present context.

- **Security:** The proxy mechanism also provides system security.

- **Speed:** It improves application performance by reducing the duplication of objects that may be large in size and memory expensive.

DISADVANTAGES

- **Slow or Delayed Response:** It is conceivable that the service will become slow or delayed.

- **The Layer of Abstraction:** This approach adds another layer of abstraction, which might be problematic if some customers access the RealSubject code directly while others access the Proxy classes.

- **Increased Complexity:** Due to the addition of many additional classes, our code may become quite complex.

APPLICABILITY

- **Virtual Proxy:** Most commonly used in databases, for example, certain high-resource-consuming data exists in the database and we require it regularly. So, in this case, we can use the Proxy Pattern to generate numerous proxies that refer to the object.

- **Protective Proxy:** It puts a protective layer over the application and may be used in schools or colleges where only a limited number of websites are permitted to be accessed through WiFi.

- **Distant Proxy:** This is very useful when the service object is on a remote server. In such circumstances, the Proxy forwards the client request across the network while managing all of the information.

Smart proxies give extra security to applications by interfering with certain activities whenever an item is accessed.

In Java, the Proxy Pattern is used as follows:

- It may be utilized in a Virtual Proxy scenario considering a case where numerous database calls are required to retrieve a large picture. Because this is a costly procedure, we can utilize the Proxy Pattern to generate many proxies that refer to the large memory-consuming object for further processing. The actual object is produced only when a client requests/accesses it, and we can then refer to the Proxy to reuse the object. This prevents the item from being duplicated, so conserving memory.

- It may utilize in a Protective Proxy scenario; it functions as an authorization layer to determine whether or not the real user has access to the proper material. For example, a Proxy server that restricts Internet access in the workplace. Only legitimate websites and material will be permitted, while the rest will be prohibited.

- It may utilize in the Remote Proxy scenario. A remote proxy can be considered the stub in the RPC call. The remote Proxy offers a local representation of the item present at each address point. Another example is providing an interface for distant resources like web services or REST resources.

- It may utilize in a Smart Proxy scenario. A smart proxy adds an extra layer of protection by performing specific actions when an item is accessed. For example, before accessing an actual object, check whether it is locked so that no other objects may modify it.

IMPLEMENTATION

- **Step 1:** Create an interface for OfficeInternetAccess.

```
public interface OfficeInternetAccess {
   public void grantInternetAccess();
}
```

- **Step 2:** Create a RealInternetAccess class that implements the OfficeInternetAccess interface to provide authorization to a specific employee.
  File: RealInternetAccess.java

```
public class RealInternetAccess implements
OfficeInternetAccess {
   private String employeeName;
   public RealInternetAccess(String empName) {
       this.employeeName = empName;
   }
   @Override
   public void grantInternetAccess() {
       System.out.println("Internet Access granted for
the employee: "+ employeeName);
   }
}
```

- **Step 3:** Create a ProxyInternetAccess class that implements the OfficeInternetAccess interface and provides the RealInternetAccess class's object.
  File: ProxyInternetAccess.java

```
public class ProxyInternetAccess implements
OfficeInternetAccess {
   private String employeeName;
   private RealInternetAccess  realaccess;
       public ProxyInternetAccess(String employeeName) {
       this.employeeName = employeeName;
   }
   @Override
```

```
public void grantInternetAccess()
{
    if (getRole(employeeName) > 4)
    {
        realaccess = new RealInternetAccess(employeeN
ame);
        realaccess.grantInternetAccess();
    }
    else
    {
        System.out.println("No Internet access is
granted. Our job level is below 5");
    }
}
public int getRole(String emplName) {
    // Check role from database based on Name and
designation
    // return the job level or job designation.
    return 9;
}
}
```

- **Step 4:** Now, create a ProxyPatternClient class that can really connect to the internet.

  File: ProxyPatternClient.java

```
public class ProxyPatternClient {
    public static void main(String[] args)
    {
        OfficeInternetAccess access = new
ProxyInternetAccess("Kashia Kaur");
        access.grantInternetAccess();
    }
}
```

C# Proxy Pattern

Participants

This pattern's classes and objects are as follows:

1. Proxy (MathProxy):

   - Keeps a reference to the actual topic that allows the Proxy to access it. If the RealSubject and Subject interfaces are the same, Proxy may refer to a Subject.

- Offers an interface that is identical to Subject's so that a proxy may be used in place of the genuine subject.

- Controls access to the actual subject and may be in charge of its creation and deletion.

- Other responsibilities vary according to the kind of proxy:

  - Remote proxies are in charge of encrypting a request and its parameters and relaying the encoded request to the true subject in another address space.

  - Virtual proxies may store extra information about the actual topic to delay access to it. The ImageProxy from Motivation, for example, caches the extent of the actual pictures.

  - Protection proxies ensure that the caller has the necessary access rights to complete a request.

2. Subject (IMath):

- Offers a standard interface for RealSubject and Proxy, allowing a Proxy to be used anywhere a RealSubject is expected.

3. RealSubject (Maths):

- Specifies the real object that the proxy represents.

C# Structural Code

The Proxy Pattern is demonstrated in this structured code, which gives a symbolic object (proxy) that controls access to another comparable object.

```csharp
using System;

namespace Proxy.Structural
{
    /// <summary> Proxy Design Pattern </summary>

    public class Program
    {
        public static void Main(string[] args)
        {
            // Create proxy and request service
```

```csharp
            Proxy proxy = new Proxy();
            proxy.Request();

            // Wait for the user

            Console.ReadKey();
        }
    }

    /// <summary> The 'Subject' abstract class </summary>

    public abstract class Subject
    {
        public abstract void Request();
    }

    /// <summary> The 'RealSubject' class </summary>

    public class RealSubject : Subject
    {
        public override void Request()
        {
            Console.WriteLine("Called RealSubject.
Request()");
        }
    }

    /// <summary> The 'Proxy' class </summary>

    public class Proxy : Subject
    {
        private RealSubject realSubject;

        public override void Request()
        {
            // Use the 'lazy initialization'

            if (realSubject == null)
            {
                realSubject = new RealSubject();
            }

            realSubject.Request();
        }
    }
}
```

Real-World C# Code

The Proxy Pattern is demonstrated in this real-world code for a Math object represented by a MathProxy object.

```
using System;

namespace Proxy.RealWorld
{
    /// <summary> Proxy Design Pattern </summary>

    public class Program
    {
        public static void Main(string[] args)
        {
            // Create the math proxy

            MathProxy proxy = new MathProxy();

            // Do math

            Console.WriteLine("5 + 2 = " + proxy.Add(5, 2));
            Console.WriteLine("5 - 2 = " + proxy.Sub(5, 2));
            Console.WriteLine("5 * 2 = " + proxy.Mul(5, 2));
            Console.WriteLine("5 / 2 = " + proxy.Div(5, 2));

            // Wait for the user

            Console.ReadKey();
        }
    }

    /// <summary> The 'Subject interface </summary>

    public interface IMath
    {
        double Add(double a, double b);
        double Sub(double a, double b);
        double Mul(double a, double b);
        double Div(double a, double b);
    }

    /// <summary> The 'RealSubject' class </summary>

    public class Math : IMath
    {
        public double Add(double a, double b)
{ return a + b; }
```

```
        public double Sub(double a, double b)
{ return a - b; }
        public double Mul(double a, double b)
{ return a * b; }
        public double Div(double a, double b)
{ return a / b; }
    }

    /// <summary> The 'Proxy Object' class </summary>

    public class MathProxy : IMath
    {
        private Math math = new Math();

        public double Add(double a, double b)
        {
            return math.Add(a, b);
        }
        public double Sub(double a, double b)
        {
            return math.Sub(a, b);
        }
        public double Mul(double a, double b)
        {
            return math.Mul(a, b);
        }
        public double Div(double a, double b)
        {
            return math.Div(a, b);
        }
    }
}
```

This chapter covered Proxy Pattern with possible implementation, UML representation, advantages, and disadvantages.

## CHAPTER 8

Bridge Pattern

IN THIS CHAPTER

> ➤ What is Bridge Pattern?

> ➤ Real-world examples

> ➤ Why is Bridge Pattern useful?

> ➤ Advantages/disadvantages

> ➤ Implementation in Python

> ➤ UML diagram

In the previous chapter, we covered Proxy Pattern, and in this chapter, we will discuss Bridge Pattern with advantages, disadvantages, UML, and its implementation.

The Bridge Pattern is a Structural Design Pattern that allows us to separate Implementation Specific Abstractions from Implementation Independent Abstractions and develop them as independent entities.

The Bridge Pattern is widely regarded as one of the most effective strategies for organizing class hierarchies.

BRIDGE DESIGN PATTERN ELEMENTS

- **Abstraction:** It is the heart of the Bridge Design Pattern and serves as a point of reference for the implementer.

DOI: 10.1201/9781003308461-8

Refined Abstraction takes the finer details one step above and hides the finer element from the implementers, extending the abstraction to a new level.

- **Implementer:** It is responsible for defining the interface for implementation classes. This interface does not have to be identical to the abstraction interface and might be rather different.

- **Concrete Implementation:** The implementer above is implemented using concrete implementation.

THE INSPIRATION FOR THE BRIDGE DESIGN PATTERN

The Bridge Pattern prevents a phenomenon known as cartesian product complexity explosion.

Using an example, the issue will become clear. Assume you're working on an Airplane. It might be either a military or a civilian jet. It can also be a passenger/soldier or cargo plane.

One way to do this is to have a MilitaryPassenger, MilitaryCargo, CommercialPassenger, and CommercialCargo aircraft.

The cartesian product complexity, in this case, is $2 \times 2 = 4$. This amount isn't groundbreaking at this size, but as additional classes and variants are added, it may rapidly become unmanageable.

The Bridge Pattern provides a link between classes (Airplane implementation) and their properties (is it a passenger or cargo plane). It prefers composition over inheritance.

We construct one class for each type in each category using the pattern. In our scenario, we'd have CommercialPlane and MilitaryPlane entities and CargoCarrier and PassengerCarrier entities.

We may not have accomplished much because we still have four courses, but consider this on a scale. We can have nPlane classes, but only CargoCarrier and PassengerCarrier can apply to these planes.

A preferable solution would be to have parent classes – Carrier and Plane. We may construct two child classes for the Carrier parent class: Cargo and Passenger. Similarly, there are two child classes for the Plane parent class: Military and Commercial.

Next, we'll need a means to link, or bridge, the Carrier and Plane subclasses. We can accomplish so by supplying one of these two classes as a parameter value to the other class's constructor. We'll be able to mix any of the subclasses by implementing the pattern.

Finally, let's look at how we can use Python to create the Bridge Design Pattern.

USING PYTHON TO IMPLEMENT THE BRIDGE DESIGN PATTERN

We will develop a Carrier parent class with two abstract methods: carry_military() and carry_passenger(). Following that, we can make a Cargo child class that inherits from the Carrier class and implements the carry_military() and carry_commercial() methods.

To avoid creating variants of classes, we'll build a Carrier with two abstract methods: carry_military() and cary_passenger().

The Carrier class will also have two child classes, Cargo and Passenger, which will inherit and implement its abstract methods:

```python
# Passenger and Cargo Carriers

class Carrier:
    def carry_military(self, items):
        pass

    def carry_commercial(self, items):
        pass

class Cargo(Carrier):
    def carry_military(self, items):
        print("Plane carries ", items," military-cargo
goods")

    def carry_commercial(self, items):
        print("Plane carries ", items," commercial-cargo
goods")

class Passenger(Carrier):
    def carry_military(self, passengers):
        print("Plane carries ", passengers, " military-
passengers")

    def carry_commercial(self, passengers):
        print("Plane carries ", passengers, " commercial-
passengers")
```

Similarly, we'll construct a Plane class with two abstract methods – display_description() and add_objects() and two child classes – Commercial and Military. We'll be supplying a Carrier to the Plane class's constructor. This is the bridge.

Cargo and Passenger will return carry commercial() if the plane is a commercial plane, and vice versa.

The number of passengers/goods is saved in the self.objects variable and supplied as a parameter to the carry commercial() method:

```python
# Military and Commercial Planes
class Plane:
    def __init__(self, Carrier):
        self.carrier = Carrier

    def display_description(self):
        pass

    def add_objects(self):
        pass

class Commercial(Plane):
    def __init__(self, Carrier, objects):
        super().__init__(Carrier)
        self.objects = objects

    def display_description(self):
        self.carrier.carry_commercial(self.objects)

    def add_objects(self, new_objects):
        self.objects += new_objects

class Military(Plane):
    def __init__(self, Carrier, objects):
        super().__init__(Carrier)
        self.objects = objects

    def display_description(self):
        self.carrier.carry_military(self.objects)

    def add_objects(self, new_objects):
        self.objects += new_objects
```

Our classes are prepped and ready. Now is the time to build some objects and bridge them with one another using the previously described constructor.

Consider the following example:

```
cargo = Cargo()
passenger = Passenger()

# Bridging-Military and Cargo-classes
military1 = Military(cargo,  110)
military1.display_description()
military1.add_objects(28)
military1.display_description()
```

We've created objects for the Cargo and Passenger classes here. The cargo object was then supplied in a constructor call to the Military class. Because it is a military plane, the cargo is classified as military cargo.

As a result, the display_description() function will print information about the military cargo. In addition, we've added 28 extra items to this load.

In a similar vein, we may cross the Military and Passenger classes:

```
cargo = Cargo()
passenger = Passenger()

# Bridging-Military and Passenger-classes
military2 = Military(passenger,  280)
military2.display_description()
military2.add_objects(12)
military2.display_description()
```

Likewise, we may bridge Commercial and Passenger:

```
# Bridging-Commercial and Passenger
commercial1 = Commercial(passenger,  420)
commercial1.display_description()
commercial1.add_objects(55)
commercial1.display_description()
```

Finally, we can bridge the Commercial and Cargo classes:

```
# Bridging-Commercial and Cargo
commercial2 = Commercial(cargo, 180)
commercial2.display_description()
commercial2.add_objects(18)
commercial2.display_description()
```

A PROBLEM

Without applying the Bridge Pattern, there is a problem.

Consider the Cuboid class, which has three elements: length, breadth, and height, as well as three methods: ProducewithAPI1(), ProduceWithAPI2(), and expand ().

Producing methods are implementation-specific since we have two production APIs, and one method, expand(), is implementation-independent.

We currently have two implementation-specific methods and one implementation-independent method. Still, when the number grows (as it would in a large-scale project), things will become difficult for the developers to manage.

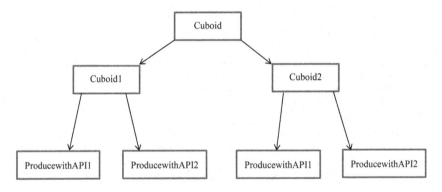

Problem of Bridge Pattern.

```
""" Without utilizing the bridge approach, write
We have a class with three attributes: length, width, and
height, as well as three methods: ProduceWithAPI1(),
ProduceWithAPI2(), and expand (). Because we have two
production APIs, several of these generating methods are
implementation-specific"""
```

```python
class Cuboid:

    class ProducingAPI1:

        """Implementation of Specific Implementation"""

        def produceCuboid(self, length, breadth, height):

            print(f'API1 is producing Cuboid with the
length = {length}, '
                    f' Breadth = {breadth} and Height =
{height}')

    class ProducingAPI2:
        """Implementation of Specific Implementation"""

        def produceCuboid(self, length, breadth, height):
            print(f'API2 is producing Cuboid with the
length = {length}, '
                    f' Breadth = {breadth} and Height =
{height}')


    def __init__(self, length, breadth, height):

        """Initialize the necessary attributes"""

        self._length = length
        self._breadth = breadth
        self._height = height

    def produceWithAPI1(self):

        """Implementation of specific Abstraction"""

        objectAPIone = self.ProducingAPI1()
        objectAPIone.produceCuboid(self._length, self._
breadth, self._height)

    def producewithAPI2(self):

        """Implementation of specific Abstraction"""

        objectAPItwo = self.ProducingAPI2()
        objectAPItwo.produceCuboid(self._length, self._
breadth, self._height)

    def expand(self, times):
```

```
        """Implementation of independent Abstraction"""

        self._length = self._length * times
        self._breadth = self._breadth * times
        self._height = self._height * times

# Instantiate a Cubiod
cuboid1 = Cuboid(2, 1, 3)

# Draw it using APIone
cuboid1.produceWithAPI1()

# Instantiate another Cuboid
cuboid2 = Cuboid(18, 22, 20)

# Draw it using APItwo
cuboid2.producewithAPI2()
```

SOLUTION USING BRIDGE PATTERN

Now consider the answer to the preceding problem. Bridge Pattern is one of the greatest solutions for such sort of difficulties. Our major objective is to split apart the codes of implementation specific abstractions and implementation independent abstractions.

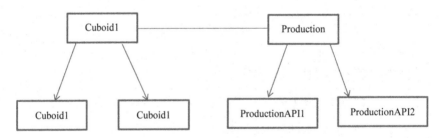

Solution of Bridge Pattern.

```
"""Bridge Method was used to implement the code.
We have a Cuboid class with three attributes: length,
width, and height, as well as three methods:
produceWithAPIOne(), produceWithAPITwo(), and expand(). Our
goal is to distinguish implementation-specific abstraction
from implementation-independent abstraction"""

class ProducingAPI1:
```

```python
    """Implementation of specific Abstraction"""

    def produceCuboid(self, length, breadth, height):

        print(f'API1 is producing Cuboid with the length =
{length}, '
              f' Breadth = {breadth} and Height = {height}')

class ProducingAPI2:

    """Implementation of specific Abstraction"""

    def produceCuboid(self, length, breadth, height):

        print(f'API2 is producing Cuboid with length =
{length}, '
              f' Breadth = {breadth} and Height = {height}')

class Cuboid:

    def __init__(self, length, breadth, height, producingAPI):

        """Initialize tnecessary attributes
           Implementation of independent Abstraction"""

        self._length = length
        self._breadth = breadth
        self._height = height

        self._producingAPI = producingAPI

    def produce(self):

        """Implementation of specific Abstraction"""

        self._producingAPI.produceCuboid(self._length,
self._breadth, self._height)

    def expand(self, times):

        """Implementation of independent Abstraction"""

        self._length = self._length * times
        self._breadth = self._breadth * times
        self._height = self._height * times

"""Instantiate cuboid and pass to it an
   object of ProducingAPIone"""
```

```
cuboid1 = Cuboid(2, 1, 3, ProducingAPI1())
cuboid1.produce()

cuboid2 = Cuboid(18, 18, 18, ProducingAPI2())
cuboid2.produce()
```

UML DIAGRAM OF BRIDGE PATTERN

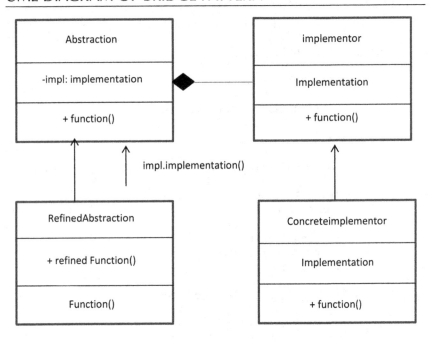

UML of Bridge Pattern.

REAL-WORLD BRIDGE DESIGN PATTERN

We can use a real-world example to understand the bridge Design Pattern better. It's very common these days. We get a charger with every smartphone we buy. The charger cable can now be separated, allowing us to use it as a USB cable to connect to other devices.

ADVANTAGES

Bridge Pattern adheres to the Single Responsibility Principle by decoupling an abstraction from its implementation such that the two can alter independently.

It does not contradict the Open/Closed Principle since we may add new abstractions and implementations separately from each other at any moment. Platform independent feature: the Bridge Pattern is a simple way to develop platform-independent functionalities.

DISADVANTAGES

- **Complexity:** Because we introduce new abstraction classes and interfaces, our code may get complex after using the Bridge technique.

- **Double Indication:** The Bridge Pattern may have a little negative influence on performance since the abstraction requires messages to be passed together with the implementation for the operation to be completed.

- **Interfaces with just one implementation:** If we only have a few interfaces, we don't have to worry, but if we have an enormous collection of interfaces with a minimum or only one implementation, it becomes difficult to manage.

APPLICABILITY

- **Run-time Binding:** Generally, the Bridge Pattern is used to provide the implementation's run-time binding; run-time binding means that we can call a method at run-time rather than compile-time.

- **Class Mapping:** To map the orthogonal class hierarchies, the Bridge Pattern is used.

- **UI Environment:** A real-world application of the Bridge Pattern is the definition of shapes in a UI Environment.

USAGE OF BRIDGE PATTERN

- When there is no need for a permanent connection between the functional abstraction and its implementation.

- When both the functional concept and its implementation need subclassing.

- It is generally utilized in situations where modifications to the implementation have no effect on the customers.

Using the Bridge Pattern in Java

- **Step 1:** Create a Question interface that allows us to go from one question to another or vice versa.

```java
// this is Question interface.
public interface Question {
    public void nextQuestion();
    public void previousQuestion();
    public void newQuestion(String q);
    public void deleteQuestion(String q);
    public void displayQuestion();
    public void displayAllQuestions();
}
// End of Question interface.
```

- **Step 2:** Make a JavaQuestions implementation class that implements the Question interface.

```java
// this is JavaQuestions class.
import java.util.ArrayList;
import java.util.List;
public class JavaQuestions implements Question {
 private List <String> questions = new
ArrayList<String>();
 private int current = 0;
 public JavaQuestions(){
    questions.add("What is the class? ");
    questions.add("What is the interface? ");
    questions.add("What is the abstraction? ");
    questions.add("How multiple polymorphism is
achieved in the java? ");
    questions.add("How many types of
exception  handling are there in the java? ");
    questions.add("Define keyword final for
the variable, method, and class in the java? ");
    questions.add("What is the abstract class? ");
    questions.add("What is the multi-threading? ");
    }
 public void nextQuestion() {
    if( current <= questions.size()-1 )
    current++;
    System.out.print(current);
    }
```

```
    public void previousQuestion() {
        if( current > 0 )
        current--;
    }

    public void newQuestion(String quest) {
        questions.add(quest);
    }

    public void deleteQuestion(String quest) {
        questions.remove(quest);
    }

    public void displayQuestion() {
        System.out.println( questions.get(current) );
    }
    public void displayAllQuestions() {
        for (String quest : questions) {
        System.out.println(quest);
    }
    }
}// End of JavaQuestions class.
```

- **Step 3:** Create a QuestionManager class that will utilize the Question interface as a bridge.

```
// this is QuestionManager class.
public class QuestionManager  {
    protected Question q1;
    public String catalog;
    public QuestionManager(String catalog) {
    this.catalog=catalog;
    }
    public void next() {
    q1.nextQuestion();
    }
    public void previous() {
    q1.previousQuestion();
    }
    public void newOne(String quest) {
    q1.newQuestion(quest);
    }
    public void delete(String quest) {
    q1.deleteQuestion(quest);
    }
```

```
    public void display() {
    q1.displayQuestion();
    }
    public void displayAll() {
        System.out.println("Question Paper:
" + catalog);
    Q1.displayAllQuestions();
    }
}// End of QuestionManager class.
```

- **Step 4:** Make a QuestionFormat class by extending the QuestionManager class.

```
// this is QuestionFormat class.
public class QuestionFormat extends QuestionManager {
    public QuestionFormat(String catalog){
        super(catalog);
    }
    public void displayAll() {
        System.out.println("\n-------------------");
        super.displayAll();
        System.out.println("-------------------");
    }
}// End of QuestionFormat class.
```

- **Step 5:** Make a class called BridgePatternDemo.

```
// this is BridgePatternDemo class.
public class BridgePatternDemo {
    public static void main(String[] args) {
    QuestionFormat questions = new
QuestionFormat("Java-Programming Language");
    questions.q1 = new JavaQuestions();
        questions.delete("what is the class?");
        questions.display();
    questions.newOne("What is the inheritance? ");

    questions.newOne("How many types of the inheritance
are there in the java?");
    questions.displayAll();
    }
}// End of BridgePatternDemo class.
```

Bridge Pattern in C#

Participants

This pattern's classes and objects are as follows:

1. Abstraction (BusinessObject):

   - Specifies the interface of the abstraction.

   - Holds a reference to an Implementor object.

2. RefinedAbstraction (CustomersBusinessObject):

   - Extends the Abstraction interface.

3. Implementor (DataObject):

   - The interface for implementation classes is defined by the Implementor (DataObject). This interface does not have to match Abstraction's interface exactly; the two interfaces might be rather different. The Implementation interface often only offers rudimentary operations, whereas Abstraction specifies higher-level operations based on these primitives.

4. CustomersDataObject ConcreteImplementor:

   - Implements the Implementor interface and describes its concrete implementation.

C# Structural Code

The Bridge Pattern is used in this structural code to separate (decouples) the interface from its implementation. The implementation can develop without altering the clients that utilize the object's abstraction.

```
using System;

namespace Bridge.Structural
{
    /// <summary> Bridge Design Pattern </summary>

    public class Program
    {
        public static void Main(string[] args)
        {
```

```
            Abstraction abs = new RefinedAbstraction();

            // Set the implementation and call

            abs.Implementor = new ConcreteImplementorA();
            abs.Operation();

            // Change the implemention and call

            abs.Implementor = new ConcreteImplementorB();
            abs.Operation();

            // Wait for the user

            Console.ReadKey();
        }
    }

    /// <summary> The 'Abstraction' class </summary>

    public class Abstraction
    {
        protected Implementor implementor;

        public Implementor Implementor
        {
            set { implementor = value; }
        }

        public virtual void Operation()
        {
            implementor.Operation();
        }
    }

    /// <summary> The 'Implementor' abstract class </
summary>

    public abstract class Implementor
    {
        public abstract void Operation();
    }

    /// <summary> The 'RefinedAbstraction' class </summary>

    public class RefinedAbstraction : Abstraction
    {
        public override void Operation()
```

```
        {
            implementor.Operation();
        }
    }

    /// <summary> The 'ConcreteImplementorX' class </summary>

    public class ConcreteImplementorX : Implementor
    {
        public override void Operation()
        {
            Console.WriteLine("ConcreteImplementorX
Operation");
        }
    }

    /// <summary> The 'ConcreteImplementorY' class </summary>

    public class ConcreteImplementorY : Implementor
    {
        public override void Operation()
        {
            Console.WriteLine("ConcreteImplementorY
Operation");
        }
    }
}
```

Real-World C# Code

This real-world code exemplifies the Bridge Pattern, which decouples a BusinessObject abstraction from its implementation in DataObject. DataObject implementations can change dynamically without affecting clients.

```
using System;
using System.Collections.Generic;

namespace Bridge.RealWorld
{
    /// <summary> Bridge Design Pattern </summary>

    public class Program
    {
```

```csharp
public static void Main(string[] args)
{
    // Create the RefinedAbstraction

    var customers = new Customers();

    // Set the ConcreteImplementor

    customers.Data = new CustomersData("Chicago");

    // Exercise bridge

    customers.Show();
    customers.Next();
    customers.Show();
    customers.Next();
    customers.Show();
    customers.Add("Lenry Belasquez");

    customers.ShowAll();

    // Wait for the user

    Console.ReadKey();
    }
}
/// <summary> The 'Abstraction' class </summary>

public class CustomersBase
{
    private DataObject dataObject;

    public DataObject Data
    {
        set { dataObject = value; }
        get { return dataObject; }
    }

    public virtual void Next()
    {
        dataObject.NextRecord();
    }

    public virtual void Prior()
    {
        dataObject.PriorRecord();
    }
```

```
        public virtual void Add(string customer)
        {
            dataObject.AddRecord(customer);
        }

        public virtual void Delete(string customer)
        {
            dataObject.DeleteRecord(customer);
        }

        public virtual void Show()
        {
            dataObject.ShowRecord();
        }

        public virtual void ShowAll()
        {
            dataObject.ShowAllRecords();
        }
}

/// <summary> The 'RefinedAbstraction' class </summary>

public class Customers : CustomersBase
{
    public override void ShowAll()
    {
        // Add the separator lines

        Console.WriteLine();
        Console.WriteLine("-------------");
        base.ShowAll();
        Console.WriteLine("-------------");
    }
}

/// <summary> The 'Implementor' abstract class </summary>

public abstract class DataObject
{
    public abstract void NextRecord();
    public abstract void PriorRecord();
    public abstract void AddRecord(string name);
    public abstract void DeleteRecord(string name);
    public abstract string GetCurrentRecord();
    public abstract void ShowRecord();
    public abstract void ShowAllRecords();
}
```

```csharp
/// <summary> The 'ConcreteImplementor' class </summary>

public class CustomersData : DataObject
{
    private readonly List<string> customers =
new List<string>();
    private int current = 0;
    private string city;

    public CustomersData(string city)
    {
        this.city = city;

        // Loaded from database

        customers.Add("Rim Tones");
        customers.Add("Ramual Lackson");
        customers.Add("Nllen Lkod");
        customers.Add("Enn Stills");
        customers.Add("Nisa Ciolani");
    }

    public override void NextRecord()
    {
        if (current <= customers.Count - 1)
        {
            current++;
        }
    }

    public override void PriorRecord()
    {
        if (current > 0)
        {
            current--;
        }
    }

    public override void AddRecord(string customer)
    {
        customers.Add(customer);
    }

    public override void DeleteRecord(string customer)
    {
        customers.Remove(customer);
    }
```

```
        public override string GetCurrentRecord()
        {
            return customers[current];
        }

        public override void ShowRecord()
        {
            Console.WriteLine(customers[current]);
        }

        public override void ShowAllRecords()
        {
            Console.WriteLine("Customer City: " + city);

            foreach (string customer in customers)
            {
                Console.WriteLine(" " + customer);
            }
        }
    }
}
```

This chapter covered Bridge Pattern with its benefits, demerits, implementation, and UML diagram.

## CHAPTER 9

Adapter and Façade Patterns

IN THIS CHAPTER

- ➤ What are Adapter and Facade Patterns?
- ➤ Real-world examples
- ➤ Why are Adapter and Facade Patterns useful?
- ➤ Advantages/disadvantages
- ➤ Implementation in Python
- ➤ UML diagram

In the previous chapter, we covered Bridge Pattern, and in this chapter, we will explain Adapter and Façade Patterns.

ADAPTER PATTERN

The Adapter Pattern is a Structural Design Pattern that allows us to adapt incompatible objects to each other. The Adapter Pattern is one of the simplest to grasp because numerous real-world examples demonstrate the analogy. The primary goal of this method is to build a link between two incompatible interfaces. This method creates a new interface for a class. We can grasp the concept more quickly if we consider the Cable Adapter, which allows us to charge our phones in locations with outlets of various shapes.

A real-world example is a card reader, which performs as an adapter between a memory card and a laptop. We insert the memory card into the card reader and the card reader into the laptop to read the memory card from the laptop. The adapter Design Pattern aids in the collaboration of classes. It converts a class's interface into another interface based on the requirements. The pattern consists of speciation, a polymorphism, and multiple forms. Consider a shape class that can use based on the requirements collected.

We can use this concept to integrate classes that could not be integrated due to interface incompatibility.

USING THE ADAPTER PATTERN TO SOLVE A PROBLEM

Assume we're developing an app that displays information about all of the vehicles on the road. It retrieves data in XML format from various vehicle organizations' APIs and displays it.

But suppose we want to upgrade our application at some point with Machine Learning algorithms that work beautifully on the data and only retrieve the important data. However, there is a limitation: it only accepts data in JSON format.

Making changes to the Machine Learning Algorithm so that it can accept data in XML format is a terrible idea.

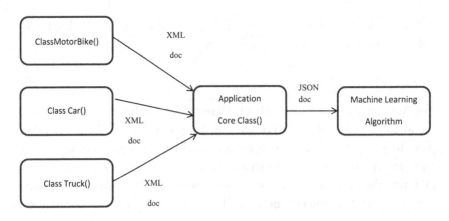

Problem without using Adapter Method.

ADAPTER PATTERN SOLUTIONS

We can use the Adapter Pattern to help solve the problem we defined above by creating an Adapter object.

In order to use an adapter in our code:

- The client should send a request to the adapter by invoking a method on the target interface.

- The Adapter should translate that request on the adaptee using the Adaptee interface.

- The client receives the result of the call and is unaware of the presence of the Adapter.

```python
# Dog - Bike
# human - Truck
# car - Car

class MotorBike:

    """Class for the MotorBike"""

    def __init__(self):
        self.name = "MotorBike"

    def TwoWheeler(self):
        return "TwoWheeler"


class Truck:

    """Class for the Truck"""

    def __init__(self):
        self.name = "Truck"

    def EightWheeler(self):
        return "EightWheeler"


class Car:

    """Class for the Car"""
```

```python
    def __init__(self):
        self.name = "Car"

    def FourWheeler(self):
        return "FourWheeler"

class Adapter:
    """
    Adapts objects by replacing the methods.
    Usage:
    motorCycle = MotorCycle()
    motorCycle = Adapter(motorCycle, wheels =
motorCycle.TwoWheeler)
    """

    def __init__(self, obj, **adapted_methods):
        """We set adapted methods in object's dict"""
        self.obj = obj
        self.__dict__.update(adapted_methods)

    def __getattr__(self, attr):
        """All non-adapted calls are passed to object"""
        return getattr(self.obj, attr)

    def original_dict(self):
        """Print original object dict"""
        return self.obj.__dict__


""" main-method """
if __name__ == "__main__":

    """list to store the objects"""
    objects = []

    motorBike = MotorBike()
    objects.append(Adapter(motorBike, wheels =
motorBike.TwoWheeler))

    truck = Truck()
    objects.append(Adapter(truck, wheels = truck.
EightWheeler))

    car = Car()
    objects.append(Adapter(car, wheels = car.
FourWheeler))

    for obj in objects:
        print("A {0} is a {1} vehicle".format(obj.name,
obj.wheels()))
```

CLASS DIAGRAM

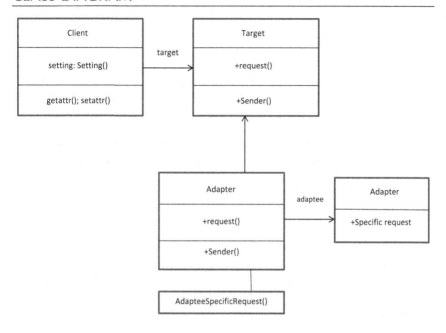

Class diagram of Adapter.

ADVANTAGES

- **Principle of Single Responsibility:** With the Adapter Method, we can achieve the principle of Single Responsibility because we can separate the concrete code from the client's primary logic.

- **Flexibility:** The Adapter Pattern aids in the code's flexibility and reusability.

- **Less Complicated Class:** Because our client class does not have to use a different interface, we can use polymorphism to switch between different adapter implementations.

- **Open/Closed principle:** The Open/Closed principle is not violated because we can incorporate the new Adapter classes into the code.

DISADVANTAGES

- **The Complexity of the Code:** As we introduce new classes, objects, and interfaces, the complexity of our code increases.

- **Adaptability:** Many adaptations with the adaptee chain are often required to achieve the desired compatibility.

APPLICABILITY

- **To make classes and interfaces compatible:** The Adapter Pattern is always used if we need to make definite classes compatible to communicate.

- **Inheritance-related:** The Adapter Pattern can be used to reuse some code, such as classes and interfaces that lack some functionality.

ADAPTER PATTERN USAGE

It is used as follows:

- When an object must use an existing class that has an incompatible interface.

- When we need to develop a reusable class that works with classes that do not have suitable interfaces.

- When we need to develop a reusable class that works with classes that do not have suitable interfaces.

An Example of the Adapter Pattern in Java

- **Step 1:** Design a CreditCard interface (Target interface)

```
public interface CreditCard {
    public void giveBankDetails();
    public String getCreditCard();
}// End of CreditCard interface.
```

- **Step 2:** Make a class called BankDetails (Adaptee class)
  File: BankDetails.java

```
// This is adapter class.
public class BankDetails{
    private String bankName;
    private String accHolderName;
    private long accNumber;
```

```
    public String getBankName() {
        return bankName;
    }
    public void setBankName(String bankName) {
        this.bankName = bankName;
    }
    public String getAccHolderName() {
        return accHolderName;
    }
    public void setAccHolderName(String accHolderName) {
        this.accHolderName = accHolderName;
    }
    public long getAccNumber() {
        return accNumber;
    }
    public void setAccNumber(long accNumber) {
        this.accNumber = accNumber;
    }
}// End of BankDetails class.
```

- **Step 3:** Create a class called BankCustomer (Adapter class)
  File: BankCustomer.java

```
// This is adapter class

import java.io.BufferedReader;
import java.io.InputStreamReader;
public class BankCustomer extends BankDetails
implements CreditCard {
 public void giveBankDetails(){
   try{
   BufferedReader br=new BufferedReader(new
InputStreamReader(System.in));

    System.out.print("Enter account holder name :");
    String customername=br.readLine();
    System.out.print("\n");

    System.out.print("Enter account number:");
    long accno=Long.parseLong(br.readLine());
    System.out.print("\n");

    System.out.print("Enter bank name :");
    String bankname=br.readLine();
```

```
    setAccHolderName(customername);
    setAccNumber(accno);
    setBankName(bankname);
    }catch(Exception e){
        e.printStackTrace();
    }
}
@Override
public String getCreditCard() {
long accno=getAccNumber();
String accholdername=getAccHolderName();
String bname=getBankName();

    return ("Account number "+accno+" of
"+accholdername+" in the "+bname+ "
                        bank is valid and
authenticated for the issuing the credit card. ");
    }
}//End of BankCustomer class.
```

- **Step 4:** Make a class called AdapterPatternDemo (client class)
  File: AdapterPatternDemo.java

```
//This is client class.
public class AdapterPatternDemo {
    public static void main(String args[]){
      CreditCard targetInterface=new BankCustomer();
      targetInterface.giveBankDetails();
      System.out.print(targetInterface.getCreditCard());
    }
}//End of BankCustomer class.
```

Adapter Pattern in C#
Participants
This pattern's classes and objects are as follows:

- **Target (ChemicalCompound):** Defines the domain-specific interface that the Client uses.

- **Adapter (Compound):** Adapts the Adaptee interface to the Target interface.

- **Adaptee (ChemicalDatabase):** Describes an existing interface that has to be modified.

- **Client (AdapterApp):** Works with objects that adhere to the Target interface.

C# Structural Code

This structure code exhibits the Adapter Pattern, which translates one class's interface onto another so that they can collaborate. These incompatible classes might be from various libraries or frameworks.

```
using System;

namespace Adapter.Structural
{
    /// <summary> Adapter Design Pattern </summary>

    public class Program
    {
        public static void Main(string[] args)
        {
            // Create the adapter and place a request

            Target target = new Adapter();
            target.Request();

            // Wait for the user

            Console.ReadKey();
        }

    }

    /// <summary> The 'Target' class </summary>

    public class Target
    {
        public virtual void Request()
        {
            Console.WriteLine("Called the Target
Request()");
        }
    }

    /// <summary> The 'Adapter' class </summary>
```

```
    public class Adapter : Target
    {
        private Adaptee adaptee = new Adaptee();

        public override void Request()
        {
            // Possibly do some other work and then call
SpecificRequest

            adaptee.SpecificRequest();
        }
    }

    /// <summary> The 'Adaptee' class </summary>

    public class Adaptee
    {
        public void SpecificRequest()
        {
            Console.WriteLine("Called the
SpecificRequest()");
        }
    }
}
```

Real-World C# Code

This real-world code shows how to use a legacy chemical databank. Chemical compound objects communicate to the databank using an Adapter interface.

```
using System;

namespace Adapter.RealWorld
{
    /// <summary> Adapter Design Pattern </summary>

    public class Program
    {
        public static void Main(string[] args)
        {
            // Non-adapted the chemical compound

            Compound unknown = new Compound();
            unknown.Display();
```

```
        // Adapted the chemical compounds

        Compound water = new RichCompound("Water");
        water.Display();

        Compound benzene = new RichCompound("Benzene");
        benzene.Display();

        Compound ethanol = new RichCompound("Ethanol");
        ethanol.Display();

        // Wait for the user

        Console.ReadKey();
    }
}

/// <summary> The 'Target' class </summary>

public class Compound
{
    protected float boilingPoint;
    protected float meltingPoint;
    protected double molecularWeight;
    protected string molecularFormula;

    public virtual void Display()
    {
        Console.WriteLine("\nCompound: Unknown --- ");
    }
}

/// <summary> The 'Adapter' class </summary>

public class RichCompound : Compound
{
    private string chemical;
    private ChemicalDatabank bank;

    // Constructor

    public RichCompound(string chemical)
    {
        this.chemical = chemical;
    }

    public override void Display()
    {
```

```
            // Adaptee

            bank = new ChemicalDatabank();

            boilingPoint = bank.GetCriticalPoint(chemical,
"B");
            meltingPoint = bank.GetCriticalPoint(chemical,
"M");
            molecularWeight = bank.
GetMolecularWeight(chemical);
            molecularFormula = bank.GetMolecularStructure(c
hemical);

            Console.WriteLine("\nCompound: {0} ------ ",
chemical);
            Console.WriteLine(" Formula is: {0}",
molecularFormula);
            Console.WriteLine(" Weight is: {0}",
molecularWeight);
            Console.WriteLine(" Melting Pt is: {0}",
meltingPoint);
            Console.WriteLine(" Boiling Pt is: {0}",
boilingPoint);
        }
    }

    /// <summary> The 'Adaptee' class </summary>

    public class ChemicalDatabank
    {
        // databank 'legacy API'

        public float GetCriticalPoint(string compound,
string point)
        {
            // Melting Point
            if (point == "M")
            {
                switch (compound.ToLower())
                {
                    case "water": return 0.1f;
                    case "benzene": return 5.4f;
                    case "ethanol": return -113.1f;
                    default: return 0f;
                }
            }

            // Boiling-Point
```

```
        else
        {
            switch (compound.ToLower())
            {
                case "water": return 101.0f;
                case "benzene": return 82.1f;
                case "ethanol": return 74.3f;
                default: return 0f;
            }
        }
    }

    public string GetMolecularStructure(string
compound)
    {
        switch (compound.ToLower())
        {
            case "water": return "H20";
            case "benzene": return "C6H6";
            case "ethanol": return "C2H5OH";
            default: return "";
        }
    }

    public double GetMolecularWeight(string compound)
    {
        switch (compound.ToLower())
        {
            case "water": return 18.035;
            case "benzene": return 77.1234;
            case "ethanol": return 45.0788;
            default: return 0d;
        }
    }
}
}
```

FACADE PATTERN

The Facade Pattern is a Structural Design Pattern that creates a more unified interface to a more complex system. The term Facade refers to the face of a building or, more specifically, the outer lying interface of a complex system composed of several subsystems. It is an important part of the Gang of Four Design Patterns. It simplifies access to methods of the underlying systems by providing a single entry point. Consider a supermarket.

An inventory management system is used to organize items. However, because the customer does not need to know about the inventory, it is preferable that the customer ask the shopkeeper for a list of items, as the shopkeeper knows where each item is located. The shopkeeper is acting as the Facade interface in this case.

Here, we create a Facade layer that allows clients to easily communicate with subsystems.

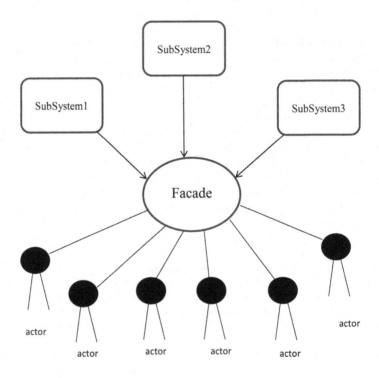

Façade Method.

A PROBLEM

Assume we have a washing machine that can wash, rinse, and spin clothes, but it does each task separately. We must abstract the complexities of the subsystems because the overall system is quite complex. We require a system that can automate the entire task without our interference.

SOLUTION BASED ON THE FACADE PATTERN

We'd like to use the Facade Pattern to solve the problem described above. It will aid us in hiding or abstracting the complexities of the subsystems listed below.

The code below was written using the Facade Pattern.

```python
"""Facade pattern with an example of the WashingMachine"""

class Washing:
    '''Subsystem # 1'''

    def wash(self):
        print("Washing")


class Rinsing:
    '''Subsystem # 2'''

    def rinse(self):
        print("Rinsing")


class Spinning:
    '''Subsystem # 3'''

    def spin(self):
        print("Spinning")


class WashingMachine:
    '''Facade'''

    def __init__(self):
        self.washing = Washing()
        self.rinsing = Rinsing()
        self.spinning = Spinning()

    def startWashing(self):
        self.washing.wash()
        self.rinsing.rinse()
        self.spinning.spin()

""" main-method """
if __name__ == "__main__":

    washingMachine = WashingMachine()
    washingMachine.startWashing()
```

CLASS DIAGRAM FOR THE FACADE METHOD

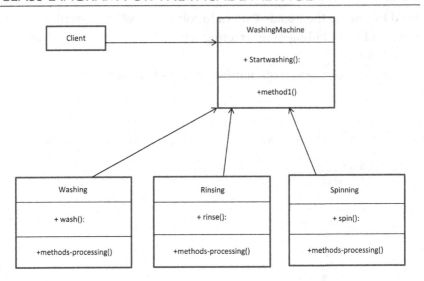

Façade Method Class Diagram.

ADVANTAGES

- **Isolation:** Our code can be easily isolated from the complexities of a subsystem.

- **Testine Process:** Using the Facade method simplifies the testing process by providing convenient methods for common testing tasks.

- **Loose Coupling:** The presence of loose coupling between clients and subsystems.

DISADVANTAGES

- **Changes in Methods:** As we know, subsequent methods in the Facade method are attached to the Facade layer, and any change in the subsequent method may cause a change in the Facade layer, which is not desirable.

- **Expensive Procedure:** Establishing the Facade method in our application for system reliability is not cheap.

- **Rules Violation:** There is always the risk of violating the Facade layer's construction.

APPLICABILITY

- **Providing a simple interface:** One of the most important applications of the Facade method is to provide a simple interface to a complex subsystem.

- **Dividing the system into layers:** It is used to provide a distinct structure to a subsystem by dividing it into layers. It also results in loose coupling between clients and subsystem.

FACADE PATTERN USAGE

It is in use:

- When we need a simple interface to a complicated subsystem.

- When there are several dependencies between clients and an abstraction's implementation classes.

Implementation in Java

- **Step 1:** Design a MobileShops interface.
  File: MobileShop.java

```java
public interface MobileShops {
    public void modelNo();
    public void prices();
}
```

- **Step 2:** Make an iPhone implementation class that implements the Mobileshops interface.
  File: Iphone.java

```java
public class Iphone implements MobileShops {
    @Override
    public void modelNo() {
        System.out.println(" Iphone 11 ");
    }
    @Override
    public void prices() {
    System.out.println(" Rs 75000.00 ");
    }
}
```

- **Step 3:** Make a Samsung implementation class that implements the Mobileshops interface.

  File: Samsung.java

```
public class Samsung implements MobileShops {
  @Override
  public void modelNo() {
  System.out.println(" Samsung galaxy 5 ");
  }
  @Override
  public void prices() {
      System.out.println(" Rs 55000.00 ");
  }
}
```

- **Step 4:** Make a Blackberry implementation class that implements the Mobileshops interface.

  File: Blackberry.java

```
public class Blackberry implements MobileShops {
  @Override
  public void modelNo() {
  System.out.println(" Blackberry 10 ");
  }
  @Override
  public void prices() {
      System.out.println(" Rs 65000.00 ");
  }
}
```

- **Step 5:** Make a concrete ShopKeeper class that implements the MobileShops interface.

  File: ShopKeeper.java

```
public class ShopKeeper {
  private MobileShops iphone;
  private MobileShops samsung;
  private MobileShops blackberry;

  public ShopKeeper(){
```

```
        iphone= new Iphone();
        samsung=new Samsung();
        blackberry=new Blackberry();
    }
    public void iphoneSale(){
        iphone.modelNo();
        iphone.prices();
    }
        public void samsungSale(){
        samsung.modelNo();
        samsung.prices();
    }
    public void blackberrySale(){
    blackberry.modelNo();
    blackberry.prices();
        }
}
```

* **Step 6:** Create a customer that can purchase mobiles from MobileShops using ShopKeeper.

    File: FacadePatternClient.java

```
import java.io.BufferedReader;
import java.io.IOException;
import java.io.InputStreamReader;

public class FacadePatternClient {
  private static int  choice;
  public static void main(String args[]) throws
NumberFormatException, IOException{
    do{
        System.out.print("======= MobileShop ======= \n");
        System.out.print("    1. IPHONE        \n");
        System.out.print("    2. SAMSUNG        \n");
        System.out.print("    3. BLACKBERRY       \n");
        System.out.print("    4. Exit           \n");
        System.out.print("Enter our choice: ");

        BufferedReader br=new BufferedReader(new
InputStreamReader(System.in));
        choice=Integer.parseInt(br.readLine());
        ShopKeeper sk=new ShopKeeper();

        switch (choice) {
        case 1:
            {
```

```
                    sk.iphoneSale();
                    }
             break;
      case 2:
             {
                 sk.samsungSale();
                 }
             break;
      case 3:
                          {
                          sk.blackberrySale();
                          }
                    break;
            default:
            {
                System.out.println("Nothing we purchased");
            }
                return;
            }

      }while(choice!=4);
}
}
```

Facade Pattern in C#

Participants

This pattern's classes and objects include:

1. Facade (MortgageApplication):

   - Understands which subsystem classes are in response to a request.

   - Delegates client requests to appropriate subsystem objects

2. Subsystem classes (Bank, Credit, Loan):

   - Subsystem functionality must implement.

   - Handle the work assigned to us by the Facade object.

   - Have no awareness of the facade and make no mention of it.

C# Structural Code

The Facade approach is demonstrated in this structural code, which gives a simpler and standard interface to a vast subsystem of classes.

```csharp
using System;

namespace Facade.Structural
{
    /// <summary> Facade Design Pattern </summary>

    public class Program
    {
        public static void Main(string[] args)
        {
            Facade facade = new Facade();

            facade.MethodX();
            facade.MethodY();

            // Wait for the user

            Console.ReadKey();
        }
    }

    /// <summary> The 'Subsystem ClassX' class </summary>

    public class SubSystemOne
    {
        public void MethodOne()
        {
            Console.WriteLine(" SubSystemOne-Method");
        }
    }

    /// <summary> The 'Subsystem ClassY' class </summary>

    public class SubSystemTwo
    {
        public void MethodTwo()
        {
            Console.WriteLine(" SubSystemTwo-Method");
        }
    }

    /// <summary> The 'Subsystem ClassC' class </summary>

    public class SubSystemThree
    {
        public void MethodThree()
        {
            Console.WriteLine(" SubSystemThree-Method");
```

```csharp
        }
    }

    /// <summary> The 'Subsystem ClassD' class </summary>

    public class SubSystemFour
    {
        public void MethodFour()
        {
            Console.WriteLine(" SubSystemFour-Method");
        }
    }

    /// <summary> The 'Facade' class </summary>

    public class Facade
    {
        SubSystemOne one;
        SubSystemTwo two;
        SubSystemThree three;
        SubSystemFour four;

        public Facade()
        {
            one = new SubSystemOne();
            two = new SubSystemTwo();
            three = new SubSystemThree();
            four = new SubSystemFour();
        }

        public void MethodA()
        {
            Console.WriteLine("\nMethodX()- ");
            one.MethodOne();
            two.MethodTwo();
            four.MethodFour();
        }

        public void MethodY()
        {
            Console.WriteLine("\nMethodY()- ");
            two.MethodTwo();
            three.MethodThree();
        }
    }
}
```

Real-World C# Code

This real-world code exhibits the Facade design as a MortgageApplication object, which gives a streamlined interface to a large subsystem of classes that assess an applicant's creditworthiness.

```csharp
using System;

namespace Facade.RealWorld
{
    /// <summary> Facade Design Pattern </summary>

    public class Program
    {
        public static void Main(string[] args)
        {
            // Facade

            Mortgage mortgage = new Mortgage();

            // Evaluate the mortgage eligibility for the
customer

            Customer customer = new Customer("Enn Kinsey");
            bool eligible = mortgage.IsEligible(customer,
145000);

            Console.WriteLine("\n" + customer.Name +
                    " has " + (eligible? "Approved" :
"Rejected"));

            // Wait for the user

            Console.ReadKey();
        }
    }

    /// <summary> The 'Subsystem ClassX' class </summary>

    public class Bank
    {
        public bool HasSufficientSavings(Customer c, int
amount)
        {
            Console.WriteLine("Check bank for the " +
c.Name);
            return true;
```

```csharp
        }
    }

    /// <summary> The 'Subsystem ClassY' class </summary>

    public class Credit
    {
        public bool HasGoodCredit(Customer c)
        {
            Console.WriteLine("Check credit for the " +
c.Name);
            return true;
        }
    }

    /// <summary> The 'Subsystem ClassC' class </summary>

    public class Loan
    {
        public bool HasNoBadLoans(Customer c)
        {
            Console.WriteLine("Check loans for " + c.Name);
            return true;
        }
    }

    /// <summary> Customer class </summary>

    public class Customer
    {
        private string name;

        // Constructor

        public Customer(string name)
        {
            this.name = name;
        }

        public string Name
        {
            get { return name; }
        }
    }

    /// <summary> The 'Facade' class </summary>

    public class Mortgage
```

```
{
    Bank bank = new Bank();
    Loan loan = new Loan();
    Credit credit = new Credit();

    public bool IsEligible(Customer cust, int amount)
    {
        Console.WriteLine("{0} applies for {1:C}
loan\n",
                cust.Name, amount);

        bool eligible = true;

        // Check the creditworthyness of the applicant

        if (!bank.HasSufficientSavings(cust, amount))
        {
            eligible = false;
        }
        else if (!loan.HasNoBadLoans(cust))
        {
            eligible = false;
        }
        else if (!credit.HasGoodCredit(cust))
        {
            eligible = false;
        }

        return eligible;
    }
}
}
```

This chapter covered Adapter and Façade Patterns with their implementation and representation.

Appraisal

A Design Pattern is a reusable solution to problems that frequently arise in software development. The pattern usually depicts the interactions and links between classes or items. The goal is to make the development process faster by providing tried-and-true development/design paradigms. Design Patterns are problem-solving methodologies that are independent of programming languages. Thus, a Design Pattern represents an idea rather than a specific implementation. We may make your code more flexible, reusable, and easily-maintained by employing Design Patterns.

Design Patterns aren't always required in projects. Design Patterns aren't supposed to be used in the creation of projects. The purpose of Design Patterns is to solve common problems. We must adopt an appropriate design whenever there is a requirement to avoid future complications. We only need to comprehend Design Patterns and their goals to figure out which pattern to use. We will only be able to choose the best one if we do this.

Goal: Identify the purpose and application of each Design Pattern so that we may select and apply the appropriate pattern as needed.

For example, in many real-world scenarios, we only want to make one instance of a class. For example, a country can only have one active president at any time. A Singleton pattern is what this pattern is called. Other software examples include a single database connection shared by several objects, as establishing a separate database connection for each item is expensive. Similarly, instead of developing many managers, an application might have a single configuration manager or error manager that handles all problems.

Once a design has been represented, it can be reused by designers other than the original designer. Individual designers could always reuse their designs or those they had learned about from others informally. On the other hand, a well-understood design representation allows a designer to communicate well-understood, well-tested designs to other practitioners dealing with similar design problems and to students learning about object-oriented design concepts.

More information than just design diagrams must include in a reusable design. For example, the problem that the design is intended to solve must be specified. This information is important because it allows potential reusers to identify available designs that are candidates for reuse when confronted with a specific problem.

Another type of information required in a reusable design is the trade-offs implied by the design. Designers must typically strike a balance between competing goals such as efficiency, flexibility, fault tolerance, and simplicity (among others). A single problem can inspire several useful designs, each with a different balance of design factors.

A Design Pattern is a suggested format for presenting reusable design elements.

A Design Pattern names, motivates, and explains a general design that addresses a recurring design problem in object-oriented systems in a systematic manner. It describes the problem, the solution, when to use it, and the consequences. It also provides implementation guidance and examples. The solution is a general arrangement of problem-solving objects and classes. The solution is tailored and implemented to address the issue in a specific context.

The first sentence of the definition expresses the intent of a Design Pattern: to present the solution to a recurring design problem consistently and coherently. The definition's next two sentences outline the content of a Design Pattern. The last two sentences explain how to use a Design Pattern. The usage makes it clear that a Design Pattern is not a program or code, but rather a design that must be tailored to the specific requirements of a specific problem and then implemented. The book "Design Patterns" contains a collection of Design Patterns, one of which is detailed below.

A Design Pattern's content consists of the twelve elements listed below:

1. **name:** Each pattern has its own distinct, short descriptive name. The collection of pattern names results in developing a specialized vocabulary that designers can use to describe and discuss design concepts.

2. **intent:** The intent is a brief description of the problem that the Design Pattern addresses. The intent is useful for browsing Design Patterns and recalling the purpose of a pattern when the name alone is insufficient.

3. **motivation:** The motive describes a typical, specific situation illustrative of the vast class of problems the pattern addresses. The reason should make it obvious that the situation is broad and serious. Class diagrams and/or object diagrams and a written description are typically included in the motivation.

4. **applicability:** This element contains a set of requirements that must be met for the pattern to be used. The criteria convey the designer's intentions (e.g., "clients should be able to overlook the distinction between compositions of objects and individual items"), complicated features of the problem (e.g., "an application employs a huge number of objects"), and limits.

5. **structure:** Here is an explanation of the pattern using class and object diagrams. The class and object names are generalizations of those found in the motivation's specific example. The Builder Pattern rationale, for example, presents an example with a base class named TextConverter and derived classes ASCIIConverter, TeXConverter, and TextWidgetConverter. The base class Builder is identified in the class diagrams in the structure section, and there is only one representative derived class entitled ConcreteBuilder.

6. **participants:** Each class in the structure section is detailed briefly. The description is a list of the roles and goals of each class in the design.

7. **collaborations:** The individuals' essential relationships and interactions are discussed. A complicated interaction sequence can be depicted using object interaction diagrams.

8. **consequences:** This section discusses the benefits and drawbacks of employing the Design Pattern. Positive consequences might include enhanced flexibility, decreased memory consumption, simpler expansion, support for a specific feature, or simplified use. Negative consequences might include inefficient behavior in certain circumstances, complicated class structure for specific issues, loss of system behavior assurances, and excessively generic design with accompanying loss of performance or storage costs. It is critical that designers present and readers comprehend both the good and negative aspects of their designs. Every design achieves a balance between numerous conflicting forces, and no design can escape having some undesirable implications.

9. **implementation:** A typical implementation is shown for the classes listed in the structure section. Because the structural part is universal, the implementation offered in this section is as well. This section is intended to provide a high-level overview of how to represent the pattern in a certain programming language.

10. **code example:** The primary code for a typical problem (typically the one stated in the rationale) is provided. This code demonstrates how the pattern might apply to the specific situation in detail.

11. **known uses:** This is a list of systems, libraries, tools, or frameworks that have addressed this Design Pattern's design issue. The sample systems may have employed a variant of the Design Pattern as a solution.

12. **similar patterns:** Other Design Patterns that are regarded to work well with this pattern are included. This collection gives designers extra assistance by pointing them to possibly relevant patterns.

DESIGN PATTERNS TYPES

Design Patterns are divided into three categories.

Creational

Class instantiation or object generation is the focus of these Design Patterns. Class-creational patterns and object-creational patterns are two subsets of these patterns. While class-creation patterns make good use of inheritance in the instantiation process, object-creation patterns use delegation.

Factory Pattern, Abstract Factory, Builder, Singleton, Object Pool, and Prototype are all Creational Design Patterns.

Use Case of the Creational Design Pattern

1. Assume a developer wants to construct an introductory DBConnection class to connect to a database and access the database from code in numerous places. Typically, the developer will create an instance of the DBConnection class and use it to perform database operations wherever needed. As each instance of the DBConnection class has a different connection to the database, numerous connections to the database are created. To cope with it, we make the DBConnection class a singleton class, which means that only one

instance of DBConnection is generated, and only one connection is made. We can regulate load balance, superfluous connections, and so on since we can manage DB Connection from a single instance.

2. We may use the Factory design if we wish to produce several instances of the same type while maintaining loose coupling. A class that implements the Factory Design Pattern acts as a link between numerous classes. Consider using several database servers, such as SQL Server and Oracle. Suppose we are developing an application with the SQL Server database as the back end, but need to change the database to Oracle in the future. In that case, we will need to modify all our code. Hence, as Factory Design Patterns maintain loose coupling and easy implementation, we should use the Factory Design Pattern to achieve loose coupling and create a similar type of object.

Structural

Structural Design Patterns involve arranging several classes and objects into bigger structures that give additional functionality.

Adapter, Bridge, Composite, Decorator, Facade, Flyweight, Private Class Data, and Proxy are Structural Design Patterns.

Use Case of Structural Design Pattern

An adapter Design Pattern is used when two interfaces are incompatible with one other and wish to build a relationship between them via an adapter. The adapter pattern translates a class's interface into another interface or class that the client expects, allowing classes that might otherwise be incompatible with operating together. So, in these incompatible cases, we may use the adapter approach.

Behavioral

Identifying and discovering shared communication patterns across items is all about behavioral patterns.

Chain of duty, Command, Interpreter, Iterator, Mediator, Memento, Null Object, Observer, State, Strategy, Template Method, and Visitor are examples of behavioral patterns.

Behavioral Design Pattern Application

The template pattern specifies the skeleton of an algorithm in an operation where some stages are delegated to subclasses. Subclasses can use the template approach to rewrite certain phases of an algorithm without affecting the algorithm's structure. For example, in our project, we could want the module's behavior to be extendable. We can make the module act in new and different ways if the application's requirements change or to satisfy the demands of new applications. However, no one is permitted to modify the source code, i.e., we can add but not change the structure in such instances when a developer can approach a template Design Pattern.

BENEFITS OF DESIGN PATTERNS REUSABILITY

- **Reusability:** By leveraging inheritance, we can make the code reusable and hence utilize it in various projects.

- **Transparent:** It enhances the code's transparency for all future developers who will utilize it.

- **Established Solution:** We can trust the solution supplied by Design Patterns since it has been well-proven and tested at important phases.

- **Established Communication:** Design Patterns facilitate communication among designers. When discussing system design, software experts may quickly visualize the high-level design in their brains when they refer to the name of the pattern employed to solve a certain issue.

- **Efficient Development:** Design Patterns aid in the creation of highly coherent modules with little coupling.

A MUST-HAVE SKILL FOR SOFTWARE DEVELOPERS

Let's start with a real-life example: imagine we are a restaurant owner. Running a restaurant entails more than just cooking food and providing it to clients. We must also take care of great food, clean dishes, and frequent issues that waiters, chefs, and other personnel face in our restaurant. As restaurant owner, we must also provide answers to those basic issues.

In software development, the same phenomenon occurs. Suppose we believe that constructing software is all about utilizing a programming language and applying logic, whether we are a newbie or an experienced programmer. In that case, we will run into many issues at the production level. Design Patterns are programming templates that provide our code with optimal flow, connectivity, and structure. It is a communication tool or a generic solution provided by experienced software developers to tackle typically recurring difficulties that developers confront during the software development phase.

As software engineer, our goal should not only be to write a lot of code, but also to decrease complexity and ensure code reusability. We will be expected to produce clean, beautiful, bug-free, and manageable code that other developers can understand and that can later be changed with minimum impact on the entire project, which is where Design Patterns come into play.

Importance in Software Development

Learning Design Patterns saves developers a lot of time. The following points describe its significance:

- It makes code reusable, bug-free, and aesthetically pleasing.

- Accelerate the development process.

- Changes or modifications become less difficult.

- Reduce the most typical issues that developers confront during the development process.

- Enhance our object-oriented skills.

- The flow of code is simple to grasp.

- Because there is less code, it is easier to maintain.

REAL-LIFE EXAMPLES HELP US UNDERSTAND THE IMPORTANCE

In software design, a Software Design Pattern is a broad, repeatable solution to an often recurring problem within a particular environment. This is Wikipedia's definition of Software Design Patterns... The preceding definition makes sense if we are experienced developer who has spent time developing code for software, but it goes right over our head and sounds uninteresting if we are a newbie who is completely unaware of it. Let us first consult with expert developers.

In software design, a Software Design Pattern is a broad, repeatable solution to an often recurring problem within a certain environment. The definition makes sense if we are experienced developer who has spent time developing code for software, but it goes right over our head and sounds uninteresting if we are a newbie who is completely unaware of it.

Real-Life Illustration

Do we enjoy eating? Which of these restaurants is our favorite? Where do we go the most? Do we prefer street food or online apps like Zomato and Swiggy? We may have experimented with different cuisines as well as different locations. If we have a favorite restaurant on our list where we frequently eat our favorite food, what is the reason for that? Of course, the expert chef at that restaurant may be preparing the meal using a specialized approach. What if we wish to make the same cuisine and do the same test at home?

What should we do now? We must employ the same strategy or method as the skilled chef. They may have tried several recipes and altered their technique to prepare that meal. Finally, they came to a halt when they acquired a precise technique for preparing that food, which tasted wonderful.

Suppose we want to produce the same food that tastes delicious as it does in our favorite restaurant. We must adopt the same approach and procedures as the expert chefs or contact a friend who cooks well and prepares dishes using a certain methodology.

Enough about food; let's get to the Design Patterns. Take heed of the terms underlined above: they tested several recipes, modified their approach, and are an experienced chef and cook. The same is true for Design Patterns. Design Patterns are similar to some of the best practices used by chefs (Gang of Four (GoF)) to prepare a meal in order for it to taste the best.

- Design Patterns are some of the design methods that experienced object-oriented software engineers employ (experienced chef or friends in our context). They are broad answers to issues encountered during software development.

- They are the results of many software engineers' trial and error (testing several recipes) over a long period of time.

LET'S GET INTO THE TECHNICAL DETAILS CONCERNING DESIGN PATTERNS

The GoF faced challenges that they overcame. They discovered that some of these solutions may be classified and that some issues are always quite prominent and common (as common as poverty). So, theoretically, Design Patterns are merely templates that provide our code with correct flow, coupling, and structure. It is a communication tool or a generic solution provided by experienced software developers to tackle typically recurring difficulties that developers confront during the software development phase.

Computing scholars and practitioners created a wide range of organizational concepts and approaches for creating high-quality object-oriented software that is brief, accurate, and reusable, describing a solution to a "typical" software design challenge. A pattern is a generic template for a solution that may use in a variety of scenarios. These templates may use millions of times to tackle particular sorts of issues.

THE GOAL OF DESIGN PATTERNS

We own and operate a restaurant. Running a restaurant entails more than just cooking food and providing it to clients. We must also take care of great cuisine, clean dishes, and frequent issues that waiters, chefs, and other personnel face in our restaurant. As restaurant owner, we must also provide answers to those basic issues.

As software engineer, our goal should not only be to write a lot of code, but also to decrease complexity and ensure code reusability.

We will be expected to produce clean, beautiful, bug-free, and manageable code that other developers can understand and that can later be changed with minimum impact on the entire project, which is where Design Patterns come into play.

- We are constructing a house without a plan. We have a basic notion of what we want or need for the house, so we begin construction on the first wall, then the second, and so on. The sooner we realize that this is not going to work, the better, and it might be even more difficult if we are building the house with numerous individuals. Without a plan, how would they know what to do? The same is true for software.

  We may construct an application in software development without first designing it. Especially if an existing design can reuse. (e.g., adding a new page to a website does not need redesigning everything.) We may just copy and paste the construction pattern from other sites. We can look for an existing solution for a similar type of problem to ours and utilize the approach or code from there to solve our own.

- Assume we are a student or a CAT candidate. Some formulae or approaches may be used to answer aptitude questions or mathematical problems. We use those formulae or strategies to tackle issues of a similar nature. We are aware that we have only saved a few words or concepts, and our efforts have been minimized. We also saved ourselves time. Design Patterns are extremely important in software development (mathematics formula or technique).

Assume we are developing some code in software development and discover that made a mistake. It needs adjustments in ten more files to be corrected. This means that our design, assuming we created it, was not excellent in the first place. What did this blunder cost us? We squandered a lot of time, resources, and efforts, and it also hampered the productivity of the other developer.

After a few days, we have ten additional courses, and we add alerts to those classes as well. When our notification system changes, we modify the code in all 10+13 classes. Our code no longer makes sense to us. We recognize that all of these classes should be disconnected from the notification system. We create a new class and place all of the notification logic within it. Then we create abstractions that allow anything to inform our system with the least amount of ripple impact and maximum reusability.

Did we note how we just created the observer or pattern for the entire program? If we had known this pattern previously, we would not have had to deal with all of those problems and would not have spent so much time. As a software engineer, we must create software that makes sense. The following points can now use to summarize the significance of Design Patterns.

- It makes code reusable, bug-free, and aesthetically pleasing.

- Accelerate the development process.

- Changes or modifications become less difficult.

- Reduce the most typical issues that developers confront during the development process.

- Enhance your object-oriented skills.

- The flow of code is simple to grasp.

- Because there is less code, it is easier to maintain.

WHY IS PYTHON A GOOD PATTERN LANGUAGE?

Patterns may be written in any programming language. Patterns should, in reality, be examined in the context of any specific programming language. Patterns, language grammar, and nature all place constraints on our programming. The limits imposed by language syntax and nature (dynamic, functional, object-oriented, and so on) might change, as can the reasons for their existence. Pattern constraints exist for a reason, and they serve a function. That is the fundamental objective of patterns: to instruct us on how to do something and how not to do it. We'll talk about patterns eventually, namely Python Design Patterns.

Python's philosophy is based on the concept of well-thought-out best practices. Python is a dynamic language. As a result, it already implements or makes it simple to implement, a number of prominent Design Patterns with just a few lines of code. Some Design Patterns are baked into Python, so we utilize them without even realizing them. Because of the nature of the language, further patterns are not required.

For instance, Factory is a structural Python Design Pattern for producing new objects while obscuring the instantiation mechanism from the user. However, because object creation in Python is designed to be dynamic, modifications such as Factory are not required. Of course, we are free to apply it if we like. There may be instances where it would be extremely beneficial, but they are the exception rather than the norm.

PATTERNS ARE FOR REUSE

Each pattern allows us to change a certain part of the system.

Redesign causes and patterns that address them:

- Specify an object's class clearly (Abstract Factory, Factory Pattern, Prototype).

- Requests that are hard-coded (Command, Chain of Responsibility).

- Platform hardware and software dependencies (Abstract Factory, Bridge).

- Object representations and implementations are required (Abstract Factory, Memento, Bridge, and Proxy).

- Dependencies in algorithms (Strategy, Builder, Iterator, Template Method, Visitor).

- Coupled tightly (Facade, Mediator, Observer, Command, Abstract Factory, and Bridge).

- Subclassing is used to increase functionality (Bridge, Composite, Decorator, Chain of Responsibility, Composite, and Strategy).

- Inability to easily switch classes (Visitor, Decorator, and Adapter).

LIST OF THE ORIGINAL 23 PATTERNS

Purpose	Design Pattern	Aspect(s) That Can Vary
Creational	Abstract Factory	families of product objects
	Builder	how a composite object gets created
	Factory	subclass of the object that is instantiated
	Prototype	class of object that is instantiated
	Singleton	the sole instance of a class
Structural	Adapter	interface to an object
	Bridge	implementation of an object
	Composite	structure and composition of an object
	Decorator	responsibilities of an object without subclassing
	façade	interface to a subsystem
	Flyweight	storage costs of objects
	Proxy	how an object is accessed; its location
Behavioral	Chain of Responsibility	an object that can fulfill request
	Command	when and how a request is fulfilled
	Interpreter	grammar and interpretation of language
	Iterator	how aggregate's elements are accessed, traversed
	Mediator	how and which objects interact with each other
	Memento	what private information is stored outside an object, and when
	Observer	number of objects that depend on another object; how the dependent objects stay up to date
	State	states of an object
	Strategy	an algorithm
	Template Method	steps of an algorithm
	Visitor	operations that can apply to an object(s) without changing their class(es)

BUILDER PATTERN

The Builder Pattern is a Creation Design Pattern that tries to "separate the building of a complicated thing from its representation in order for the same production process to produce diverse representations." It enables you to build complicated items step by step. Using the same building code, we can simply generate alternative kinds and representations of the object.

It is primarily intended to increase the flexibility of solutions to different object creation difficulties in object-oriented programming.

The Problem if the Builder Pattern Is Not Used

Imagine we want to join one of the exclusive batches of PeeksforPeeks without utilizing the Builder Pattern. So we will go there and inquire about the fee structure, available hours, and batches for the course we wish to enroll in. After inspecting the system, they will inform us about the courses, their fee structures, available timings, and batches.

Our fundamental goal is to create a system that is adaptable, trustworthy, structured, and lubricious. Unexperienced developers will construct a different and unique lesson for each and every course offered by PeeksforPeeks. Then, for each class, they will construct a separate object instantiation, which is not always necessary. The primary issue will occur when PeeksforPeeks launches new courses and developers are forced to implement additional classes since their code is not very flexible.

```python
# concrete-course
class DSA():

    """Class for the Data Structures and Algorithms"""

    def Fee(self):
        self.fee = 9200

    def available_batches(self):
        self.batches = 6

    def __str__(self):
        return "DSA"

# concrete-course
class SDE():

    """Class for the Software development Engineer"""

    def Fee(self):
        self.fee = 20000
```

```
    def available_batches(self):
        self.batches = 3

    def __str__(self):
        return "SDE"

# concrete-course
class STL():

    """class for the Standard Template Library of C++"""

    def Fee(self):
        self.fee = 8000

    def available_batches(self):
        self.batches = 5

    def __str__(self):
        return "STL"


# main-method
if __name__ == "__main__":

    sde = SDE()    # object for the SDE
    dsa = DSA()    # object for the DSA
    stl = STL()    # object for the STL

    print(f'Name of the Course: {sde} and its Fee: {sde.fee}')
    print(f'Name of the Course: {stl} and its Fee: {stl.fee}')
    print(f'Name of the Course: {dsa} and its Fee: {dsa.fee}')
```

Solution Using Builder Pattern

Our final result should be any PeeksforPeeks course. It might be SDE, STL, or DSA. Before selecting a certain course, we must first gather information about the courses, curriculum, cost structure, schedules, and batches. Using the same procedure, we may pick other courses from PeeksforPeeks. That is the advantage of employing the Builder Pattern.

```
# Abstract-course
class Course:

    def __init__(self):
        self.Fee()
        self.available_batches()
```

```python
    def Fee(self):
        raise NotImplementedError

    def available_batches(self):
        raise NotImplementedError

    def __repr__(self):
        return 'Fee : {0.fee} | Batches Available :
{0.batches}'.format(self)

# concrete-course
class DSA(Course):

    """Class for the Data Structures and Algorithms"""

    def Fee(self):
        self.fee = 9200

    def available_batches(self):
        self.batches = 6

    def __str__(self):
        return "DSA"

# concrete course
class SDE(Course):

    """Class for the Software Development Engineer"""

    def Fee(self):
        self.fee = 20000

    def available_batches(self):
        self.batches = 3

    def __str__(self):
        return "SDE"

# concrete course
class STL(Course):

    """Class for Standard Template Library"""

    def Fee(self):
        self.fee = 5000

    def available_batches(self):
        self.batches = 7

    def __str__(self):
        return "STL"
```

```
# Complex Course
class ComplexCourse:

    def __repr__(self):
        return 'Fee : {0.fee} | available_batches:
{0.batches}'.format(self)

# Complex-course
class Complexcourse(ComplexCourse):

    def Fee(self):
        self.fee = 8000

    def available_batches(self):
        self.batches = 5

# construct-course
def construct_course(cls):

    course = cls()
    course.Fee()
    course.available_batches()

    return course     # return course object

# main-method
if __name__ == "__main__":

    dsa = DSA()   # object for the DSA course
    sde = SDE()   # object for the SDE course
    stl = STL()   # object for the STL course

    complex_course = construct_course(Complexcourse)
    print(complex_course)
```

Benefits of Using the Builder Pattern

- **Reusability:** When creating the different product representations, we may reuse the same building code for additional representations.

- **Single Responsibility Principle:** The Single Responsibility Principle states that we may isolate the business logic from the complicated building code.

- **Object Construction:** Here, we build our object step by step, delay construction phases, or repeat steps recursively.

The following are the disadvantages of utilizing the Builder Pattern: Because the Builder Pattern necessitates the creation of numerous new classes, the complexity of our code increases.

- **Mutability:** The builder class must be changeable.

- **Initialization:** The class's data members are not guaranteed to be initialized.

Applicability

- **Building Complex Objects:** The Builder Pattern enables you to build the items step by step. We can even postpone the execution of some processes without affecting the final outcome. It is convenient to call the stages recursively while creating an object tree. Because it does not enable the exposing of an unfinished object, it stops the client code from getting the partial data.

- **Differentiate by Representations:** The Builder Pattern is used when the building of numerous product representations comprises identical stages that change only in the specifics. The base builder interface is used to describe all building steps, which are then carried out by concrete builders.

In Java, an Example of the Builder Design Pattern

To create a simple example of the Builder Design Pattern, follow the six steps below:

- Make two abstract classes. The CD and Company

- Create two company implementation classes: Apple and Samsung.

- Make a CDType class.

- Make a CDBuilder class.

- Make a BuilderDemo class.

1. **Make a Packing interface**
   File: Packing.java

```
public interface Packing {
    public String pack();
    public int prices();
}
```

2. **Design two abstract classes: CD and Company:** Create an abstract class CD that implements the Packing interface.
   File: CD.java

```
public abstract class CD implements Packing{
    public abstract String pack();
}
```

File: Company.java

```
public abstract class Company extends CD{
    public abstract int prices();
}
```

3. **Create two company implementation classes: Apple and Samsung**
   File: Apple.java

```
public class Apple extends Company{
    @Override
        public int prices(){
                    return 23;
    }
    @Override
    public String pack(){
            return "Apple CD";
        }
}//End of Apple class.
```

File: Samsung.java

```java
public class Apple extends Company {
    @Override
        public int prices(){
                            return 18;
    }
    @Override
    public String pack(){
            return "Samsung CD";
        }
}//End of Samsung class.
```

4. Design the CDType class
File: CDType.java

```java
import java.util.ArrayList;
import java.util.List;
public class CDType {
            private List<Packing> items=new
ArrayList<Packing>();
            public void addItem(Packing packs) {
                    items.add(packs);
            }
            public void getCost(){
              for (Packing packs : items) {
                        packs.prices();
              }
            }
            public void showItems(){
              for (Packing packing : items){
                System.out.print("CD-name : "+packing.
pack());
                System.out.println(", Prices : "+packing.
prices());
              }
            }
}//End of CDType class.
```

5. Make a CDBuilder class
File: CDBuilder.java

```java
public class CDBuilder {
    public CDType buildAppleCD(){
```

```
        CDType cds=new CDType();
        cds.addItem(new Apple());
        return cds;
}
public CDType buildSamsungCD(){
CDType cds=new CDType();
cds.addItem(new Samsung());
return cds;
}
}// End of CDBuilder class.
```

6. Make a BuilderDemo class
File: BuilderDemo.java

```
public class BuilderDemo{
    public static void main(String args[]){
        CDBuilder cdBuilder=new CDBuilder();
        CDType cdType1=cdBuilder.buildAppleCD();
        cdType1.showItems();

        CDType cdType2=cdBuilder.buildSamsungCD();
        cdType2.showItems();
    }
}
```

A REAL-WORLD APPLICATION OF THE BUILDER PATTERN

Let's look at a real-world example of the Builder Design Pattern step by step.

- **Step 1:** Create an interface Item representing the Pizza and Cold-drink.
  File: Item.java

```
public interface Item
{
    public String name();
    public String size();
    public float prices();
}// End of interface Item.
```

- **Step 2:** Create an abstract class Pizza that implements the Item interface.
  File: Pizza.java

```
public abstract class Pizza implements Item{
    @Override
    public abstract float prices();
}
```

- **Step 3:** Create an abstract ColdDrink class that implements the Item interface.
  File: ColdDrink.java

```
public abstract class ColdDrink implements Item{
    @Override
    public abstract float prices();
```

- **Step 4:** Develop an abstract class VegPizza that extends the abstract class Pizza.
  File: VegPizza.java

```
public abstract class VegPizza extends Pizza{
    @Override
    public abstract float prices();
    @Override
    public abstract  String name();
    @Override
    public abstract  String size();
}// End of abstract class VegPizza
```

- **Step 5:** Develop an abstract class NonVegPizza that extends the abstract class Pizza.
  File: NonVegPizza.java

```
public abstract class NonVegPizza extends Pizza{
    @Override
    public abstract float prices();
    @Override
```

```
public abstract String name();
@Override
public abstract String size();
}// End of abstract class NonVegPizza.
```

- **Step 6:** Now, extend the abstract class VegPizza with concrete sub-classes SmallCheezePizza, MediumCheezePizza, LargeCheezePizza, and ExtraLargeCheezePizza.

  File: SmallCheezePizza.java

```
public class SmallCheezePizza extends VegPizza{
    @Override
    public float prices() {
        return 180.0f;
    }
    @Override
    public String name() {
        return "Cheeze Pizza";
    }
    @Override
    public String size() {
        return "Small size";
    }
}// End of  SmallCheezePizza class.
```

  File: MediumCheezePizza.java

```
public class MediumCheezePizza extends VegPizza{
    @Override
    public float prices() {
        return  220.f;
    }
    @Override
    public String name() {
        return "Cheeze Pizza";
    }
    @Override
    public String size() {
        return "Medium Size";
    }
}// End of MediumCheezePizza class.
</textaera></div>
```

```
<div id="filename">File: LargeCheezePizza.java</div>
<div class="codeblock"><textarea  name="code"
class="java">
public class LargeCheezePizza extends VegPizza{
    @Override
    public float prices() {
        return 290.0f;
    }
    @Override
    public String name() {
        return "Cheeze Pizza";
    }
    @Override
    public String size() {
        return "Large Size";
    }
}// End of LargeCheezePizza class.
```

File: ExtraLargeCheezePizza.java

```
public class ExtraLargeCheezePizza extends VegPizza{
    @Override
    public float prices() {
        return 320.f;
    }
    @Override
    public String name() {
        return "Cheeze Pizza";
    }
    @Override
    public String size() {
        return "Extra-Large Size";
    }
}// End of ExtraLargeCheezePizza class.
```

- **Step 7:** Now, extend the abstract class VegPizza with concrete subclasses SmallOnionPizza, MediumOnionPizza, LargeOnionPizza,
  and ExtraLargeOnionPizza.
  File: SmallOnionPizza.java

```
public class SmallOnionPizza extends VegPizza {
    @Override
```

```
    public float prices() {
        return 140.0f;
    }
    @Override
    public String name() {
        return  "Onion Pizza";
    }
    @Override
    public String size() {
        return  "Small Size";
    }
}// End of SmallOnionPizza class.
```

File: MediumOnionPizza.java

```
public class MediumOnionPizza extends VegPizza {
    @Override
    public float prices() {
        return 180.0f;
    }
    @Override
    public String name() {
        return  "Onion Pizza";
    }
    @Override
    public String size() {
        return "Medium Size";
    }
}// End of MediumOnionPizza class.
```

File: LargeOnionPizza.java

```
public class LargeOnionPizza extends  VegPizza{
    @Override
    public float prices() {
        return 190.0f;
    }
    @Override
    public String name() {
        return "Onion Pizza";
    }
    @Override
```

```
public String size() {
    return "Large size";
}
}// End of LargeOnionPizza class.
```

File: ExtraLargeOnionPizza.java

```
public class ExtraLargeOnionPizza extends VegPizza {
    @Override
    public float prices() {
        return 220.0f;
    }
    @Override
    public String name() {
        return "Onion Pizza";
    }
    @Override
    public String size() {
        return "Extra-Large Size";
    }
}// End of ExtraLargeOnionPizza class
```

- **Step 8:** Now, extend the abstract class VegPizza with concrete sub-classes SmallMasalaPizza, MediumMasalaPizza, LargeMasalaPizza, and ExtraLargeMasalaPizza.

  File: SmallMasalaPizza.java

```
public class SmallMasalaPizza extends VegPizza{
    @Override
    public float prices() {
        return 120.0f;
    }
    @Override
    public String name() {
        return "Masala Pizza";
    }
    @Override
    public String size() {
        return "Samll Size";
    }
}// End of SmallMasalaPizza class
```

File: MediumMasalaPizza.java

```java
public class MediumMasalaPizza extends VegPizza {

    @Override
    public float prices() {
        return 130.0f;
    }

    @Override
    public String name() {

        return "Masala Pizza";

    }

    @Override
    public String size() {
       return  "Medium Size";
    }
```

File: LargeMasalaPizza.java

```java
public class LargeMasalaPizza extends  VegPizza{
    @Override
    public float prices() {
        return 170.0f;
    }

    @Override
    public String name() {

        return "Masala Pizza";

    }

    @Override
    public String size() {
       return "Large Size";
    }
} //End of LargeMasalaPizza class
```

File: ExtraLargeMasalaPizza.java

```
public class ExtraLargeMasalaPizza extends VegPizza {
    @Override
    public float prices() {
        return 190.0f;
    }

    @Override
    public String name() {

        return "Masala Pizza";

    }

    @Override
    public String size() {
        return "Extra-Large Size";
    }
}// End of ExtraLargeMasalaPizza class
```

- **Step 9:** Now, extend the abstract class NonVegPizza with concrete subclasses SmallNonVegPizza, MediumNonVegPizza, LargeNonVegPizza, and ExtraLargeNonVegPizza.
  File: SmallNonVegPizza.java

```
public class SmallNonVegPizza extends NonVegPizza {

    @Override
    public float prices() {
        return 190.0f;
    }

    @Override
    public String name() {
        return "Non-Veg Pizza";
    }

    @Override
    public String size() {
        return "Samll Size";
    }

}// End of SmallNonVegPizza class
```

File: MediumNonVegPizza.java

```java
public class MediumNonVegPizza extends NonVegPizza{

    @Override
    public float prices() {
        return 220.0f;
    }

    @Override
    public String name() {
        return "Non-Veg Pizza";
    }

    @Override
    public String size() {
        return "Medium Size";
    }
```

File: LargeNonVegPizza.java

```java
public class LargeNonVegPizza extends NonVegPizza{

    @Override
    public float price() {
        return 230.0f;
    }

    @Override
    public String name() {
        return "Non-Veg Pizza";
    }

    @Override
    public String size() {
        return "Large Size";
    }
}// End of LargeNonVegPizza class
```

File: ExtraLargeNonVegPizza.java

```java
public class ExtraLargeNonVegPizza extends NonVegPizza {
    @Override
```

```
public float prices() {
    return 260.0f;
}

@Override
public String name() {
    return "Non-Veg Pizza";
}

@Override
public String size() {
    return "Extra-Large Size";
}

}

// End of ExtraLargeNonVegPizza class
```

- **Step 10:** Create two abstract classes, Pepsi and Coke, which will extend the abstract class ColdDrink.
  File: Pepsi.java

```
public abstract class Pepsi extends ColdDrink {

    @Override
    public abstract String name();

    @Override
    public abstract String size();

    @Override
    public abstract float prices();

}// End of Pepsi class
```

File: Coke.java

```
public abstract class Coke  extends ColdDrink {

    @Override
    public abstract String name();
```

```
    @Override
    public abstract  String size();

    @Override
    public abstract  float price();

}// End of Coke class

</textaea></div>

<p>Step 11:<b>Create concrete sub-classes SmallPepsi,
MediumPepsi, LargePepsi that will extend to abstract
class Pepsi.</b></p>
<div id="filename">File: SmallPepsi.java</div>
<div class="codeblock"><textarea  name="code"
class="java">
public class SmallPepsi  extends Pepsi{

    @Override
    public String name() {
        return "320 ml Pepsi";
    }

    @Override
    public float prices() {
        return 27.0f;
    }

    @Override
    public String size() {
        return "Small Size";
    }
}// End of SmallPepsi class
```

File: MediumPepsi.java

```
public class MediumPepsi extends Pepsi {

    @Override
    public String name() {
        return "400 ml Pepsi";
    }
```

```
    @Override
    public String size() {
        return "Medium Size";
    }

    @Override
    public float prices() {
        return 38.0f;
    }
}// End of MediumPepsi class
```

File: LargePepsi.java

```
public class LargePepsi extends Pepsi{
    @Override
    public String name() {
        return "780 ml Pepsi";
    }

    @Override
    public String size() {
        return "Large Size";
    }

    @Override
    public float prices() {
        return 52.0f;
    }
}// End of LargePepsi class
```

- **Step 12:** Now, extend the abstract class Coke with concrete subclasses SmallCoke, MediumCoke, and LargeCoke.
  File: SmallCoke.java

```
public class SmallCoke extends Coke{

    @Override
    public String name() {
        return "320 ml Coke";
    }

    @Override
    public String size() {
```

```
        return "Small Size";
    }

    @Override
    public float prices() {

        return  27.0f;
    }
}// End of SmallCoke class
```

File: MediumCoke.java

```
public class MediumCoke extends Coke{

    @Override
    public String name() {
        return "400 ml Coke";
    }

    @Override
    public String size() {

        return "Medium Size";
    }

    @Override
    public float prices() {

        return  38.0f;
    }
}// End of MediumCoke class
```

File: LargeCoke.java

```
public class LargeCoke extends Coke {
    @Override
    public String name() {
        return "780 ml Coke";
    }

    @Override
    public String size() {
```

```
        return "Large Size";
    }

    @Override
    public float prices() {

        return 55.0f;
    }
}// End of LargeCoke class
```

</textrea>

Step 13:Create OrderedItems class that are having Item objects defined above.
File: OrderedItems.java
<textarea name="code" class="java">

```
import java.util.ArrayList;
import java.util.List;
public class OrderedItems {

    List<Item> items=new ArrayList<Item>();

    public void addItems(Item item){

        items.add(item);
    }
    public float getCost(){

        float cost=0.0f;
            for (Item item : items) {
                cost+=item.prices();
            }
        return cost;
    }
    public void showItems(){

        for (Item item : items) {
            System.out.println("Item is:" +item.name());
            System.out.println("Size is:" +item.size());
            System.out.println("Prices is: " +item.
prices());

        }
    }

}// End of OrderedItems class
```

- **Step 14:** Create an OrderBuilder class that will be responsible for creating OrderedItems class objects.

  File: OrdereBuilder.java

```java
import java.io.BufferedReader;
import java.io.IOException;
import java.io.InputStreamReader;
public class OrderBuilder {
    public OrderedItems preparePizza() throws
IOException{

        OrderedItems itemsOrder=new OrderedItems();
        BufferedReader br =new BufferedReader(new
InputStreamReader(System.in));

        System.out.println(" Enter choice of Pizza ");
        System.out.println("===================");
        System.out.println("1. Veg-Pizza");
        System.out.println("2. Non-Veg Pizza");
        System.out.println("3. Exit");
        System.out.println("===================");

        int pizzaandcolddrinkchoice=Integer.parseInt
(br.readLine());
        switch(pizzaandcolddrinkchoice)
        {
         case 1:{

            System.out.println("We ordered Veg
Pizza");
            System.out.println("\n\n");
            System.out.println("Enter types of
Veg-Pizza");
            System.out.println("--------------");
            System.out.println("1.Cheeze Pizza");
            System.out.println("2.Onion Pizza");
            System.out.println("3.Masala Pizza");
            System.out.println("4.Exit");
            System.out.println("--------------");
            int vegpizzachoice=Integer
.parseInt(br.readLine());
            switch(vegpizzachoice)
            {
```

```
                    case 1:
                    {
                        System.out.println("We ordered
Cheeze Pizza");
                        System.out.println("Enter
cheeze pizza size");
                        System.out.println("-------");
                        System.out.println("1.Small
Cheeze Pizza");
                        System.out.println("2.Medium
Cheeze Pizza");
                        System.out.println("3.Large
Cheeze Pizza");
                        System.out.println("4.Extra-
Large Cheeze Pizza");
                        System.out.println("-------");
                        int heezepizzasize=Integer.
parseInt(br.readLine());
                    switch(cheezepizzasize)
                        {
                        case 1:
                            itemsOrder.addItems(new
SmallCheezePizza());
                                break;
                        case 2:
                            itemsOrder.addItems(new
MediumCheezePizza());
                                break;
                        case 3:
                            itemsOrder.addItems(new
LargeCheezePizza());
                                break;
                        case 4:
                            itemsOrder.addItems(new
ExtraLargeCheezePizza());
                                break;
                        case 2:
                            {
                            System.out.println("We
ordered Onion Pizza");
                            System.out.println
("Enter Onion pizza size");
                            System.out.println
("---------------------");
                            System.out.println
("1. Small Onion Pizza");
```

```
                          System.out.println
("2. Medium Onion Pizza");
                          System.out.println
("3. Large Onion Pizza");
                          System.out.println
("4. Extra-Large Onion Pizza");
                          System.out.println
("---------------------");
                          int onionpizzasize
=Integer.parseInt(br.readLine());
                          switch(onionpizzasize)
                          {
                            case 1:
                              itemsOrder
.addItems(new SmallOnionPizza());
                              break;

                            case 2:
                              itemsOrder.
addItems(new MediumOnionPizza());
                              break;

                            case 3:
                              itemsOrder.
addItems(new LargeOnionPizza());
                              break;

                            case 4:
                              itemsOrder
.addItems(new ExtraLargeOnionPizza());
                              break;

                          }
                          }
                          break;
                        case 3:
                          {
                          System.out.println
("We ordered Masala Pizza");
                          System.out.println
("Enter Masala pizza size");
                          System.out.println
("---------------------");
                          System.out.println
("1. Small Masala Pizza");
```

```
                            System.out.println
("2. Medium Masala Pizza");
                            System.out.println
("3. Large Masala Pizza");
                            System.out.println
("4. Extra-Large Masala Pizza");
                            System.out.println
(---------------------");
                            int masalapizzasize=
Integer.parseInt(br.readLine());
                            switch(masalapizzasize)
                            {
                            case 1:
                            itemsOrder.addItems
(new SmallMasalaPizza());

                                break;

                            case 2:
                            itemsOrder.addItems
(new MediumMasalaPizza());

                                break;

                            case 3:
                            itemsOrder.addItems
(new LargeMasalaPizza());

                                break;

                            case 4:
                            itemsOrder.addItems
(new ExtraLargeMasalaPizza());

                                break;

                            }

                            }
                            break;

                    }

                    }
                    break;// Veg-pizza choice complete

            case 2:
            {
                System.out.println("We ordered
Non-Veg Pizza");
```

```
                    System.out.println("\n\n");

                    System.out.println("Enter Non-Veg
pizza size");
                    System.out.println
("----------------------");
                    System.out.println("1. Small
Non-Veg Pizza");
                    System.out.println("2. Medium
Non-Veg Pizza");
                    System.out.println("3. Large
Non-Veg Pizza");
                    System.out.println("4. Extra-Large
Non-Veg Pizza");
                    System.out.println
("----------------------");


                    int nonvegpizzasize=Integer
.parseInt(br.readLine());

                    switch(nonvegpizzasize)
                    {

                    case 1:
                    itemsOrder.addItems(new
SmallNonVegPizza());
                        break;

                    case 2:
                      itemsOrder.addItems(new
MediumNonVegPizza());
                        break;

                    case 3:
                        itemsOrder.addItems
(new LargeNonVegPizza());
                        break;

                    case 4:
                        itemsOrder.addItems
(new ExtraLargeNonVegPizza());
                        break;
                    }

            }
```

```
               break;
          default:
            {
            break;


            }

    }//end of the main Switch

//continued?
System.out.println("Enter choice of ColdDrink");
System.out.println("======================");
System.out.println("          1. Pepsi");
System.out.println("          2. Coke");
System.out.println("          3. Exit");
System.out.println("======================");
int coldDrink=Integer.parseInt(br.readLine());
switch (coldDrink)
  {
   case 1:
     {
     System.out.println("We ordered Pepsi");
     System.out.println("Enter PepsiSize");
     System.out.println("----------------");
     System.out.println("1. Small Pepsi");
     System.out.println("2. Medium Pepsi");
     System.out.println("3. Large Pepsi");
     System.out.println("----------------");
     int pepsisize=Integer.parseInt(br.readLine());
     switch(pepsisize)
       {
         case 1:
          itemsOrder.addItems(new SmallPepsi());
          break;

         case 2:
          itemsOrder.addItems(new MediumPepsi());
          break;

         case 3:
          itemsOrder.addItems(new LargePepsi());
          break;

         }
       }
       break;
```

```
         case 2:
                          {
         System.out.println("We ordered Coke");
         System.out.println("Enter Coke Size");
         System.out.println("---------------");
         System.out.println("1. Small Coke");
         System.out.println("2. Medium Coke");
         System.out.println("3. Large Coke");
         System.out.println("4. Extra-Large Coke");
         System.out.println("---------------");

         int cokesize=Integer.parseInt
(br.readLine());
             switch(cokesize)
             {
                 case 1:
                   itemsOrder.addItems
(new SmallCoke());
                     break;

                 case 2:
                   itemsOrder.addItems(new
MediumCoke());
                     break;

                 case 3:
                   itemsOrder.addItems
(new LargeCoke());
                     break;

             }
             }
             break;
           default:
             {
                break;
             }

             }//End of Cold-Drink switch
         return itemsOrder;
         } //End of the preparePizza() method
```

- **Step 15:** Make a BuilderDemo class that will make use of the OrderBuilder class.

    File: Prototype.java

```
import java.io.IOException;
public class BuilderDemo {

    public static void main(String[] args) throws
IOException {
        // here TODO code application logic

        OrderBuilder builder=new OrderBuilder();

        OrderedItems orderedItems=builder.
preparePizza();

        orderedItems.showItems();

        System.out.println("\n");
        System.out.println("Total Cost is : "+
orderedItems.getCost());


    }
}// End of BuilderDemo class
```

C# Builder Pattern

Participants

This pattern's classes and objects are as follows:

1. Builder (VehicleBuilder):

- Defines an abstract interface for creating Product object parts.

2. ConcreteBuilder (MotorCycleBuilder, CarBuilder, ScooterBuilder):

- Builds and assembles product parts by utilizing the Builder interface.

- Defines and maintains the representation it creates.

- Provides a means of retrieving the product.

3. Director (Shop):

- Uses the Builder interface to create an object.

4. Vehicle (Product):

- Represents the complex object under construction. ConcreteBuilder creates the internal representation of the product and defines the assembly process.

- Includes classes that define the constituent parts, as well as interfaces for putting the parts together to form the final result.

C# Structural Code

This structural code demonstrates the Builder Pattern, which is used to create complex objects step by step. The construction process can generate various object representations and provides a high level of control over object assembly.

```csharp
using System;
using System.Collections.Generic;

namespace DoFactory.GangOfFour.Builder.Structural
{
    /// <summary> MainApp startup class for the Structural
    /// Builder Design Pattern </summary>

    public class MainApp
    {
        /// <summary> Entry point into the console
application. </summary>

        public static void Main()
        {
            // Create the director and builders

            Director director = new Director();

            Builder b1 = new ConcreteBuilder1();
            Builder b2 = new ConcreteBuilder2();

            // Construct the two products

            director.Construct(b1);
            Product p1 = b1.GetResult();
            p1.Show();

            director.Construct(b2);
            Product p2 = b2.GetResult();
            p2.Show();
```

```
            // Wait for the user

            Console.ReadKey();
        }
    }

    /// <summary> The 'Director' class </summary>

    class Director
    {
        // Builder uses complex series of the steps

        public void Construct(Builder builder)
        {
            builder.BuildPartX();
            builder.BuildPartY();
        }
    }

    /// <summary> The 'Builder' abstract class </summary>

    abstract class Builder
    {
        public abstract void BuildPartX();
        public abstract void BuildPartY();
        public abstract Product GetResult();
    }

    /// <summary> The 'ConcreteBuilder1' class </summary>

    class ConcreteBuilder1 : Builder
    {
        private Product _product = new Product();

        public override void BuildPartX()
        {
            _product.Add("PartX");
        }

        public override void BuildPartY()
        {
            _product.Add("PartY");
        }

        public override Product GetResult()
        {
            return _product;
        }
```

```
        }
    }

    /// <summary> The 'ConcreteBuilder2' class </summary>

    class ConcreteBuilder2 : Builder
    {
        private Product _product = new Product();

        public override void BuildPartX()
        {
            _product.Add("PartA");
        }

        public override void BuildPartY()
        {
            _product.Add("PartB");
        }

        public override Product GetResult()
        {
            return _product;
        }
    }

    /// <summary> The 'Product' class </summary>

    class Product
    {
        private List<string> _parts = new List<string>();

        public void Add(string part)
        {
            _parts.Add(part);
        }

        public void Show()
        {
            Console.WriteLine("\nProduct Parts---");
            foreach (string part in _parts)
                Console.WriteLine(part);
        }
    }
}
```

Real-World C# Code

This real-world code demonstrates the Builder Pattern, in which various vehicles are assembled step by step. VehicleBuilders are used in the Shop to build a variety of Vehicles in a series of sequential steps.

```csharp
using System;
using System.Collections.Generic;

namespace DoFactory.GangOfFour.Builder.RealWorld
{
    /// <summary> MainApp startup class for the Real-World
    Builder Design Pattern. </summary>

    public class MainApp
    {
        /// <summary> Entry point into console application.
    </summary>

        public static void Main()
        {
            VehicleBuilder builder;

            // Create shop with the vehicle builders

            Shop shop = new Shop();

            // Construct and display the vehicles

            builder = new ScooterBuilder();
            shop.Construct(builder);
            builder.Vehicle.Show();

            builder = new CarBuilder();
            shop.Construct(builder);
            builder.Vehicle.Show();

            builder = new MotorCycleBuilder();
            shop.Construct(builder);
            builder.Vehicle.Show();

            // Wait for the user

            Console.ReadKey();
        }
    }

    /// <summary> The 'Director' class </summary>
```

```csharp
class Shop
{
    // Builder uses complex series of the steps

    public void Construct(VehicleBuilder
vehicleBuilder)
    {
        vehicleBuilder.BuildFrame();
        vehicleBuilder.BuildEngine();
        vehicleBuilder.BuildWheels();
        vehicleBuilder.BuildDoors();
    }
}

/// <summary> The 'Builder' abstract class </summary>

abstract class VehicleBuilder
{
    protected Vehicle vehicle;

    // Gets the vehicle instance

    public Vehicle Vehicle
    {
        get { return vehicle; }
    }

    // Abstract the build methods

    public abstract void BuildFrame();
    public abstract void BuildEngine();
    public abstract void BuildWheels();
    public abstract void BuildDoors();
}

/// <summary> The 'ConcreteBuilder1' class </summary>

class MotorCycleBuilder : VehicleBuilder
{
    public MotorCycleBuilder()
    {
        vehicle = new Vehicle("MotorCycle");
    }

    public override void BuildFrame()
    {
        vehicle["frame"] = "MotorCycle-Frame";
    }
```

```
public override void BuildEngine()
{
    vehicle["engine"] = "520 cc";
}

public override void BuildWheels()
{
    vehicle["wheels"] = "2";
}

public override void BuildDoors()
{
    vehicle["doors"] = "0";
}
}

/// <summary> The 'ConcreteBuilder2' class </summary>

class CarBuilder : VehicleBuilder
{
    public CarBuilder()
    {
        vehicle = new Vehicle("Car");
    }

    public override void BuildFrame()
    {
        vehicle["frame"] = "Car-Frame";
    }

    public override void BuildEngine()
    {
        vehicle["engine"] = "2800 cc";
    }

    public override void BuildWheels()
    {
        vehicle["wheels"] = "4";
    }

    public override void BuildDoors()
    {
        vehicle["doors"] = "4";
    }
}

/// <summary> The 'ConcreteBuilder3' class </summary>
```

```csharp
class ScooterBuilder : VehicleBuilder
{
    public ScooterBuilder()
    {
        vehicle = new Vehicle("Scooter");
    }

    public override void BuildFrame()
    {
        vehicle["frame"] = "Scooter-Frame";
    }

    public override void BuildEngine()
    {
        vehicle["engine"] = "52 cc";
    }

    public override void BuildWheels()
    {
        vehicle["wheels"] = "2";
    }

    public override void BuildDoors()
    {
        vehicle["doors"] = "0";
    }
}

/// <summary> The 'Product' class </summary>

class Vehicle
{
    private string _vehicleType;
    private Dictionary<string, string> _parts =
      new Dictionary<string, string>();
    // Constructor

    public Vehicle(string vehicleType)
    {
        this._vehicleType = vehicleType;
    }

    // Indexer

    public string this[string key]
    {
        get { return _parts[key]; }
        set { _parts[key] = value; }
    }
```

```
public void Show()
{
        Console.WriteLine("\n--------------");
        Console.WriteLine("Vehicle Type is: {0}",
_vehicleType);
        Console.WriteLine(" Frame is: {0}",
_parts["frame"]);
        Console.WriteLine(" Engine is: {0}",
_parts["engine"]);
        Console.WriteLine(" #Wheels is: {0}",
_parts["wheels"]);
        Console.WriteLine(" #Doors is: {0}",
_parts["doors"]);
    }
}
}
```

PROTOTYPE PATTERN

The Prototype Pattern is a Creational Design Pattern that seeks to minimize the number of classes needed in an application. It enables you to duplicate existing objects regardless of how their classes are implemented in practice. In general, the object is formed here by running-time cloning of a prototype instance.

It is strongly advised to utilize the Prototype Pattern when creating an item is a time-consuming and resource-intensive operation when a similar object already exists. This approach allows us to replicate the original object and then alter it to meet our needs.

Problems We Confront in the Absence of the Prototype Pattern

Assume we have a Shape class that generates various forms like as circles, rectangles, squares, and so on, and we already have one object of it. Now we want to make an identical duplicate of this item. How would a typical developer fare?

He or she will build a new object of the same class, applying all of the original objects' functions and properties. However, we cannot replicate every field of the original object since some may be secret or protected and not accessible from the outside of the object.

The difficulties do not end here. We also become reliant on the code of another class, which is never a good thing in software development.

For a better understanding, consider the example of Courses at PeeksforPeeks, which offers courses such as SDE, DSA, STL, and so on. Creating objects for similar courses again and over is not a suitable activity for improved resource use.

```python
# concrete-course
class DSA():
    """Class for the Data Structures and Algorithms"""

    def Type(self):
        return "Data-Structures and Algorithms"

    def __str__(self):
        return "DSA"


# concrete-course
class SDE():
    """Class for the Software development Engineer"""

    def Type(self):
        return "Software-Development Engineer"

    def __str__(self):
        return "SDE"


# concrete course
class STL():
    """class for the Standard Template Library of C++"""

    def Type(self):
        return "Standard-Template Library"

    def __str__(self):
        return "STL"


# main method
if __name__ == "__main__":
    sde = SDE()  # object for the SDE
    dsa = DSA()  # object for the DSA
    stl = STL()  # object for the STL
```

```
    print(f'Name of the Course: {sde} and its type:
{sde.Type()}')
    print(f'Name of the Course: {stl} and its type:
{stl.Type()}')
    print(f'Name of the Course: {dsa} and its type:
{dsa.Type()}')
```

Prototype Pattern Solution

To address such issues, we employ the Prototype Pattern. We'd make distinct classes for Courses_At_PFP and Course_At_PFP Cache, which would allow us to make an identical replica of an existing object with the same field attributes. This method delegated the cloning operation to the actual copied objects. In this section, we create a common interface or class that enables object cloning, allowing us to clone the object without attaching our code to the class of that function.

A prototype is an object that allows for cloning.

```
# import required modules

from abc import ABCMeta, abstractmethod
import copy


# class - Courses at PeeksforPeeks
class Courses_At_PFP(metaclass = ABCMeta):

    # constructor
    def __init__(self):
        self.id = None
        self.type = None

    @abstractmethod
    def course(self):
        pass

    def get_type(self):
        return self.type

    def get_id(self):
        return self.id
```

```python
    def set_id(self, sid):
        self.id = sid

    def clone(self):
        return copy.copy(self)

# class - DSA course
class DSA(Courses_At_PFP):
    def __init__(self):
        super().__init__()
        self.type = "Data-Structures and Algorithms"

    def course(self):
        print("Inside the DSA::course() method")

# class - SDE Course
class SDE(Courses_At_PFP):
    def __init__(self):
        super().__init__()
        self.type = "Software-Development Engineer"

    def course(self):
        print("Inside SDE::course() method.")

# class - STL Course
class STL(Courses_At_PFP):
    def __init__(self):
        super().__init__()
        self.type = "Standard-Template Library"

    def course(self):
        print("Inside STL::course() method.")

# class - Courses At PeeksforPeeks Cache
class Courses_At_PFP_Cache:

    # cache to store the useful information
    cache = {}

    @staticmethod
    def get_course(sid):
        COURSE = Courses_At_PFP_Cache.cache.get(sid, None)
        return COURSE.clone()

    @staticmethod
    def load():
```

```
sde = SDE()
sde.set_id("1")
Courses_At_PFP_Cache.cache[sde.get_id()] = sde

dsa = DSA()
dsa.set_id("2")
Courses_At_PFP_Cache.cache[dsa.get_id()] = dsa

stl = STL()
stl.set_id("3")
Courses_At_PFP_Cache.cache[stl.get_id()] = stl

# main function
if __name__ == '__main__':
    Courses_At_PFP_Cache.load()

    sde = Courses_At_PFP_Cache.get_course("1")
    print(sde.get_type())

    dsa = Courses_At_PFP_Cache.get_course("2")
    print(dsa.get_type())

    stl = Courses_At_PFP_Cache.get_course("3")
    print(stl.get_type())
```

Advantages

- **Less Subclasses:** All of the other Creational Design Patterns introduce a slew of new subclasses, which can be difficult to manage
  when working on a large project. We may avoid this by adopting the
  Prototype Design Pattern.

- **Gives different values to new objects:** All highly dynamic systems
  allow us to implement new behavior through object composition by
  declaring values for an object's variables rather than by establishing
  new classes.

- **Gives new objects varied structure:** Generally, all programs construct objects from parts and subparts. For our convenience, such
  apps frequently allow us to create sophisticated, user-defined structures to reuse a specific subcircuit.

Drawbacks

- **Abstraction:** It aids in abstraction by concealing the specific implementation details of the class.

- **Lower-Level Resource Waste:** It may be proven to be an overload of resources for a project that employs very few objects.

Applicability

- **Independence from Concrete Class:** The prototype Pattern allows us to implement new objects without relying on the concrete implementation of the class.

- **Recurring Difficulties:** The prototype technique is often used to handle recurring and complicated software development challenges.

Prototype Pattern Usage

- At runtime, when the classes are instantiated.

- When the cost of producing an object is high or complicated.

- When you want to keep the number of classes in an application as low as possible.

- When the client application must be unaware of the creation and representation of objects.

In Java, an Example of the Prototype Design Pattern

Let's look at an example of the Prototype Design Pattern.

File: Prototype.java

```
interface Prototype {

    public Prototype getClone();

}//End of the Prototype interface.
```

File: EmployeeRecord.java

```java
class EmployeeRecord implements Prototype{

    private int id;
    private String names, designation;
    private double salary;
    private String address;

    public EmployeeRecord(){
            System.out.println(" Employee Records of
Oracle Corporation ");
            System.out.println("-----------------------");
            System.out.
println("Eid"+"\t"+"Enames"+"\t"+"Edesignation"+"\
t"+"Esalary"+"\t\t"+"Eaddress");

    }

    public EmployeeRecord(int id, String names, String
designation, double salary, String address) {

            this();
            this.id = id;
            this.names = names;
            this.designation = designation;
            this.salary = salary;
            this.address = address;
    }

    public void showRecord(){

            System.out.
println(id+"\t"+names+"\t"+designation+"\t"+salary+"\
t"+address);
    }

        @Override
        public Prototype getClone() {

            return new EmployeeRecord(id,names,designation,
salary,address);
    }
}//End of the EmployeeRecord class.
```

File: PrototypeDemo.java

```
import java.io.BufferedReader;
import java.io.IOException;
import java.io.InputStreamReader;

class PrototypeDemo{
    public static void main(String[] args) throws
IOException {

        BufferedReader br =new BufferedReader(new
InputStreamReader(System.in));
        System.out.print("Enter the Employee Id: ");
        int eid=Integer.parseInt(br.readLine());
        System.out.print("\n");

        System.out.print("Enter the Employee Names: ");
        String ename=br.readLine();
        System.out.print("\n");

        System.out.print("Enter the Employee Designation: ");
        String edesignation=br.readLine();
        System.out.print("\n");

        System.out.print("Enter the Employee Address: ");
        String eaddress=br.readLine();
        System.out.print("\n");

        System.out.print("Enter the Employee Salary: ");
        double esalary= Double.parseDouble(br.readLine());
        System.out.print("\n");

        EmployeeRecord e1=new EmployeeRecord(eid,enames,
edesignation,esalary,eaddress);

        e1.showRecord();
        System.out.println("\n");
        EmployeeRecord e2=(EmployeeRecord) e1.getClone();
        e2.showRecord();
    }
}//End of ProtoypeDemo class.
```

Prototype Pattern in C#

The Prototype Design Pattern specifies the type of objects to create by using a prototypical instance and then copying this prototype to create new objects.

Participants

This pattern's classes and objects are as follows:

1. Prototype (ColorPrototype):

   - Declares an interface for cloning itself.

2. ConcretePrototype (Color):

   - Implements a cloning operation.

3. Client (ColorManager):

   - Makes a new object by requesting that a prototype clone itself.

C# Structural Code

This structural code demonstrates the Prototype pattern, which involves creating new objects by copying preexisting objects (prototypes) of the same class.

```csharp
using System;

namespace Prototype.Structural
{
    /// <summary> Prototype Design Pattern </summary>

    public class Program
    {
        public static void Main(string[] args)
        {
            // Create the two instances and clone each

            ConcretePrototype1 p1 = new
ConcretePrototype1("I");
            ConcretePrototype1 c1 = (ConcretePrototype1)
p1.Clone();
            Console.WriteLine("Cloned: {0}", c1.Id);

            ConcretePrototype2 p2 = new
ConcretePrototype2("II");
            ConcretePrototype2 c2 = (ConcretePrototype2)
p2.Clone();
            Console.WriteLine("Cloned: {0}", c2.Id);

            // Wait for the user
```

```
        Console.ReadKey();
    }
}

/// <summary> The 'Prototype' abstract class </summary>

public abstract class Prototype
{
    string id;

    // Constructor

    public Prototype(string id)
    {
        this.id = id;
    }

    // Gets-id

    public string Id
    {
        get { return id; }
    }

    public abstract Prototype Clone();
}

/// <summary> A 'ConcretePrototype' class </summary>

public class ConcretePrototype1 : Prototype
{
    // Constructor

    public ConcretePrototype1(string id)
        : base(id)
    {
    }

    // Returns shallow copy

    public override Prototype Clone()
    {
        return (Prototype)this.MemberwiseClone();
    }
}

/// <summary> A 'ConcretePrototype' class </summary>
```

```
public class ConcretePrototype2 : Prototype
{
    // Constructor

    public ConcretePrototype2(string id)
        : base(id)
    {
    }

    // Returns shallow copy

    public override Prototype Clone()
    {
        return (Prototype)this.MemberwiseClone();
    }
}
}
```

Real-World Code in C#

This code demonstrates the Prototype pattern, which creates new Color objects by copying preexisting, user-defined Colors of the same type.

```
using System;
using System.Collections.Generic;

namespace Prototype.RealWorld
{
    /// <summary> Prototype Design Pattern </summary>

    public class Program
    {
        public static void Main(string[] args)
        {
            ColorManager colormanager = new ColorManager();

            // Initialize with the standard colors

            colormanager["red"] = new Color(255, 0, 0);
            colormanager["green"] = new Color(0, 255, 0);
            colormanager["blue"] = new Color(0, 0, 255);

            // User adds the personalized colors
```

```
          colormanager["angry"] = new Color(255, 54, 0);
          colormanager["peace"] = new Color(128, 211, 128);
          colormanager["flame"] = new Color(211, 34, 20);

          // User clones the selected colors

          Color color1 = colormanager["red"].Clone() as
Color;
          Color color2 = colormanager["peace"].Clone() as
Color;
          Color color3 = colormanager["flame"].Clone() as
Color;

          // Wait for the user

          Console.ReadKey();
      }
  }

  /// <summary> The 'Prototype' abstract class </summary>

  public abstract class ColorPrototype
  {
      public abstract ColorPrototype Clone();
  }

  /// <summary> The 'ConcretePrototype' class </summary>

  public class Color : ColorPrototype
  {
      int red;
      int green;
      int blue;

      // Constructor

      public Color(int red, int green, int blue)
      {
          this.red = red;
          this.green = green;
          this.blue = blue;
      }

      // Create shallow copy

      public override ColorPrototype Clone()
      {
          Console.WriteLine(
```

```
            "Cloning color RGB: {0,3},{1,3},{2,3}",
            red, green, blue);
        return this.MemberwiseClone() as ColorPrototype;
    }
}


/// <summary> Prototype manager </summary>

public class ColorManager
{
    private Dictionary<string, ColorPrototype> colors =
        new Dictionary<string, ColorPrototype>();

    // Indexer

    public ColorPrototype this[string key]
    {
        get { return colors[key]; }
        set { colors.Add(key, value); }
    }
}
}
```

ABSTRACT FACTORY PATTERN

The Abstract Factory Pattern is a Creational Design pattern that allows us to create families of linked items without having to describe their particular classes. We have the simplest technique to make a comparable kind of numerous objects by using the abstract Factory Pattern.

It allows us to encapsulate a collection of separate factories. Essentially, we are attempting to abstract the development of objects based on logic, business, platform selection, and so on.

Problems We Confront in the Absence of the Abstract Factory Pattern

Assume we want to be a part of one of the exclusive batches of PeeksforPeeks. So we'll go there and inquire about the offered Courses, their Fee Structure, their Timings, and other vital details. They will just examine their system and provide us with all the information we want. Does it appear simple? Consider how the developers structure the system and make their website so lubricious.

Developers will create distinct classes for each course, each with its own set of attributes such as fee structure, timings, etc. But how will they call them and instantiate their objects?

Here's the issue: imagine there were just three-four courses offered at PeeksforPeeks at first, but they added five additional courses.

As a result, we must manually initialize their objects, which is undesirable from the developer's perspective.

```python
# Python Code for the object
# oriented concepts without using
# the Abstract factory
# method in the class

class DSA:

    """ Class for the Data Structure and Algorithms """

    def price(self):
        return 13000

    def __str__(self):
        return "DSA"

class STL:

    """Class for the Standard Template Library"""

    def price(self):
        return 9000

    def __str__(self):
        return "STL"

class SDE:

    """Class for the Software Development Engineer"""

    def price(self):
        return 19000

    def __str__(self):
        return 'SDE'

# main method
if __name__ == "__main__":

    sde = SDE()      # object for the SDE class
    dsa = DSA()      # object for the DSA class
    stl = STL()      # object for the STL class
```

```
    print(f'Name of course is {sde} and its price is
{sde.price()}')
    print(f'Name of course is {dsa} and its price is
{dsa.price()}')
    print(f'Name of course is {stl} and its price is
{stl.price()}')
```

Solution Based on the Abstract Factory Pattern

Its answer is to replace the plain object formation calls with calls to the specific abstract factory function. There will be no change in the object's construction, but they will call within the factory function.

We will construct a new class called Course_At_PFP that will automatically handle all object initialization. We no longer have to be concerned about how many courses we will add over time.

```
# Python Code for the object
# oriented concepts using the
# abstract factory design pattern

import random

class Course_At_PFP:

    """ PeeksforPeeks portal for the courses """

    def __init__(self, courses_factory = None):
        """course-factory is out abstract-factory"""

        self.course_factory = courses_factory

    def show_course(self):

        """creates and shows courses using abstract
factory"""

        course = self.course_factory()

        print(f'We have course named {course}')
        print(f'its price is {course.Fee()}')


class DSA:


    """Class for the Data Structure and Algorithms"""
```

```
    def Fee(self):
        return 13000

    def __str__(self):
        return "DSA"

class STL:

    """Class for the Standard Template Library"""

    def Fee(self):
        return 9000

    def __str__(self):
        return "STL"

class SDE:

    """Class for Software Development Engineer"""

    def Fee(self):
        return 19000

    def __str__(self):
        return 'SDE'

def random_course():

    """A random class for the choosing the course"""

    return random.choice([SDE, STL, DSA])()


if __name__ == "__main__":

    course = Course_At_PFP(random_course)

    for i in range(6):
        course.show_course()
```

Advantages of Using the Abstract Factory Pattern

- This pattern is especially useful when the client is unsure what type to create.

- Introducing new product variants without breaking the existing client code is simple.

- The products we receive from the Factory are unquestionably compatible with one another.

Disadvantages of Using Abstract Factory Pattern

- Due to the existence of many classes, our simple code may become complicated.
- We end up with many small files, resulting in file clutter.

Applicability

- Abstract Factory patterns are most commonly found in sheet metal stamping equipment used to manufacture automobiles.
- It can use in a system that must process reports from various categories, such as input, output, and intermediate exchanges.

Abstract Factory Pattern Usage

- When the system must be self-contained in terms of how its objects are created, composed, and represented.
- This constraint must be enforced when a family of related objects must be used together.
- When we want to provide an object library that does not show implementations but only exposes interfaces.
- When the system must be configured with one of several families of objects.

In Java, an Example of the Abstract Factory Pattern

We calculate loan payments for various banks such as DFC, ICICI, and BI.

- **Step 1:** Design a bank interface.

```
import java.io.*;
interface Bank{
        String getBankName();
}
```

- **Step 2:** Implement the Bank interface in concrete classes.

```
class DFC implements Bank{
    private final String BNAME;
    public HDFC(){
            BNAME="DFC BANK";
    }
    public String getBankName() {
            return BNAME;
    }
}
```

```
class ICCI implements Bank{
    private final String BNAME;
    ICCI(){
            BNAME="ICCI BANK";
    }
    public String getBankName() {
            return BNAME;
    }
}
```

```
class BI implements Bank{
    private final String BNAME;
    public BI(){
            BNAME="BI BANK";
    }
    public String getBankName(){
            return BNAME;
    }
}
```

- **Step 3:** Create the abstract class Loan.

```
abstract class Loan{
    protected double rate;
    abstract void getInterestRate(double rate);
    public void calculateLoanPayment(double loanamount,
int years)
    {
        /* to calculate monthly loan payment i.e., EMI

            rate=annual interest rate/12*100;
            n=number of the monthly installments;
            1year=12 months.
            so, n=years*12;
```

```
*/
        double EMI;
        int n;

        n=years*12;
        rate=rate/1200;
    EMI=((rate*Math.pow((1+rate),n))/((Math.
    pow((1+rate),n))-1))*loanamount;

    System.out.println("our monthly EMI is "+ EMI +" for
    amount"+loanamount+" we have borrowed");
    }
    }// end of Loan abstract class.
```

- **Step 4:** Design concrete classes that extend the abstract Loan class.

```
class HomeLoan extends Loan{
    public void getInterestRate(double r1){
        rate=r1;
    }
}//End of HomeLoan class.


class BussinessLoan extends Loan{
    public void getInterestRate(double r1){
        rate=r1;
    }
}//End of BusssinessLoan class.


class EducationLoan extends Loan{
    public void getInterestRate(double r1){
        rate=r1;
    }
}//End of EducationLoan class.
```

- **Step 5:** Create an abstract class (i.e., AbstractFactory) to obtain the factories for Bank and Loan Objects.

```
abstract class AbstractFactory{
    public abstract Bank getBank(String bank);
    public abstract Loan getLoan(String loan);
}
```

- **Step 6:** Create factory classes that inherit from the AbstractFactory class in order to produce concrete class objects based on the information provided.

```
class BankFactory extends AbstractFactory{
    public Bank getBank(String bank){
        if(bank == null){
            return null;
        }
        if(bank.equalsIgnoreCase("DFC")){
            return new DFC();
        } else if(bank.equalsIgnoreCase("ICCI")){
            return new ICCI();
        } else if(bank.equalsIgnoreCase("BI")){
            return new BI();
        }
        return null;
    }
    public Loan getLoan(String loan) {
        return null;
    }
}//End of BankFactory class.
```

```
class LoanFactory extends AbstractFactory{
    public Bank getBank(String bank){
        return null;
    }

public Loan getLoan(String loan){
if(loan == null){
  return null;
}
if(loan.equalsIgnoreCase("Home")){
  return new HomeLoan();
} else if(loan.equalsIgnoreCase("Business")){
  return new BussinessLoan();
} else if(loan.equalsIgnoreCase("Education")){
  return new EducationLoan();
}
return null;
} }
```

- **Step 7:** Create a FactoryCreator class to obtain factories by passing information like Bank or Loan.

```
class FactoryCreator {
    public static AbstractFactory getFactory(String
choice){
        if(choice.equalsIgnoreCase("Bank")){
            return new BankFactory();
        } else if(choice.equalsIgnoreCase("Loan")){
            return new LoanFactory();
        }
        return null;
    }
}//End of FactoryCreator.
```

- **Step 8:** Use the FactoryCreator to obtain AbstractFactory in order to obtain concrete class factories by passing information such as type.

```
import java.io.*;
class AbstractFactoryPatternExample {
    public static void main(String args[])throws
IOException {

        BufferedReader br=new BufferedReader(new
InputStreamReader(System.in));

        System.out.print("Enter name of Bank from where
we want to take loan amount: ");
        String bankName=br.readLine();

System.out.print("\n");
System.out.print("Enter type of loan e.g. home loan or
business loan or education loan : ");

String loanName=br.readLine();
AbstractFactory bankFactory = FactoryCreator.
getFactory("Bank");
Bank b=bankFactory.getBank(bankName);

System.out.print("\n");
System.out.print("Enter interest rate for "+b.
getBankName()+ ": ");

double rate=Double.parseDouble(br.readLine());
System.out.print("\n");
System.out.print("Enter loan amount we want to take: ");
```

```
double loanAmount=Double.parseDouble(br.readLine());
System.out.print("\n");
System.out.print("Enter number of years to pay our
entire loan amount: ");
int years=Integer.parseInt(br.readLine());

System.out.print("\n");
System.out.println("we are taking loan from "+
b.getBankName());

AbstractFactory loanFactory = FactoryCreator.
getFactory("Loan");
        Loan l=loanFactory.getLoan(loanName);
        l.getInterestRate(rate);
        l.calculateLoanPayment(loanAmount,years);
    }
}//End of AbstractFactoryPatternExample
```

Abstract Factory Pattern in C#

The Abstract Factory Pattern provides an interface for generating families of linked or dependent items without describing their concrete classes.

Participants

This pattern's classes and objects are as follows:

1. AbstractFactory (ContinentFactory):

   - Specifies an interface for operations that produce abstract products.

2. ConcreteFactory (AfricaFactory, AmericaFactory):

   - Carries out activities to produce concrete product items.

3. AbstractProduct (Herbivore, Carnivore):

   - Defines an interface for a product object type.

4. Product (Wildebeest, Lion, Bison, Wolf):

   - A product object defined by the relevant concrete factory.

   - AbstractProduct interface is implemented.

5. Client (AnimalWorld):

- Uses interfaces specified by the AbstractFactory and AbstractProduct classes.

C# Structural Code

The Abstract Factory pattern creates parallel hierarchies of objects in this structured code. Object generation has been abstracted, so client code has no requirement to include hard-coded class names.

```csharp
using System;

namespace DoFactory.GangOfFour.Abstract.Structural
{
    /// <summary> MainApp startup class for Structural
    /// Abstract Factory Design Pattern. </summary>

    class MainApp
    {
        /// <summary> Entry point into the console
application. </summary>

        public static void Main()
        {
            // Abstract-factory #1

            AbstractFactory factory1 =
new ConcreteFactory1();
            Client client1 = new Client(factory1);
            client1.Run();

            // Abstract-factory #2

            AbstractFactory factory2 =
new ConcreteFactory2();
            Client client2 = new Client(factory2);
            client2.Run();

            // Wait for the user input

            Console.ReadKey();
        }
    }

    /// <summary> The 'AbstractFactory' abstract class
    /// </summary>
```

```csharp
abstract class AbstractFactory
{
    public abstract AbstractProductX CreateProductX();
    public abstract AbstractProductY CreateProductY();
}


/// <summary> The 'ConcreteFactory1' class
/// </summary>

class ConcreteFactory1 : AbstractFactory
{
    public override AbstractProductX CreateProductX()
    {
        return new ProductX1();
    }
    public override AbstractProductY CreateProductY()
    {
        return new ProductY1();
    }
}


/// <summary> The 'ConcreteFactory2' class
/// </summary>

class ConcreteFactory2 : AbstractFactory
{
    public override AbstractProductX CreateProductX()
    {
        return new ProductX2();
    }
    public override AbstractProductY CreateProductY()
    {
        return new ProductY2();
    }
}

/// <summary> The 'AbstractProductX' abstract class
/// </summary>

abstract class AbstractProductX
{
}


/// <summary> The 'AbstractProductY' abstract class
/// </summary>

abstract class AbstractProductY
{
```

```
      public abstract void Interact(AbstractProductX a);
}


/// <summary> The 'ProductA1' class
/// </summary>

class ProductX1 : AbstractProductX
{
}


/// <summary> The 'ProductY1' class
/// </summary>

class ProductY1 : AbstractProductY
{
    public override void Interact(AbstractProductX a)
    {
        Console.WriteLine(this.GetType().Name +
          " interacts with " + a.GetType().Name);
    }
}

/// <summary> The 'ProductX2' class
/// </summary>

class ProductX2 : AbstractProductX
{
}


/// <summary> The 'ProductB2' class
/// </summary>

class ProductY2 : AbstractProductY
{
    public override void Interact(AbstractProductX a)
    {
        Console.WriteLine(this.GetType().Name +
          " interacts with " + a.GetType().Name);
    }
}

/// <summary> The 'Client' class. Interaction
environment for the products.
/// </summary>

class Client
{
    private AbstractProductX _abstractProductX;
    private AbstractProductY _abstractProductY;
```

```
            // Constructor

            public Client(AbstractFactory factory)
            {
                _abstractProductY = factory.CreateProductY();
                _abstractProductX = factory.CreateProductX();
            }

            public void Run()
            {
                _abstractProductY.Interact(_abstractProductX);
            }
        }
    }
```

Real-World C# Code

This real-world code explains how to use several factories to create diverse animal worlds for a computer game. Although the creatures made by the Continent factories varied, their interactions with one another do not.

```
using System;

namespace DoFactory.GangOfFour.Abstract.RealWorld
{
    /// <summary> MainApp startup class for Real-World
    /// Abstract Factory Design Pattern. </summary>

    class MainApp
    {
        /// <summary> Entry point into the console
application.
        /// </summary>

        public static void Main()
        {
            // Create and run the African animal world

            ContinentFactory africa = new AfricaFactory();
            AnimalWorld world = new AnimalWorld(africa);
            world.RunFoodChain();

            // Create and run the American animal world
```

```
        ContinentFactory america = new AmericaFactory();
        world = new AnimalWorld(america);
        world.RunFoodChain();

        // Wait for the user input

        Console.ReadKey();
    }
}

/// <summary> The 'AbstractFactory' abstract class
/// </summary>

abstract class ContinentFactory
{
    public abstract Herbivore CreateHerbivore();
    public abstract Carnivore CreateCarnivore();
}

/// <summary> The 'ConcreteFactory1' class
/// </summary>

class AfricaFactory : ContinentFactory
{
    public override Herbivore CreateHerbivore()
    {
        return new Wildebeest();
    }
    public override Carnivore CreateCarnivore()
    {
        return new Lion();
    }
}

/// <summary> The 'ConcreteFactory2' class
/// </summary>

class AmericaFactory : ContinentFactory
{
    public override Herbivore CreateHerbivore()
    {
        return new Bison();
    }
    public override Carnivore CreateCarnivore()
    {
        return new Wolf();
    }
}
```

```csharp
/// <summary> The 'AbstractProductA' abstract class
/// </summary>

abstract class Herbivore
{
}


/// <summary> The 'AbstractProductB' abstract class
/// </summary>

abstract class Carnivore
{
    public abstract void Eat(Herbivore h);
}

/// <summary> The 'ProductA1' class
/// </summary>

class Wildebeest : Herbivore
{
}

/// <summary> The 'ProductB1' class
/// </summary>

class Lion : Carnivore
{
    public override void Eat(Herbivore h)
    {
        // Eat-Wildebeest

        Console.WriteLine(this.GetType().Name +
            " eats " + h.GetType().Name);
    }
}

/// <summary> The 'ProductA2' class
/// </summary>

class Bison : Herbivore
{
}

/// <summary> The 'ProductB2' class
/// </summary>

class Wolf : Carnivore
{
```

```
        public override void Eat(Herbivore h)
        {
            // Eat Bison

            Console.WriteLine(this.GetType().Name +
                " eats " + h.GetType().Name);
        }
    }

    /// <summary> The 'Client' class
    /// </summary>

    class AnimalWorld
    {
        private Herbivore _herbivore;
        private Carnivore _carnivore;

        // Constructor

        public AnimalWorld(ContinentFactory factory)
        {
            _carnivore = factory.CreateCarnivore();
            _herbivore = factory.CreateHerbivore();
        }

        public void RunFoodChain()
        {
            _carnivore.Eat(_herbivore);
        }
    }
}
```

COMPOSITE PATTERN

The Composite Pattern is a Structural Design Pattern that describes a group of objects that are handled in the same manner as a single instance of the same type of object. The Composite Method's goal is to compose items into Tree type structures to express whole-partial hierarchies.

One of the primary benefits of utilizing the Composite Pattern is that it allows us first to compose the objects into the Tree Structure and then operate with these structures as a single object or entity.

The procedures available on all composite objects frequently have a least common denominator connection.

Four groups are participating with the Composite Pattern:

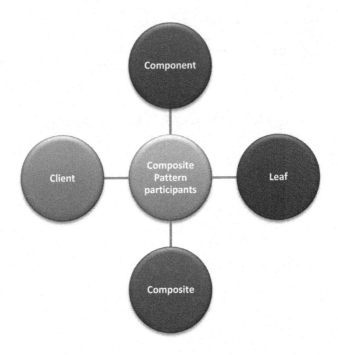

Participants of Composite Pattern.

1. **Component:** A component aids in implementing the default behavior for the interface shared by all classes as needed. It specifies the interface of the composition's objects and the methods for accessing and controlling its child components.

2. **Leaf:** It determines the behavior of the composition's primitive items. It represents the composition's leaf item.

3. **Composite:** It holds the child component and performs child-related activities in the component interface.

4. **Client:** It manipulates the composition's objects via the component interface.

The Problem without the Use of the Composite Pattern

Assume we are investigating an organizational structure comprised of General Managers, Managers, and Developers. A General Manager may have numerous Managers reporting to him, while a Manager may have many developers reporting.

Assume we need to figure out the total compensation of all workers. So, how would you go about doing that?

An average developer would almost certainly take the direct technique, going through each person and calculating the overall wage. It looks simple, doesn't it? Not so when it comes to implementation. Because we need to know the classes of all the workers, including the General Manager, Manager, and Developers.

In a tree-based structure, it appears to be an impossible problem to solve using a direct method.

Composite Pattern Solution

One of the most satisfactory answers to the difficulty above is to work with a standard interface that provides a function for computing the total salary.

When we have "composites that contain components, each of which may be a composite," we often employ the Composite Pattern.

```
"""Here we attempt to make organizational hierarchy with
the sub-organization,
which may have subsequent sub-organizations, like:
GeneralManager                      [Composite]
    Manager1                        [Composite]
        Developer11                 [Leaf]
        Developer12                 [Leaf]
    Manager2                        [Composite]
        Developer21                 [Leaf]
        Developer22                 [Leaf]"""


class LeafElement:

    '''Class representing objects at bottom or Leaf of the
hierarchy tree'''

    def __init__(self, *args):

        ''''Takes first positional argument and assigns to
the member variable "position".'''
        self.position = args[0]

    def showDetails(self):
```

```python
        '''Prints position of the child element.'''
        print("\t", end ="")
        print(self.position)


class CompositeElement:

    '''Class represents objects at any level of the
hierarchy
    tree except for the bottom or leaf level. Maintains
child
    objects by adding and removing them from the tree
structure'''

    def __init__(self, *args):

        '''Takes first positional argument and assigns to
member
        variable "position". Initializes list of children
elements'''
        self.position = args[0]
        self.children = []

    def add(self, child):

        '''Adds supplied child element to list of children
        elements "children".'''
        self.children.append(child)

    def remove(self, child):

        '''Removes supplied child element from list of
        children elements "children".'''
        self.children.remove(child)

    def showDetails(self):

        '''Prints details of component element first. Then,
        iterates over each of its children, prints their
details by
        calling their showDetails() method'''
        print(self.position)
        for child in self.children:
            print("\t", end ="")
            child.showDetails()


"""main-method"""

if __name__ == "__main__":
```

```
topLevelMenu = CompositeElement("GeneralManager")
subMenuItem1 = CompositeElement("Manager-1")
subMenuItem2 = CompositeElement("Manager2")
subMenuItem11 = LeafElement("Developer-11")
subMenuItem12 = LeafElement("Developer-12")
subMenuItem21 = LeafElement("Developer-21")
subMenuItem22 = LeafElement("Developer-22")
subMenuItem1.add(subMenuItem-11)
subMenuItem1.add(subMenuItem-12)
subMenuItem2.add(subMenuItem-22)
subMenuItem2.add(subMenuItem-22)

topLevelMenu.add(subMenuItem-1)
topLevelMenu.add(subMenuItem-2)
topLevelMenu.showDetails()
```

Advantages

The Open/Closed Principle is followed because introducing new components, classes, and interfaces into the program are permitted without damaging the client's current code.

- **Less Memory Consumption:** In this technique, we must construct fewer objects than in the traditional manner, decreasing memory consumption and keeping us safe from memory mistakes.

- **Improved Execution Time:** Although creating an object in Python takes little time, we may minimize the execution time of our application by sharing objects.

It gives structural flexibility with manageable classes or interfaces by creating class hierarchies that comprise basic and complicated objects.

Disadvantages

- **Component Restriction:** The Composite Pattern makes limiting the kind of composite components more challenging. It should not use if we do not intend to depict a complete or partial hierarchy of objects.

- Once the structure of the tree is determined, the Composite Pattern will construct the overall general tree.

- **Language Type-System:** Because it is not permitted to utilize the programming language's type system, our program must rely on run-time checks to enforce the limitations.

Applicability

- **Nested Tree Structure is required:** When creating a hierarchical tree structure, which includes leaves objects and other object containers, the Composite Pattern is strongly recommended.

- **Graphic Designer:** A shape can be classified as basic (e.g., a straight line) or complicated (e.g., a rectangle). Because all shapes share similar activities, such as displaying the shape on screen, a composite pattern can be utilized to allow the computer to deal with all shapes equally.

Use of a Composite Pattern

It is used as follows:

- When we wish to depict an entire or partial object hierarchy.

- When responsibilities must dynamically assigned to particular objects without impacting other objects. Where the object's duty may change from time to time.

Elements of the Composite Pattern: Let's look at the four elements of the composite pattern:

1. **Component:**

   - Declares the interface for the items in the composition.

   - As appropriate, implements default behavior for the interface shared by all classes.

   - Declares an interface for controlling and accessing its child components.

2. **Leaf:**

   - In composition, this item represents a leaf. A leaf has no offspring.

   - Defines the behavior of the composition's basic objects.

3. **Composite:**

- Defines the behavior of components with children.

- Saves the child component.

- In the component interface, it implements child-related operations.

4. **Client:**

- The component interface is used to manipulate items in the composition.

In Java, an Example of a Composite Pattern

- **Step 1:** Design an Employee interface that will be used as a component.

```
// this is Employee interface i.e. Component.
public interface Employee {
    public  int getId();
    public String getNames();
    public double getSalary();
      public void print();
    public void add(Employee employee);
      public void remove(Employee employee);
      public Employee getChild(int x);
}// End of Employee interface.
```

- **Step 2:** Create a BankManager class that will use as a Composite and will implement the Employee interface.
  File: BankManager.java

```
// this is BankManager class i.e. Composite.
import java.util.ArrayList;
import java.util.Iterator;
import java.util.List;
public class BankManager implements Employee {
      private int id;
      private String names;
      private double salary;
```

```java
    public BankManager(int id, String names, double
salary) {
      this.id=id;
      this.names = names;
      this.salary = salary;
    }
        List<Employee> employees = new
ArrayList<Employee>();
    @Override
    public void add(Employee employee) {
       employees.add(employee);
    }
       @Override
    public Employee getChild(int x) {
     return employees.get(x);
    }
    @Override
    public void remove(Employee employee) {
     employees.remove(employee);
    }
    @Override
    public int getId()   {
     return id;
    }
    @Override
    public String getNames() {
     return names;
    }
    @Override
    public double getSalary() {
     return salary;
    }
    @Override
    public void print() {
     System.out.println("=================");
     System.out.println("Id ="+getId());
     System.out.println("Names ="+getNames());
     System.out.println("Salary ="+getSalary());
     System.out.println("=================");

     Iterator<Employee> it = employees.iterator();

        while(it.hasNext())   {
           Employee employee = it.next();
           employee.print();
        }
    }
}// End of BankManager class.
```

* **Step 3:** Create a Cashier class that acts as a leaf and implements the Employee interface.
  File: Cashier.java

```java
public class Cashier implements Employee{
    /*
        In this class, some methods do not apply to
cashiers because
        it is leaf node.
    */
    private int id;
        private String names;
    private double salary;
    public Cashier(int id,String names,double
salary)    {
            this.id=id;
            this.names = names;
            this.salary = salary;
    }
    @Override
    public void add(Employee employee) {
        //this is a leaf node, so this method is
not applicable to this class.
    }
    @Override
    public Employee getChild(int x) {
        //this is a leaf node, so this method is
not applicable to this class.
        return null;
    }
    @Override
    public int getId() {
        // TODO Auto-generated the method stub
        return id;
    }
    @Override
    public String getNames() {
        return names;
    }
    @Override
    public double getSalary() {
        return salary;
    }
    @Override
    public void print() {
        System.out.println("===================");
        System.out.println("Id ="+getId());
```

```
            System.out.println("Names ="+getNames());
            System.out.println("Salary
="+getSalary());
            System.out.println("===================");
      }
      @Override
      public void remove(Employee employee) {
            //this is a leaf node, so this method is
not applicable to this class.
      }
}
```

- **Step 4:** Create an Accountant class, which will be considered as a leaf and will implement the Employee interface.

  File: Accountant.java

```
public class Accountant implements Employee{
    /*
        In this class, some methods are not applicable
to cashiers because
        it is a leaf node.
    */
        private int id;
        private String names;
        private double salary;
        public Accountant(int id,String names,double
salary)  {
            this.id=id;
            this.names = names;
            this.salary = salary;
        }
        @Override
        public void add(Employee employee) {
            //this is a leaf node, so this method is
not applicable to this class.
        }
        @Override
        public Employee getChild(int i) {
            //this is a leaf node, so this method is
not applicable to this class.
            return null;
        }
```

```
        @Override
        public int getId() {
            // TODO Auto-generated the method stub
            return id;
        }
        @Override
        public String getNames() {
            return names;
        }
        @Override
        public double getSalary() {
            return salary;
        }
        @Override
        public void print() {
            System.out.println("================");
            System.out.println("Id ="+getId());
            System.out.println("Names ="+getNames());
            System.out.println("Salary ="+getSalary());
            System.out.println("================");
        }
        @Override
        public void remove(Employee employee) {
            //this is a leaf node, so this method is
not applicable to this class.
        }
    }
```

- **Step 5:** Create a CompositePatternDemo class that will be used as a Client and will implement the Employee interface.
  File: CompositePatternDemo.java

```
public class CompositePatternDemo {
    public static void main(String args[]){
        Employee emp1=new Cashier(201,"Rohan Kumar",
23000.0);
        Employee emp2=new Cashier(202,"Sohan Sharma",
29000.0);
        Employee emp3=new Accountant(203,"Reema
Malhotra", 35000.0);
        Employee manager1=new
BankManager(200,"Pshwani Kehsav",120000.0);
```

```
            manager1.add(emp1);
            manager1.add(emp2);
            manager1.add(emp3);
            manager1.print();
        }

    }
```

Composite Pattern in C#

The Composite Design Pattern composes elements into tree structures to describe part-whole hierarchies. This pattern allows clients to handle individual objects and object compositions equally.

Participants

This pattern's classes and objects are as follows:

1. Component (DrawingElement):

   • Defines the interface for the composition's objects

   • As appropriate, implements default behavior for the interface shared by all classes.

   • Specifies an interface for controlling and accessing its child components.

   • (Optional) specifies and implements an interface for accessing a component's parent in the recursive structure.

2. Leaf (PrimitiveElement):

   • Represents the composition's leaf objects. A leaf has no offspring.

   • Describes the behavior of the composition's basic objects.

3. Composite (CompositeElement):

   • Describes the behavior of components with children.

   • Keeps child components.

   In the Component interface, it implements child-related operations.

4. Client (CompositeApp):

   • Manipulates composition items using the Component interface.

C# Structural Code

This structural code exemplifies the Composite pattern, which enables the development of a tree structure in which individual nodes are accessible consistently regardless of whether they are leaf nodes or branch (composite) nodes.

```csharp
using System;
using System.Collections.Generic;

namespace Composite.Structural
{
    /// <summary> Composite Design Pattern </summary>

    public class Program
    {
        public static void Main(string[] args)
        {
            // Create tree structure

            Composite root = new Composite("root");
            root.Add(new Leaf("Leaf X"));
            root.Add(new Leaf("Leaf Y"));

            Composite comp = new Composite("Composite A");
            comp.Add(new Leaf("Leaf AX"));
            comp.Add(new Leaf("Leaf AY"));

            root.Add(comp);
            root.Add(new Leaf("Leaf Z"));

            // Add and remove leaf

            Leaf leaf = new Leaf("Leaf E");
            root.Add(leaf);
            root.Remove(leaf);

            // Recursively display tree

            root.Display(1);

            // Wait for the user

            Console.ReadKey();
        }
    }
```

```
/// <summary> The 'Component' abstract class
/// </summary>

public abstract class Component
{
    protected string names;

    // Constructor

    public Component(string name)
    {
        this.names = names;
    }

    public abstract void Add(Component c);
    public abstract void Remove(Component c);
    public abstract void Display(int depth);
}

/// <summary> The 'Composite' class
/// </summary>

public class Composite : Component
{
    List<Component> children = new List<Component>();

    // Constructor

    public Composite(string names)
        : base(names)
    {
    }

    public override void Add(Component component)
    {
        children.Add(component);
    }

    public override void Remove(Component component)
    {
        children.Remove(component);
    }

    public override void Display(int depth)
    {
        Console.WriteLine(new String('-', depth) + names);

        // Recursively display child nodes
```

```
        foreach (Component component in children)
        {
            component.Display(depth + 2);
        }
    }
}

/// <summary> The 'Leaf' class
/// </summary>

public class Leaf : Component
{
    // Constructor

    public Leaf(string name)
        : base(name)
    {
    }

    public override void Add(Component c)
    {
        Console.WriteLine("Cannot add to leaf");
    }

    public override void Remove(Component c)
    {
        Console.WriteLine("Cannot remove from leaf");
    }

    public override void Display(int depth)
    {
        Console.WriteLine(new String('-', depth) + names);
    }
}
}
```

Real-World C# Code

This real-world code displays the Composite pattern, which is used to construct a graphical tree structure composed of primitive nodes (lines, circles, and so on) and composite nodes (groups of drawing elements that make up more complex elements).

```
using System;
using System.Collections.Generic;
```

```
namespace Composite.RealWorld
{
    /// <summary> Composite Design Pattern
    /// </summary>

    public class Program
    {
        public static void Main(string[] args)
        {
            // Create tree structure

            CompositeElement root = new
CompositeElement("Picture");
            root.Add(new PrimitiveElement("Red-Line"));
            root.Add(new PrimitiveElement("Blue-Circle"));
            root.Add(new PrimitiveElement("Green-Box"));

            // Create branch

            CompositeElement comp = new
CompositeElement("Two-Circles");
            comp.Add(new PrimitiveElement("Black-Circle"));
            comp.Add(new PrimitiveElement("White-Circle"));
            root.Add(comp);

            // Add and remove the PrimitiveElement

            PrimitiveElement pe = new
PrimitiveElement("Yellow-Line");
            root.Add(pe);
            root.Remove(pe);

            // Recursively display the nodes

            root.Display(1);

            // Wait for the user

            Console.ReadKey();
        }
    }

    /// <summary> 'Component' Treenode
    /// </summary>

    public abstract class DrawingElement
    {
        protected string names;
```

```
    // Constructor

    public DrawingElement(string names)
    {
        this.names = names;
    }

    public abstract void Add(DrawingElement d);
    public abstract void Remove(DrawingElement d);
    public abstract void Display(int indent);
}

/// <summary> The 'Leaf' class
/// </summary>

public class PrimitiveElement : DrawingElement
{
    // Constructor

    public PrimitiveElement(string names)
        : base(names)
    {
    }

    public override void Add(DrawingElement c)
    {
        Console.WriteLine(
            "Cannot add to a PrimitiveElement");
    }

    public override void Remove(DrawingElement c)
    {
        Console.WriteLine(
            "Cannot remove from PrimitiveElement");
    }

    public override void Display(int indent)
    {
        Console.WriteLine(
            new String('-', indent) + " " + names);
    }
}

/// <summary> 'Composite' class
/// </summary>

public class CompositeElement : DrawingElement
{
```

```
        List<DrawingElement> elements = new
    List<DrawingElement>();

        // Constructor

        public CompositeElement(string names)
            : base(names)
        {
        }

        public override void Add(DrawingElement d)
        {
            elements.Add(d);
        }

        public override void Remove(DrawingElement d)
        {
            elements.Remove(d);
        }

        public override void Display(int indent)
        {
            Console.WriteLine(new String('-', indent) +
                "+ " + names);

            // Display the each child element on this node

            foreach (DrawingElement d in elements)
            {
                d.Display(indent + 2);
            }
        }
    }
}
```

DECORATOR PATTERN

The Decorator Pattern is a Structural Design Pattern that allows us to dynamically attach new behaviors to objects without affecting their implementation by enclosing these objects within the wrapper objects that contain the behaviors.

Because of its built-in functionality, the Decorator Pattern is significantly easier to implement in Python. It is not equal to Inheritance since the new functionality is added to that specific object rather than the entire subclass.

The Problem without Using Decorator Pattern

Imagine we're working with a formatting tool that includes capabilities like bolding and underlining text. However, after some time, our formatting tools were well-known within the intended audience. We learned from feedback that our audience desires additional capabilities in the program, such as the ability to make text Italic and many other features.

Does it seem simple? Because we must adhere to the Single Responsibility Principle, it is not a simple process to implement this or modify our classes to add new features without disrupting the current client code.

Decorator Pattern Solution

Let's look at the answer we have to prevent such situations. At first, we just had WrittenText, but we must add filters such as BOLD, ITALIC, and UNDERLINE. As a result, we'll create distinct wrapper classes for each function, such as BoldWrapperClass, ItalicWrapperClass, and UnderlineWrapperClass.

```python
class WrittenText:

    """Represents Written text """

    def __init__(self, text):
        self._text = text

    def render(self):
        return self._text

class UnderlineWrapper(WrittenText):

    """Wraps tag in <u>"""

    def __init__(self, wrapped):
        self._wrapped = wrapped

    def render(self):
        return "<u>{}</u>".format(self._wrapped.render())

class ItalicWrapper(WrittenText):

    """Wraps tag in <i>"""

    def __init__(self, wrapped):
        self._wrapped = wrapped
```

```
    def render(self):
        return "<i>{}</i>".format(self._wrapped.render())

class BoldWrapper(WrittenText):

    """"Wraps tag in <b>"""

    def __init__(self, wrapped):
        self._wrapped = wrapped

    def render(self):
        return "<b>{}</b>".format(self._wrapped.render())

""" main-method """

if __name__ == '__main__':

    before_pfp = WrittenText("PeeksforPeeks")
    after_pfp = ItalicWrapper(UnderlineWrapper(BoldWrapper(
before_pfp)))

    print("before :", before_pfp.render())
    print("after :", after_pfp.render())
```

Advantages

- **Single Responsibility Principle:** Using the Decorator approach, it is simple to separate a monolithic class that implements several different versions of behavior into many classes.

- **Runtime Responsibilities:** At runtime, we may simply add or remove responsibilities from an object.

- **Subclassing:** Subclassing is an alternative to the decorator technique. Subclassing adds functionality at compile-time, affecting all instances of the original class; decorating might offer additional behavior for particular objects during runtime.

Disadvantages

- **Removing Wrapper:** It is quite difficult to remove a specific wrapper from the wrapper's stack.

- **Complicated Decorators:** Having decorators maintain track of other decorators may be difficult since looking back into numerous levels of the decorator chain begins to stretch the decorator pattern beyond its real goal.

- **Ugly Configuration:** A large number of layers' code may cause the configurations to be ugly.

Applicability

- **Incapable Inheritance:** When it is not feasible to extend the functionality of an object using Inheritance, the Decorator technique is used.

- **Runtime Assignment:** One of the most essential features of the Decorator Pattern is the ability to give varied and unique behaviors to the object during runtime.

Decorator Pattern Usage

- When we want to assign responsibilities to objects openly and dynamically without affecting other objects.

- When we want to assign responsibilities to an object that we may wish to modify in the future.

- Subclassing is no longer a viable method of extending functionality.

Implementation of Decorator Pattern in Java

- **Step 1:** Develop a Food interface.

```
public interface Food {
    public String prepareFood();
    public double foodPrices();
}// End of Food interface.
```

- **Step 2:** Develop a VegFood class that implements the Food interface and overrides all of its functions.
File: VegFood.java

```
public class VegFood implements Food {
    public String prepareFood(){
        return "Veg Food";
    }
```

```
        public double foodPrices(){
        return 60.0;
    }
}
```

- **Step 3:** Create a FoodDecorator abstract class that implements the Food interface, overrides all of its methods and can decorate additional foods.

  File: FoodDecorator.java

```
public abstract class FoodDecorator implements Food{
    private Food newFood;
    public FoodDecorator(Food newFood)  {
        this.newFood=newFood;
    }
    @Override
    public String prepareFood(){
        return newFood.prepareFood();
    }
    public double foodPrices(){
        return newFood.foodPrices();
    }
}
```

- **Step 4:** Develop a NonVegFood concrete class that extends the FoodDecorator class and overrides all of its methods.

  File: NonVegFood.java

```
public class NonVegFood extends FoodDecorator{
    public NonVegFood(Food newFood) {
        super(newFood);
    }
    public String prepareFood(){
        return super.prepareFood() +" With the Roasted
Chiken and Chiken Curry  ";
    }
    public double foodPrices()   {
        return super.foodPrices()+160.0;
    }
}
```

- **Step 5:** Create a concrete class called ChineseFood that extends the FoodDecorator class and overrides all of its functions.
  File: ChineeseFood.java

```
public class ChineeseFood extends FoodDecorator{
    public ChineeseFood(Food newFood)    {
        super(newFood);
    }
    public String prepareFood(){
        return super.prepareFood() +" With the Fried
Rice and Manchurian  ";
    }
    public double foodPrices()    {
        return super.foodPrices()+75.0;
    }
}
```

- **Step 6:** Create a DecoratorPatternCustomer class that will utilize the Food interface to determine what sort of food the client wants (Decorates).
  File: DecoratorPatternCustomer.java

```
import java.io.BufferedReader;
import java.io.IOException;
import java.io.InputStreamReader;
public class DecoratorPatternCustomer {
    private static int  choice;
    public static void main(String args[]) throws
NumberFormatException, IOException    {
        do{
            System.out.print("====== Food-Menu ====== \n");
            System.out.print("           1. Vegetarian
Food.    \n");
            System.out.print("           2. Non-Vegetarian
Food.\n");
            System.out.print("           3. Chineese
Food.      \n");
            System.out.print("           4. Exit
\n");
            System.out.print("Enter our choice: ");
            BufferedReader br=new BufferedReader(new
InputStreamReader(System.in));
```

```
        choice=Integer.parseInt(br.readLine());
        switch (choice) {
        case 1:{
                VegFood vf=new VegFood();
            System.out.println(vf.prepareFood());
            System.out.println( vf.foodPrices());
            }
            break;

            case 2:{
            Food f1=new NonVegFood((Food) new
VegFood());
                System.out.println(f1.
prepareFood());
                System.out.println( f1.foodPrices());
            }
            break;
        case 3:{
                Food f2=new ChineeseFood((Food) new
VegFood());
                System.out.println(f2.
prepareFood());
                System.out.println(
f2.foodPrices());
                }
            break;

        default:{
            System.out.println("Other than these no
food is available");
            }
        return;
        }//end of the switch

}while(choice!=4);
    }
}
```

Decorator Pattern in C#

The Decorator Design Pattern dynamically assigns new responsibilities to an object. This pattern provides a more flexible option for adding functionality than subclassing.

Participants
This pattern's classes and objects are as follows:

1. Component (LibraryItem):

   - Specifies the interface for objects that can have responsibilities dynamically assigned to them.

2. ConcreteComponent (Book, Video):

   - Identifies an object to which extra responsibilities can be assigned

3. Decorator (Decorator):

   - Holds a reference to a Component object and specifies an interface that adheres to the interface of the Component.

4. ConcreteDecorator (Borrowable):

   - Responsibilities are added to the component.

C# Structural Code

This structured code showcases the Decorator pattern, which adds more functionality to an existing object dynamically.

```
using System;

namespace Decorator.Structural
{
    /// <summary> Decorator Design Pattern
    /// </summary>

    public class Program
    {
        public static void Main(string[] args)
        {
            // Create the ConcreteComponent and two
Decorators

            ConcreteComponent c1 = new ConcreteComponent();
            ConcreteDecoratorA d1 = new ConcreteDecoratorX();
            ConcreteDecoratorB d2 = new ConcreteDecoratorY();

            // Link-decorators

            d1.SetComponent(c1);
            d2.SetComponent(d1);
```

```
        d2.Operation();

        // Wait for the user

        Console.ReadKey();
    }
}

/// <summary> The 'Component' abstract class
/// </summary>

public abstract class Component
{
    public abstract void Operation();
}

/// <summary> The 'ConcreteComponent' class
/// </summary>

public class ConcreteComponent : Component
{
    public override void Operation()
    {
        Console.WriteLine("ConcreteComponent.
Operation()");
    }
}

/// <summary>
/// The 'Decorator' abstract class
/// </summary>

public abstract class Decorator : Component
{
    protected Component component;

    public void SetComponent(Component component)
    {
        this.component = component;
    }

    public override void Operation()
    {
        if (component != null)
        {
            component.Operation();
        }
    }
}
```

```
/// <summary> The 'ConcreteDecoratorX' class
/// </summary>

public class ConcreteDecoratorX : Decorator
{
    public override void Operation()
    {
        base.Operation();
        Console.WriteLine("ConcreteDecoratorX.
Operation()");
    }
}

/// <summary> The 'ConcreteDecoratorY' class
/// </summary>

public class ConcreteDecoratorY : Decorator
{
    public override void Operation()
    {
        base.Operation();
        AddedBehavior();
        Console.WriteLine("ConcreteDecoratorY
.Operation()");
    }

    void AddedBehavior()
    {
    }
}
}
```

Real-World C# Code

This real-world code exemplifies the Decorator Pattern, which adds "borrowable" functionality to existing library objects (books and videos).

```
using System;
using System.Collections.Generic;

namespace Decorator.RealWorld
{
```

```csharp
/// <summary> Decorator Design Pattern
/// </summary>

public class Program
{
    public static void Main(string[] args)
    {
        // Create-book

        Book book = new Book("Lorley", "Inside.NET",
20);
        book.Display();

        // Create-video

        Video video = new Video("Pielberg", "Laws",
24, 82);
        video.Display();

        // Make the video borrowable, then borrow and
display

        Console.WriteLine("\nMaking the video
borrowable:");

        Borrowable borrowvideo = new Borrowable(video);
        borrowvideo.BorrowItem("Customer #1");
        borrowvideo.BorrowItem("Customer #2");

        borrowvideo.Display();

        // Wait for the user

        Console.ReadKey();
    }
}
/// <summary> The 'Component' abstract class
/// </summary>

public abstract class LibraryItem
{
    private int numCopies;

    public int NumCopies
    {
        get { return numCopies; }
        set { numCopies = value; }
    }
```

```csharp
    public abstract void Display();
}

/// <summary> The 'ConcreteComponent' class
/// </summary>

public class Book : LibraryItem
{
    private string author;
    private string title;

    // Constructor

    public Book(string author, string title, int
numCopies)
    {
        this.author = author;
        this.title = title;
        this.NumCopies = numCopies;
    }

    public override void Display()
    {
        Console.WriteLine("\nBook --- ");
        Console.WriteLine(" The Author is: {0}",
author);
        Console.WriteLine(" The Title is: {0}", title);
        Console.WriteLine(" # The Copies is: {0}",
NumCopies);
    }
}

/// <summary> The 'ConcreteComponent' class
/// </summary>

public class Video : LibraryItem
{
    private string director;
    private string title;
    private int playTime;

    // Constructor

    public Video(string director, string title, int
numCopies, int playTime)
    {
        this.director = director;
        this.title = title;
```

```
          this.NumCopies = numCopies;
          this.playTime = playTime;
      }

      public override void Display()
      {
          Console.WriteLine("\nVideo --- ");
          Console.WriteLine(" The Director is: {0}",
director);
          Console.WriteLine(" The Title is: {0}", title);
          Console.WriteLine(" # The Copies is: {0}",
NumCopies);
          Console.WriteLine(" The Playtime is: {0}\n",
playTime);
      }
  }

  /// <summary> The 'Decorator' abstract class
  /// </summary>

  public abstract class Decorator : LibraryItem
  {
      protected LibraryItem libraryItem;

      // Constructor

      public Decorator(LibraryItem libraryItem)
      {
          this.libraryItem = libraryItem;
      }

      public override void Display()
      {
          libraryItem.Display();
      }
  }

  /// <summary> The 'ConcreteDecorator' class
  /// </summary>

  public class Borrowable : Decorator
  {
      protected readonly List<string> borrowers = new
List<string>();

      // Constructor

      public Borrowable(LibraryItem libraryItem)
```

```
        : base(libraryItem)
    {
    }

    public void BorrowItem(string name)
    {
        borrowers.Add(name);
        libraryItem.NumCopies--;
    }

    public void ReturnItem(string name)
    {
        borrowers.Remove(name);
        libraryItem.NumCopies++;
    }

    public override void Display()
    {
        base.Display();

        foreach (string borrower in borrowers)
        {
            Console.WriteLine(" borrower: " + borrower);
        }
    }
    }
}
```

FLYWEIGHT PATTERN

The Flyweight Pattern is a Structural Design Pattern that focuses on reducing the number of objects needed by the application at run-time. It essentially produces a Flyweight object that is shared by many contexts. It is designed in such a way that it is impossible to tell the difference between an item and a Flyweight Object. The fact that Flyweight objects are immutable is a significant feature. This implies that they cannot alter after they have been built.

To implement the Flyweight Pattern in Python, we utilize a Dictionary, which maintains references to previously constructed objects, each of which is connected with a key.

Why Are We Concerned with the Number of Objects in Our Program?

A smaller number of objects minimizes memory utilization and keeps us safe from memory-related issues.

Despite the fact that generating an object in Python is rapid, we may lower the execution time of our application by sharing objects.

The Problem without Using Flyweight Pattern

Assume we are a game developer who enjoy racing games and want to create a racing game for ourselves and a buddy. We made one and began playing the game since we are excellent game creators. Then we gave the game to our buddies, although they didn't like it since the game kept crashing every few minutes.

But why is that? (If we believe we're a Pro Game Developer, guess why.) After many hours of troubleshooting, you discovered that the problem is a shortage of RAM on our friend's machine. Because our system is considerably more powerful than our friend's system, the game ran smoothly on our system but not on our friend's.

Solution Based on the Flyweight Pattern

So, as a developer, what will we do to boost performance? (Obviously! We're not planning to boost my RAM). The underlying issue is with automobile objects since each car is represented by individual objects that include a wealth of data like its color, size, seats, maximum speed, and so on. When our RAM is full and we are unable to add any additional objects that are now necessary, our game will crash. To prevent such circumstances in applications, it is the developer's responsibility to adopt the Flyweight Pattern, which enables us to fit more objects into the available RAM by sharing common sections of the objects.

The Flyweight Pattern is used in the following code:

```
class ComplexCars(object):

    """Separate class for the Complex Cars"""

    def __init__(self):

        pass

    def cars(self, car_name):

        return "ComplexPattern[% s]" % (car_name)

class CarFamilies(object):
```

```
"""dictionary to store ids of car"""

car_family = {}

def __new__(cls, name, car_family_id):
    try:
        id = cls.car_family[car_family_id]
    except KeyError:
        id = object.__new__(cls)
        cls.car_family[car_family_id] = id
    return id

def set_car_info(self, car_info):

    """set car information"""

    cg = ComplexCars()
    self.car_info = cg.cars(car_info)

def get_car_info(self):

    """return car information"""

    return (self.car_info)


if __name__ == '__main__':
    car_data = (('a', 1, 'Audi23'), ('a', 2, 'Ferrari32'),
('b', 1, 'Audi54'))
    car_family_objects = []
    for c in car_data:
        obj = CarFamilies(c[0], c[1])
        obj.set_car_info(c[2])
        car_family_objects.append(obj)

    """similar id's says that they are same objects """

    for c in car_family_objects:
        print("id = " + str(id(c)))
        print(c.get_car_info())
```

Advantages

- **Reduced RAM Usage:** When we have a lot of identical objects in our application, it is always advisable to utilize the Flyweight Pattern to save a lot of RAM space.

- **Improved Data Caching:** When a client or user requires a fast response time, it is usually preferable to employ the Flyweight Pattern since it aids in data caching.

- **Improved Performance:** Because we are employing fewer heavy items, our performance will eventually improve.

Disadvantages

- **Encapsulation Breaking:** When we attempt to transfer the state outside the object, we break encapsulation and may become less efficient than retaining the state within the object.

- Flyweight Pattern is difficult to use depending on the language we use; it is simple to use in languages like Python and Java where all object variables are references, but it is common in languages like C and C++ where objects can be allocated as local variables on the stack and destroyed as a result of programmer action.

- **Complicated Code:** Using the Flyweight Pattern always increases the complexity of the code for novice developers to grasp.

Applicability

- **To Reduce the Number of Objects:** When our program has a large number of heavy-weight objects, we apply the Flyweight approach to eliminate excessive memory usage.

- **Independent Object Applications:** When our program is not dependent on the object produced, we may utilize this way to save a lot of computer space.

- **Reduced Project Costs:** When it is necessary to lower the cost of a project in terms of space and time complexity, the Flyweight approach is always favored.

Flyweight Pattern Usage

- When a program employs a large number of objects.

- When the cost of storage is significant due to the number of objects.

- When the program does not rely on the identification of the object.

Implementation of Flyweight Pattern in Java

- **Step 1:** Design an interface.
  Filename: Shape.java

```java
public interface Shape {
    void draw();
}
```

- **Step 2:** Make a concrete class that implements the same interface.
  Filename: Circle.java

```java
public class Circle implements Shape {
    private String color;
    private int c;
    private int d;
    private int radius;

    public Circle(String color){
        this.color = color;
    }

    public void setX(int c) {
        this.c = c;
    }

    public void setY(int d) {
        this.y = d;
    }

    public void setRadius(int radius) {
        this.radius = radius;
    }

    @Override
    public void draw() {
        System.out.println("Circle: Draw() [Color : " +
color + ", c : " + c + ", d :" + d + ", radius :" +
radius);
    }
}
```

- **Step 3:** Create a factory to produce concrete class objects depending on the information provided.

  Filename: ShapeFactory.java

```java
import java.util.HashMap;

public class ShapeFactory {

    // Uncomment compiler directive line and javac
*.java will compile properly.
    // @SuppressWarnings("unchecked")
    private static final HashMap circleMap = new
HashMap();

    public static Shape getCircle(String color) {
        Circle circle = (Circle)circleMap.get(color);

        if(circle == null) {
            circle = new Circle(color);
            circleMap.put(color, circle);
            System.out.println("Creating the circle of
color : " + color);
        }
        return circle;
    }
}
```

- **Step 4:** Invoke the factory to obtain an object of a concrete class by providing details such as color.

  Filename: FlyweightPatternDemo.java

```java
public class FlyweightPatternDemo {
    private static final String colors[] = { "Pink",
"Grey", "Red", "Blue", "Black" };
    public static void main(String[] args) {

        for(int x=0; x < 20; ++x) {
            Circle circle = (Circle)ShapeFactory.
getCircle(getRandomColor());
            circle.setX(getRandomX());
            circle.setY(getRandomY());
            circle.setRadius(100);
            circle.draw();
        }
    }
```

```
    private static String getRandomColor() {
        return colors[(int)(Math.random()*colors.
    length)];
    }
    private static int getRandomX() {
        return (int)(Math.random()*100 );
    }
    private static int getRandomY() {
        return (int)(Math.random()*100);
    }
}
```

Flyweight Pattern in C#

The Flyweight Design Pattern makes effective use of sharing to accommodate a large number of fine-grained objects.

Participants

This pattern's classes and objects are as follows:

1. Flyweight (Character):

   - Defines an interface for flyweights to receive and operate in an extrinsic state.

2. ConcreteFlyweight (CharacterA, CharacterB, . . ., CharacterZ):

   - Implements the Flyweight interface and, if applicable, adds storage for the intrinsic state. A ConcreteFlyweight object must be able to be shared. Any state it stores must intrinsic, that seems to be, it must be independent of the ConcreteFlyweight object's context.

3. UnsharedConcreteFlyweight (not used):

   - It is not necessary to share all Flyweight categories. The Flyweight interface allows for sharing but does not enforce it. It is common for UnsharedConcreteFlyweight objects to have ConcreteFlyweight objects as children at some level in the flyweight object structure (as the Row and Column classes have).

4. FlyweightFactory (CharacterFactory):

   - Builds and manages flyweight objects ensure correct flyweight sharing When a client requests a flyweight, the FlyweightFactory object either assets an existing instance or builds one if none already exists.

5. Client (FlyweightApp):

- Keeps a reference to flyweight (s).
- Computes or saves the flyweight's extrinsic state (s).

C# Structural Code

This structure code exemplifies the Flyweight pattern, in which a limited number of objects are shared several times by various clients.

```csharp
using System;
using System.Collections.Generic;

namespace Flyweight.Structural
{
    /// <summary> Flyweight Design Pattern
    /// </summary>

    public class Program
    {
        public static void Main(string[] args)
        {
            // Arbitrary extrinsic state

            int extrinsicstate = 24;

            FlyweightFactory factory = new
FlyweightFactory();

            // Work with different flyweight instances

            Flyweight fx = factory.GetFlyweight("A");
            fx.Operation(--extrinsicstate);

            Flyweight fy = factory.GetFlyweight("B");
            fy.Operation(--extrinsicstate);

            Flyweight fz = factory.GetFlyweight("C");
            fz.Operation(--extrinsicstate);

            UnsharedConcreteFlyweight fu = new
                UnsharedConcreteFlyweight();
```

```
        fu.Operation(--extrinsicstate);

        // Wait for the user

        Console.ReadKey();
    }
}
/// <summary> The 'FlyweightFactory' class
/// </summary>

public class FlyweightFactory
{
    private Dictionary<string, Flyweight> flyweights {
get; set; } = new Dictionary<string, Flyweight>();

    // Constructor

    public FlyweightFactory()
    {
        flyweights.Add("A", new ConcreteFlyweight());
        flyweights.Add("B", new ConcreteFlyweight());
        flyweights.Add("C", new ConcreteFlyweight());
    }

    public Flyweight GetFlyweight(string key)
    {
        return ((Flyweight)flyweights[key]);
    }
}

/// <summary> The 'Flyweight' abstract class
/// </summary>

public abstract class Flyweight
{
    public abstract void Operation(int extrinsicstate);
}

/// <summary> The 'ConcreteFlyweight' class
/// </summary>

public class ConcreteFlyweight : Flyweight
{
    public override void Operation(int extrinsicstate)
    {
        Console.WriteLine("ConcreteFlyweight: " +
extrinsicstate);
    }
}
```

```
/// <summary> The 'UnsharedConcreteFlyweight' class
/// </summary>

public class UnsharedConcreteFlyweight : Flyweight
{
    public override void Operation(int extrinsicstate)
    {
        Console.WriteLine("UnsharedConcreteFlyweight: " +
            extrinsicstate);
    }
}
}
```

Real-World C# Code

This real-world code exemplifies the Flyweight Pattern, in which a limited number of Character objects are shared several times by a document with possibly many characters.

```
using System;
using System.Collections.Generic;

namespace Flyweight.RealWorld
{
    /// <summary> Flyweight Design Pattern
    /// </summary>

    public class Program
    {
        public static void Main(string[] args)
        {
            // Build document with the text

            string document = "AAZZBBZB";
            char[] chars = document.ToCharArray();

            CharacterFactory factory = new
CharacterFactory();

            // extrinsic-state

            int pointSize = 12;

            // For each character use a flyweight object
```

```csharp
                foreach (char c1 in chars)
                {
                    pointSize++;
                    Character character = factory.
GetCharacter(c1);
                    character.Display(pointSize);
                }

                // Wait for the user

                Console.ReadKey();
            }
        }

        /// <summary> The 'FlyweightFactory' class
        /// </summary>

        public class CharacterFactory
        {
            private Dictionary<char, Character> characters =
new Dictionary<char, Character>();

            public Character GetCharacter(char key)
            {
                // Uses the "lazy initialization"

                Character character = null;

                if (characters.ContainsKey(key))
                {
                    character = characters[key];
                }
                else
                {
                    switch (key)
                    {
                        case 'A': character = new CharacterA();
break;
                        case 'B': character = new CharacterB();
break;
                        //...
                        case 'Z': character = new CharacterZ();
break;
                    }
                    characters.Add(key, character);
                }
                return character;
            }
        }
    }
```

```
/// <summary> The 'Flyweight' abstract class
/// </summary>

public abstract class Character
{
    protected char symbol;
    protected int width;
    protected int height;
    protected int ascent;
    protected int descent;
    protected int pointSize;

    public abstract void Display(int pointSize);
}

/// <summary> A 'ConcreteFlyweight' class
/// </summary>

public class CharacterA : Character
{
    // Constructor
    public CharacterA()
    {
        symbol = 'A';
        height = 120;
        width = 130;
        ascent = 80;
        descent = 0;
    }

    public override void Display(int pointSize)
    {
        this.pointSize = pointSize;
        Console.WriteLine(symbol +
            " (pointsize " + this.pointSize + ")");
    }
}

/// <summary> A 'ConcreteFlyweight' class
/// </summary>

public class CharacterB : Character
{
    // Constructor

    public CharacterB()
    {
        symbol = 'B';
        height = 120;
```

```
            width = 150;
            ascent = 82;
            descent = 0;
        }

        public override void Display(int pointSize)
        {
            this.pointSize = pointSize;
            Console.WriteLine(this.symbol +
                " (pointsize " + this.pointSize + ")");
        }
    }

    // ... C, D, E, etc.

    /// <summary>
    /// A 'ConcreteFlyweight' class
    /// </summary>

    public class CharacterZ : Character
    {
        // Constructor

        public CharacterZ()
        {
            symbol = 'Z';
            height = 120;
            width = 120;
            ascent = 78;
            descent = 0;
        }

        public override void Display(int pointSize)
        {
            this.pointSize = pointSize;
            Console.WriteLine(this.symbol +
                " (pointsize " + this.pointSize + ")");
        }
    }
}
```

CHAIN OF RESPONSIBILITY

The Chain of Responsibility Pattern is a Behavioral Design Pattern that is the object-oriented counterpart of if... elif... elif... else that allows us to dynamically rearrange the condition-action blocks at run-time. It enables us to route requests via the handler chain. The processing is simple; whenever a handler receives a request, it has two options: process it or transmit it to the next handler in the chain.

This pattern attempts to decouple request senders from receivers by allowing the request to pass through chained receivers until it is processed.

The Problem without Using the Chain of Responsibility Pattern

Assume we are creating a basic website that accepts input strings and reports on various features of the strings, such as whether the string is a palindrome. Is the string in upperCase? Is lowerCase a string? And several other characteristics. After careful consideration, you conclude that these tests for the input string should do in the order listed. As a result, the developer is faced with creating an application that can pick which action to take next at runtime.

Solution Using Chain of Responsibility Pattern

The Chain of Responsibility Pattern solves the difficulty above. It generates a new Abstract handler to handle the sequential activities that must execute dynamically. For example, we may build four handlers called FirstConcreteHandler, SecondConcreteHandler, ThirdConcreteHandler, and Defaulthandler and call them successively from the user class.

```python
class AbstractHandler(object):

    """Parent class of all the concrete handlers"""

    def __init__(self, nxt):

        """change or increase local variable using nxt"""

        self._nxt = nxt

    def handle(self, request):

        """It calls the processRequest through given
request"""

        handled = self.processRequest(request)

        """case when it is not handled"""
```

```
        if not handled:
            self._nxt.handle(request)

    def processRequest(self, request):

        """throws a NotImplementedError"""

        raise NotImplementedError('First implement it !')


class FirstConcreteHandler(AbstractHandler):

    """Concrete Handler # 1: Child class of
AbstractHandler"""

    def processRequest(self, request):

        '''return True if the request is handled '''

        if 'a' < request <= 'e':
            print("This is {} handling the request '{}'".
format(self.__class__.__name__, request))
            return True


class SecondConcreteHandler(AbstractHandler):

    """Concrete Handler # 2: Child class of the
AbstractHandler"""

    def processRequest(self, request):

        '''return True if request is handled'''

        if 'e' < request <= 'l':
            print("This is {} handling request '{}'".
format(self.__class__.__name__, request))
            return True

class ThirdConcreteHandler(AbstractHandler):

    """Concrete Handler # 3: Child class of the
AbstractHandler"""

    def processRequest(self, request):

        '''return True if request is handled'''

        if 'l' < request <= 'z':
```

```
            print("This is {} handling request '{}'".
format(self.__class__.__name__, request))
            return True

class DefaultHandler(AbstractHandler):

    """Default Handler: child class from AbstractHandler"""

    def processRequest(self, request):

        """Gives message that th request is not handled and
returns true"""

        print("This is {} telling us that request '{}' has
no handler right now.".format(self.__class__.__name__,

request))
        return True


class User:

    """User-Class"""

    def __init__(self):

        """Provides sequence of handles for the users"""

        initial = None

        self.handler = FirstConcreteHandler(SecondConcreteH
andler(ThirdConcreteHandler(DefaultHandler(initial))))

    def agent(self, user_request):

        """Iterates over each request and sends them to the
specific handles"""

        for request in user_request:
            self.handler.handle(request)

"""main-method"""

if __name__ == "__main__":

    """Create client object"""
    user = User()

    """Create requests to process"""
```

```
string = "GeeksforGeeks"
requests = list(string)

"""Send requests one by one, to handlers as per the
sequence of handlers defined in the Client class"""
user.agent(requests)
```

Advantages

- **Single Responsibility Principle:** It is simple to separate the classes that initiate operations from the classes that conduct operations here.

- The open/closed approach states that we may add new code classes without disrupting current client code.

- **Increases Flexibility:** As responsibilities are assigned to objects, the code becomes more flexible.

Disadvantages

- **Uncertain about the Request:** This pattern provides no guarantee that the item will be received or not.

- **Spotting Characteristics:** Because of debugging, seeing operation characteristics becomes tough.

- **System Performance Depreciation:** It may have an impact on system performance owing to constant cycle calls.

Applicability

- **Processing many handlers in the following order:** Because linking is possible in any sequence, the Chain of Responsibility Pattern is very useful when it is necessary to process numerous handlers in a certain order.

- **Requests for Decoupling:** This pattern is often used when you wish to separate the sender and recipient of a request.

- **Unknown Handlers:** When you don't want to define handlers in the code, the Chain of Responsibility is always chosen.

Usage of the Chain of Responsibility Pattern

It is used as follows:

- When there are many objects that can handle a request and the handler is uncertain.

- When the group of objects capable of handling the request must be defined dynamically.

Java Implementation

- **Step 1:** Create an abstract class called Logger.

```java
public abstract class Logger {
    public static int OUTPUTINFO=1;
    public static int ERRORINFO=2;
    public static int DEBUGINFO=3;
    protected int levels;
    protected Logger nextLevelLogger;
    public void setNextLevelLogger(Logger
nextLevelLogger) {
        this.nextLevelLogger = nextLevelLogger;
    }
        public void logMessage(int levels, String msg)
{
        if(this.levels<=levels){
            displayLogInfo(msg);
        }
        if (nextLevelLogger!=null) {
            nextLevelLogger.logMessage(levels, msg);
        }
    }
    protected abstract void displayLogInfo
(String msg);
}
```

- **Step 2:** Create ConsoleBasedLogger class
  File: ConsoleBasedLogger.java

```java
public class ConsoleBasedLogger extends Logger {
    public ConsoleBasedLogger(int levels) {
        this.levels=levels;
    }
```

```
    @Override
    protected void displayLogInfo(String msg) {
        System.out.println("CONSOLE-LOGGER INFO:
"+msg);
    }
}
```

- **Step 3:** Create a class called DebugBasedLogger.
  File: DebugBasedLogger.java

```
public class DebugBasedLogger extends Logger {
    public DebugBasedLogger(int levels) {
        this.levels=levels;
    }
    @Override
    protected void displayLogInfo(String msg) {
        System.out.println("DEBUG-LOGGER INFO: "+msg);
    }
}// End of DebugBasedLogger class.
```

- **Step 4:** Create a class called ErrorBasedLogger.
  File: ErrorBasedLogger.java

```
public class ErrorBasedLogger extends Logger {
    public ErrorBasedLogger(int levels) {
        this.levels=levels;
    }
    @Override
    protected void displayLogInfo(String msg) {
        System.out.println("ERROR-LOGGER INFO: "+msg);
    }
}// End of ErrorBasedLogger class.
```

- **Step 5:** Create a class called ChainOfResponsibilityClient.
  File: ChainofResponsibilityClient.java

```
public class ChainofResponsibilityClient {
    private static Logger doChaining(){
        Logger consoleLogger = new
ConsoleBasedLogger(Logger.OUTPUTINFO);
```

```
                Logger errorLogger = new
ErrorBasedLogger(Logger.ERRORINFO);
                consoleLogger.setNextLevelLogger(errorLog
ger);

                Logger debugLogger = new
DebugBasedLogger(Logger.DEBUGINFO);
                errorLogger.setNextLevelLogger(debugLogger);

                return consoleLogger;
                }
                public static void main(String args[]){
                Logger chainLogger= doChaining();

                chainLogger.logMessage(Logger.
OUTPUTINFO, "Enter sequence of values ");
                chainLogger.logMessage(Logger.ERRORINFO,
"Error is occured now");
                chainLogger.logMessage(Logger.DEBUGINFO,
"This was error now debugging is compeled");
                }
}
```

Chain of Responsibility Pattern in C#

By allowing many objects to handle a request, the Chain of Responsibility Design Pattern avoids tying the sender of a request to its recipient. This pattern connects the receiving objects and transmits the request down the chain until it is handled by an object.

Participants

This pattern's classes and objects are as follows:

1. Handler (Approver):

   • Offers an interface for processing requests.

   • Implements the successor link (optional).

2. ConcreteHandler (Director, VicePresident, President):

   • Processes requests for which it is accountable.

   • Can get access to its successor.

- If the ConcreteHandler is capable of handling the request, it does so; otherwise, the request is sent to its successor.

3. Client (ChainApp):

- Sends a request to a ConcreteHandler object on the chain.

C# Structural Code

This structural code shows the Chain of Responsibility Pattern, in which several connected objects (the Chain) can react to a request or pass it on to the next item in the line.

```
using System;

namespace Chain.Structural
{
    /// <summary> Chain of Responsibility Design Pattern
    /// </summary>

    public class Program
    {
        public static void Main(string[] args)
        {
            // Setup Chain of Responsibility

            Handler h1 = new ConcreteHandler1();
            Handler h2 = new ConcreteHandler2();
            Handler h3 = new ConcreteHandler3();
            h1.SetSuccessor(h2);
            h2.SetSuccessor(h3);

            // Generate and process request

            int[] requests = { 12, 15, 19, 23, 19, 30, 29,
26 };

            foreach (int request in requests)
            {
                h1.HandleRequest(request);
            }

            // Wait for the user

            Console.ReadKey();
        }
    }
```

```csharp
/// <summary> The 'Handler' abstract class
/// </summary>

public abstract class Handler
{
    protected Handler successor;

    public void SetSuccessor(Handler successor)
    {
        this.successor = successor;
    }

    public abstract void HandleRequest(int request);
}

/// <summary> The 'ConcreteHandler1' class
/// </summary>

public class ConcreteHandler1 : Handler
{
    public override void HandleRequest(int request)
    {
        if (request >= 0 && request < 10)
        {
            Console.WriteLine("{0} handled
request {1}",
                this.GetType().Name, request);
        }
        else if (successor != null)
        {
            successor.HandleRequest(request);
        }
    }
}

/// <summary> The 'ConcreteHandler2' class
/// </summary>

public class ConcreteHandler2 : Handler
{
    public override void HandleRequest(int request)
    {
        if (request >= 12 && request < 22)
        {
            Console.WriteLine("{0} handled
request {1}",
                this.GetType().Name, request);
        }
```

```
                else if (successor != null)
                {
                    successor.HandleRequest(request);
                }
            }
        }

        /// <summary> The 'ConcreteHandler3' class
        /// </summary>

        public class ConcreteHandler3 : Handler
        {
            public override void HandleRequest(int request)
            {
                if (request >= 22 && request < 32)
                {
                    Console.WriteLine("{0} handled
request {1}",
                        this.GetType().Name, request);
                }
                else if (successor != null)
                {
                    successor.HandleRequest(request);
                }
            }
        }
    }
```

Real-World C# Code

This real-world code exemplifies the Chain of Responsibility Pattern, in which various linked managers and executives can reply to a purchase request or forward it to a superior. Each job can have its own set of regulations that it must follow in order to approve instructions.

```
using System;

namespace Chain.RealWorld
{
    /// <summary> Chain of Responsibility Design Pattern
    /// </summary>

    public class Program
    {
        public static void Main(string[] args)
```

```
        {
            // Chain of Responsibility Setup

            Approver larry = new Director();
            Approver sam = new VicePresident();
            Approver tammy = new President();

            larry.SetSuccessor(sam);
            sam.SetSuccessor(tammy);

            // Generate and process the purchase requests

            Purchase p1 = new Purchase(2094, 380.00,
"Supplies");
            larry.ProcessRequest(p);

            p1 = new Purchase(2075, 42990.10, "Project X");
            larry.ProcessRequest(p);

            p1 = new Purchase(2026, 129100.00, "Project Y");
            larry.ProcessRequest(p);

            // Wait for the user

            Console.ReadKey();
        }
    }
    /// <summary> The 'Handler' abstract class
    /// </summary>

    public abstract class Approver
    {
        protected Approver successor;

        public void SetSuccessor(Approver successor)
        {
            this.successor = successor;
        }

        public abstract void ProcessRequest(Purchase
purchase);
    }

    /// <summary> The 'ConcreteHandler' class
    /// </summary>

    public class Director : Approver
    {
```

```
        public override void ProcessRequest(Purchase
purchase)
        {
            if (purchase.Amount < 11000.0)
            {
                Console.WriteLine("{0} approved request#
{1}",
                    this.GetType().Name, purchase.Number);
            }
            else if (successor != null)
            {
                successor.ProcessRequest(purchase);
            }
        }
    }


    /// <summary> The 'ConcreteHandler' class
    /// </summary>

    public class VicePresident : Approver
    {
        public override void ProcessRequest(Purchase
purchase)
        {
            if (purchase.Amount < 28000.0)
            {
                Console.WriteLine("{0} approved
request# {1}",
                    this.GetType().Name, purchase.Number);
            }
            else if (successor != null)
            {
                successor.ProcessRequest(purchase);
            }
        }
    }


    /// <summary> The 'ConcreteHandler' class
    /// </summary>

    public class President : Approver
    {
        public override void ProcessRequest(Purchase
purchase)
        {
            if (purchase.Amount < 110000.0)
            {
                Console.WriteLine("{0} approved request# {1}",
```

```
                            this.GetType().Name, purchase.Number);
            }
            else
            {
                Console.WriteLine(
                    "Request# {0} requires an executive
meeting!",
                    purchase.Number);
            }
        }
    }

    /// <summary> Class holding request details
    /// </summary>

    public class Purchase
    {
        int number;
        double amount;
        string purpose;

        // Constructor

        public Purchase(int number, double amount, string
purpose)
        {
            this.number = number;
            this.amount = amount;
            this.purpose = purpose;
        }

        // Gets or sets the purchase number

        public int Number
        {
            get { return number; }
            set { number = value; }
        }

        // Gets or sets the purchase amount

        public double Amount
        {
            get { return amount; }
            set { amount = value; }
        }

        // Gets or sets the purchase purpose
```

```
public string Purpose
{
    get { return purpose; }
    set { purpose = value; }
}
}
}
```

COMMAND PATTERN

The Command Pattern is a Behavioral Design Pattern that encapsulates a request as an object, allowing for the customization of clients with various demands as well as the queuing or tracking of requests. In our scenario, parameterizing additional objects with various demands implies that the button used to turn on the lights may subsequently be used to turn on the radio or open the garage door. It aids in elevating "method invocation on an object" to complete object status. Essentially, it contains all of the information required to execute an action or trigger an event.

The Problem without Utilizing the Command Pattern

Consider ourselves to be working on a code editor. Our current objective is to add additional buttons to the editor's toolbar for various actions. It is quite simple to construct a single Button Class that can be used for all of the buttons. Given that all of the buttons in the editor seem to be the same, what should we do? Should we create several subclasses for each location where the button is used?

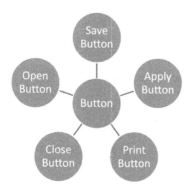

Problem without using Command Pattern.

Solution via Using the Command Pattern

Let's have a look at the answer to the difficulty outlined above. It is usually a good idea to partition the program into multiple levels to facilitate development and debugging. According to the command pattern, objects should not submit these requests directly. Instead, we should isolate all request data, such as the object being called, the method name, and the list of arguments, into a distinct command class with a single function that triggers this request.

```python
"""Use built-in abc to implement the Abstract classes and
methods"""
from abc import ABC, abstractmethod

"""Class Dedicated to Command"""
class Command(ABC):

    """constructor-method"""
    def __init__(self, receiver):
        self.receiver = receiver

    """process-method"""
    def process(self):
        pass

"""Class dedicated to the Command Implementation"""
class CommandImplementation(Command):

    """constructor-method"""
    def __init__(self, receiver):
        self.receiver = receiver

    """process-method"""
    def process(self):
        self.receiver.perform_action()

"""Class dedicated to the Receiver"""
class Receiver:

    """perform action method"""
    def perform_action(self):
        print('Action performed in receiver.')

"""Class dedicated to the Invoker"""
class Invoker:
```

```
"""command-method"""
def command(self, cmd):
    self.cmd = cmd

"""execute-method"""
def execute(self):
    self.cmd.process()

"""main-method"""
if __name__ == "__main__":

    """create the Receiver object"""
    receiver = Receiver()
    cmd = CommandImplementation(receiver)
    invoker = Invoker()
    invoker.command(cmd)
    invoker.execute()
```

Advantages

- The Open/Closed Principle states that we may bring new commands into the program without damaging the current client's code.

- **Single Responsibility Principle:** It is quite simple to decouple the classes that call operations from other classes in this case.

- **Implementable UNDO/REDO:** The Command Pattern may be used to implement the functions of UNDO/REDO.

- **Encapsulation:** It aids in encapsulating all of the information required to carry out an action or occurrence.

Disadvantages

- **Complexity Increases:** As we include further layers between senders and receivers, the code's complexity grows.

- **Class Quantity Grows:** The number of classes grows with each individual command.

- Each command is a ConcreteCommand class, which increases the number of classes for implementation and maintenance.

Applicability

- **Implementing Reversible Operations:** Because the Command Pattern supports UNDO/REDO operations, we may potentially reverse the operations.

- **Parameterization:** When we need to parameterize objects with operations, we should always utilize the Command Pattern.

Command Pattern Usage

- It is utilized when you need to parameterize objects based on an action.

- When requests must be created and executed at various times.

- When rollback, logging, or transaction functionality is required.

Example of Command Pattern in Java

- **Step 1:** Create an ActionListernerCommand interface to serve as a Command.

```
public interface ActionListenerCommand {
    public void execute();
}
```

- **Step 2:** Make a Document class that will serve as a Receiver.
  File: Document.java

```
public class Document {
    public void open(){
        System.out.println("Document-Opened");
    }
    public void save(){
        System.out.println("Document-Saved");
    }
}
```

- **Step 3:** Make an ActionOpen class that will serve as a ConcreteCommand.
  File: ActionOpen.java

```
public class ActionOpen implements
ActionListenerCommand{
    private Document doc;
```

```
public ActionOpen(Document doc) {
    this.doc = doc;
}
@Override
public void execute() {
    doc.open();
}
}
```

- **Step 4:** Make an ActionSave class that will serve as a ConcreteCommand.

  File: AdapterPatternDemo.java

```
public class ActionSave implements
ActionListenerCommand{
    private Document doc;
    public ActionSave(Document doc) {
        this.doc = doc;
    }
    @Override
    public void execute() {
        doc.save();
    }
}
```

- **Step 5:** Make a MenuOptions class to serve as an Invoker.

  File: ActionSave.java

```
public class ActionSave implements
ActionListenerCommand{
    private Document doc;
    public ActionSave(Document doc) {
        this.doc = doc;
    }
    @Override
    public void execute() {
        doc.save();
    }
}
```

- **Step 6:** Make a CommanPatternClient class to serve as a client.
  File: AdapterPatternDemo.java

```
public class CommandPatternClient {
    public static void main(String[] args) {
        Document doc = new Document();

        ActionListenerCommand clickOpen = new
ActionOpen(doc);
        ActionListenerCommand clickSave = new
ActionSave(doc);

        MenuOptions menu = new MenuOptions(clickOpen,
clickSave);

        menu.clickOpen();
        menu.clickSave();
    }
}
```

Command Pattern in C#

The Command Design Pattern encapsulates a request as an entity, allowing us to parameterize clients, queue or log requests, and offer undoable activities.

Participants

This pattern's classes and objects are as follows:

1. Command (Command):

   - Specifies an interface for carrying out an action.

2. ConcreteCommand (CalculatorCommand):

   - Describes the relationship between a Receiver object and an action.

   - Execute is implemented by calling the relevant operation(s) on Receiver.

3. Client (CommandApp):

   - Constructs a ConcreteCommand object and assigns it a receiver.

4. Invoker (User):

- Requests that the command carries out the request.

5. Recipient (Calculator):

- Understands how to carry out the activities linked with carrying out the request.

C# Structural Code

The Command Pattern is demonstrated in this structured code, which saves requests as objects and allows clients to execute or replay the requests.

```
using System;

namespace Command.Structural
{
    /// <summary> Command Design Pattern
    /// </summary>

    public class Program
    {
        public static void Main(string[] args)
        {
            // Create receiver, command, and invoker

            Receiver receiver = new Receiver();
            Command command = new
ConcreteCommand(receiver);
            Invoker invoker = new Invoker();

            // Set and execute the command

            invoker.SetCommand(command);
            invoker.ExecuteCommand();

            // Wait for the user

            Console.ReadKey();
        }
    }

    /// <summary> The 'Command' abstract class
    /// </summary>

    public abstract class Command
```

```
{
    protected Receiver receiver;

    // Constructor

    public Command(Receiver receiver)
    {
        this.receiver = receiver;
    }

    public abstract void Execute();
}

/// <summary> The 'ConcreteCommand' class
/// </summary>

public class ConcreteCommand : Command
{
    // Constructor

    public ConcreteCommand(Receiver receiver) :
        base(receiver)
    {
    }

    public override void Execute()
    {
        receiver.Action();
    }
}

/// <summary> The 'Receiver' class
/// </summary>

public class Receiver
{
    public void Action()
    {
        Console.WriteLine("Called Receiver.Action()");
    }
}

/// <summary> The 'Invoker' class
/// </summary>

public class Invoker
{
    Command command;
```

```
    public void SetCommand(Command command)
    {
        this.command = command;
    }

    public void ExecuteCommand()
    {
        command.Execute();
    }
}
}
```

Real-World C# Code

This real-world code shows the Command Pattern in action in a basic cal-culator with an infinite number of undo and redo. It's worth noting that the word "operator" is a keyword in C#. It may be used as an identifier by prefixing it with "@".

```csharp
using System;
using System.Collections.Generic;

namespace Command.RealWorld
{
    /// <summary> Command Design Pattern
    /// </summary>

    public class Program
    {
        public static void Main(string[] args)
        {
            // Create a user and let compute

            User user = new User();

            // User presses the calculator buttons

            user.Compute('+', 120);
            user.Compute('-', 90);
            user.Compute('*', 14);
            user.Compute('/', 21);

            // Undo the 4 commands

            user.Undo(4);
```

```
            // Redo the 3 commands

            user.Redo(3);

            // Wait for the user

            Console.ReadKey();
        }
    }

/// <summary> The 'Command' abstract class
/// </summary>

public abstract class Command
{
    public abstract void Execute();
    public abstract void UnExecute();
}

/// <summary> The 'ConcreteCommand' class
/// </summary>

public class CalculatorCommand : Command
{
    char @operator;
    int operand;
    Calculator calculator;

    // Constructor

    public CalculatorCommand(Calculator calculator,
        char @operator, int operand)
    {
        this.calculator = calculator;
        this.@operator = @operator;
        this.operand = operand;
    }

    // Gets-operator

    public char Operator
    {
        set { @operator = value; }
    }

    // Get-operand

    public int Operand
```

```
{
    set { operand = value; }
}

// Execute the new command

public override void Execute()
{
    calculator.Operation(@operator, operand);
}

// Unexecute the last command

public override void UnExecute()
{
    calculator.Operation(Undo(@operator), operand);
}

// Returns the opposite operator for given operator

private char Undo(char @operator)
{
    switch (@operator)
    {
        case '+': return '-';
        case '-': return '+';
        case '*': return '/';
        case '/': return '*';
        default:
            throw new
        ArgumentException("@operator");
    }
}
}

/// <summary> The 'Receiver' class
/// </summary>

public class Calculator
{
    int curr = 0;

    public void Operation(char @operator, int operand)
    {
        switch (@operator)
        {
            case '+': curr += operand; break;
            case '-': curr -= operand; break;
```

```
                case '*': curr *= operand; break;
                case '/': curr /= operand; break;
            }
            Console.WriteLine(
                "Current value = {0,3} (following {1} {2})",
                curr, @operator, operand);
        }
    }

    /// <summary> The 'Invoker' class
    /// </summary>

    public class User
    {
        // Initializers

        Calculator calculator = new Calculator();
        List<Command> commands = new List<Command>();
        int current = 0;

        public void Redo(int levels)
        {
            Console.WriteLine("\n---- Redo {0} levels ",
levels);
            // Perform redo operations
            for (int x = 0; x < levels; x++)
            {
                if (current < commands.Count - 1)
                {
                    Command command = commands[current++];
                    command.Execute();
                }
            }
        }

        public void Undo(int levels)
        {
            Console.WriteLine("\n-- Undo {0} levels ",
levels);

            // Perform the undo operations

            for (int x = 0; x < levels; x++)
            {
                if (current > 0)
                {
                    Command command = commands[--current]
as Command;
```

```
                    command.UnExecute();
            }
        }
    }

    public void Compute(char @operator, int operand)
    {
        // Create the command operation and execute it

        Command command = new
CalculatorCommand(calculator, @operator, operand);
        command.Execute();

        // Add the command to undo list

        commands.Add(command);
        current++;
    }
}
```

INTERPRETER PATTERN

One of the Behavioral Design Patterns is the Interpreter Design Pattern. The interpreter pattern is used to specify a language's grammatical representation and to offer an interpreter to deal with this grammar.

- This pattern entails developing an expression interface that instructs how to comprehend a certain situation. This pattern is utilized in SQL parsing, symbol processing engines, and other applications.

- This pattern is used to a hierarchy of expressions. Each expression in this list is either terminal or non-terminal.

- The Interpreter Design Pattern's tree structure is similar to that of the Composite Design Pattern, with terminal expressions being leaf objects and non-terminal expressions being composites.

- A parser generates the tree, which includes the expressions to be evaluated. The interpreter pattern does not include the parser.

Components of Design

- **AbstractExpression (Expression):** Defines an interpret() action that is overridden by all nodes (terminal and nonterminal) in the AST.

- **TerminalExpression (NumberExpression):** This class implements the interpret() method for terminal expressions.

- **NonterminalExpression:** Implements the interpret() procedure for all nonterminal expressions (AdditionExpression, SubtractionExpression, and MultiplicationExpression).

- **Context (String):** Contains global information for the interpreter. This String expression using Postfix notation must be evaluated and processed.

- **Client (ExpressionParser):** Creates (or receives) the AST composed of TerminalExpression and NonTerminalExpression. The interpret() procedure is called by the Client.

Let's look at an Interpreter Design Pattern sample.

```
// Expression interface used to check interpreter.
interface Expression
{
    boolean interpreter(String con);
}

// TerminalExpression class implementing
// above interface. This interpreter
// just check if data is same as the
// interpreter data.
class TerminalExpression implements Expression
{
    String data;

    public TerminalExpression(String data)
    {
        this.data = data;
    }

    public boolean interpreter(String con)
    {
        if(con.contains(data))
        {
            return true;
        }
        else
        {
            return false;
        }
```

```
        }
    }
    // OrExpression class implementing the
    // above interface. This interpreter returns
    // the or condition of the data
    // is same as the interpreter data.
    class OrExpression implements Expression
    {
        Expression expr1;
        Expression expr2;

        public OrExpression(Expression expr1, Expression expr2)
        {
            this.expr1 = expr1;
            this.expr2 = expr2;
        }
        public boolean interpreter(String con)
        {
            return expr1.interpreter(con) || expr2
    .interpreter(con);
        }
    }

    // AndExpression class implementing the above interface.
    // This interpreter just returns the
    // And condition of the
    // data is same as interpreter data.
    class AndExpression implements Expression
    {
        Expression expr1;
        Expression expr2;

        public AndExpression(Expression expr1, Expression expr2)
        {
            this.expr1 = expr1;
            this.expr2 = expr2;
        }
        public boolean interpreter(String con)
        {
            return expr1.interpreter(con) && expr2.
    interpreter(con);
        }
    }

    // Driver-class
    class InterpreterPattern
    {
        public static void main(String[] args)
        {
```

```
        Expression person1 = new TerminalExpression
("Pushagra");
        Expression person2 = new
TerminalExpression("Nokesh");
        Expression isSingle = new OrExpression(person1,
person2);

        Expression vikram = new
TerminalExpression("Kiram");
        Expression committed = new TerminalExpression
("Committed");
        Expression isCommitted = new AndExpression(vikram,
committed);

        System.out.println(isSingle.
interpreter("Pushagra"));
        System.out.println(isSingle.interpreter("Nokesh"));
        System.out.println(isSingle.interpreter("Pchint"));

        System.out.println(isCommitted.
interpreter("Committed, Kiram"));
        System.out.println(isCommitted.interpreter("Single,
Kiram"));

    }
}
```

In the preceding code, we create an interface Expression and concrete classes that implement the Expression interface. TerminalExpression is defined as the primary interpreter, while the classes OrExpression and AndExpression are used to generate combinational expressions.

Advantages

It is simple to modify and expand the grammar. Because the pattern uses classes to describe grammatical rules, inheritance may be used to modify or expand the grammar. Existing expressions may be progressively updated, and new expressions can be created as variants of existing ones.

It is also simple to put the grammar into practice. The implementations of classes that define nodes in the abstract syntax tree are comparable. These classes are simple to build, and their production is often automated by a compiler or parser generator.

Disadvantages

Complex grammars are difficult to maintain. The Interpreter pattern specifies at least one class for each grammatical rule. As a result, grammar with
a large number of rules might be difficult to administer and maintain.

Implementation of Interpreter Pattern in Java

- **Step 1:** Create Pattern interface.

```java
public interface Pattern {
    public String conversion(String exp);
}
```

- **Step 2:** Create InfixToPostfixPattern class that will allow what kind
  of pattern us want to convert.
  File: InfixToPostfixPattern.java

```java
import java.util.Stack;
public class InfixToPostfixPattern implements Pattern{
    @Override
    public String conversion(String exp) {
        int priority = 0;// for the priority of
operators.
        String postfix = "";
        Stack stl = new Stack();
        for (int x = 0; x < exp.length(); x++)
        {
            char ch = exp.charAt(i);
            if (ch == '+' || ch == '-' || ch == '*' ||
ch == '/'||ch=='%')
            {
                // check the precedence
                if (stl.size() <= 0)
                    stl.push(ch);
            }
            else
            {
                Character chTop = (Character) stl.
peek();
                if (chTop == '*' || chTop == '/')
                    priority = 1;
                else
                    priority = 0;
```

```
                    if (priority == 1)
                    {
                        if (ch == '*' || ch ==
'/'||ch=='%')
                        {
                            postfix += st1.pop();
                                                        i--;
                        }
                        else
                        { // Same
                            postfix += st1.pop();
                            i--;
                        }
                    }
                    else
                    {
                        if (ch == '+' || ch == '-')
                        {
                            postfix += st1.pop();
                            st1.push(ch);
                        }
                        else
                            st1.push(ch);
                    }
                }
            }
            else
            {
                postfix += ch;
            }
        }
        int len = st1.size();
        for (int y = 0; y < len; y++)
            postfix += st1.pop();
        return postfix;

    }
}// End of InfixToPostfixPattern class.
```

- **Step 3:** Create InterpreterPatternClient class that will use InfixToPostfix Conversion.

    File: InterpreterPatternClient.java

```
public class InterpreterPatternClient {
    public static void main(String[] args)
```

```
    {
        String infix = "c+d*e";

        InfixToPostfixPattern ip=new
InfixToPostfixPattern();

        String postfix = ip.conversion(infix);
        System.out.println("Infix is:    " + infix);
        System.out.println("Postfix is: " +
postfix);
    }
}
```

Interpreter Pattern in C#

The Interpreter Design Pattern, given a language, specifies a representation for its grammar as well as an interpreter that utilizes the representation to understand sentences in the language.

C# Structural Code

This structured code exhibits the Interpreter Patterns, which offer an interpreter that interprets parsed sentences by utilizing a given grammar.

```
using System;
using System.Collections.Generic;

namespace Interpreter.Structural
{
    /// <summary> Interpreter Design Pattern
    /// </summary>

    public class Program
    {
        public static void Main(string[] args)
        {
            Context context = new Context();

            // Usually tree

            List<AbstractExpression> list = new
List<AbstractExpression>();
```

```
        // Populate the 'abstract syntax tree'

        list.Add(new TerminalExpression());
        list.Add(new NonterminalExpression());
        list.Add(new TerminalExpression());
        list.Add(new TerminalExpression());

        // Interpret

        foreach (AbstractExpression exp in list)
        {
            exp.Interpret(context);
        }

        // Wait for the user

        Console.ReadKey();
    }
}

/// <summary> The 'Context' class
/// </summary>

public class Context
{
}

/// <summary> The 'AbstractExpression' abstract class
/// </summary>

public abstract class AbstractExpression
{
    public abstract void Interpret(Context context);
}

/// <summary> The 'TerminalExpression' class
/// </summary>

public class TerminalExpression : AbstractExpression
{
    public override void Interpret(Context context)
    {
        Console.WriteLine("Called Terminal.Interpret()");
    }
}

/// <summary> The 'NonterminalExpression' class
/// </summary>
```

```
public class NonterminalExpression : AbstractExpression
{
    public override void Interpret(Context context)
    {
        Console.WriteLine("Called Nonterminal.
Interpret()");
    }
}
}
```

Real-World C# Code

This real-world code shows how to utilize the Interpreter pattern to convert a Roman number to a decimal.

```
using System.Collections.Generic;

namespace Interpreter.RealWorld
{
    /// <summary> Interpreter Design Pattern
    /// </summary>

    public class Program
    {
        public static void Main(string[] args)
        {
            string roman = "MCMXXVIII";
            Context context = new Context(roman);

            // Build 'parse tree'

            List<Expression> tree = new List<Expression>();
            tree.Add(new ThousandExpression());
            tree.Add(new HundredExpression());
            tree.Add(new TenExpression());
            tree.Add(new OneExpression());

            // Interpret

            foreach (Expression exp in tree)
            {
                exp.Interpret(context);
            }

            Console.WriteLine("{0} = {1}",
                roman, context.Output);
```

```
            // Wait for the user

            Console.ReadKey();
        }
    }

    /// <summary> The 'Context' class
    /// </summary>

    public class Context
    {
        string input;
        int output;

        // Constructor

        public Context(string input)
        {
            this.input = input;
        }

        public string Input
        {
            get { return input; }
            set { input = value; }
        }

        public int Output
        {
            get { return output; }
            set { output = value; }
        }
    }

    /// <summary> The 'AbstractExpression' class
    /// </summary>

    public abstract class Expression
    {
        public void Interpret(Context context)
        {
            if (context.Input.Length == 0)
                return;

            if (context.Input.StartsWith(Nine()))
            {
                context.Output += (9 * Multiplier());
                context.Input = context.Input.Substring(2);
```

```
        }
        else if (context.Input.StartsWith(Four()))
        {
            context.Output += (4 * Multiplier());
            context.Input = context.Input.Substring(2);
        }
        else if (context.Input.StartsWith(Five()))
        {
            context.Output += (5 * Multiplier());
            context.Input = context.Input.Substring(1);
        }

        while (context.Input.StartsWith(One()))
        {
            context.Output += (1 * Multiplier());
            context.Input = context.Input.Substring(1);
        }
    }

    public abstract string One();
    public abstract string Four();
    public abstract string Five();
    public abstract string Nine();
    public abstract int Multiplier();
}

/// <summary> A 'TerminalExpression' class
/// <remarks> Thousand checks for the Roman Numeral M
</remarks>
/// </summary>

public class ThousandExpression : Expression
{
    public override string One() { return "M"; }
    public override string Four() { return " "; }
    public override string Five() { return " "; }
    public override string Nine() { return " "; }
    public override int Multiplier() { return 1000; }
}

/// <summary> A 'TerminalExpression' class
/// <remarks> Hundred checks C, CD, D or CM
/// </remarks></summary>

public class HundredExpression : Expression
{
    public override string One() { return "C"; }
    public override string Four() { return "CD"; }
```

```
        public override string Five() { return "D"; }
        public override string Nine() { return "CM"; }
        public override int Multiplier() { return 100; }
}


/// <summary>
/// A 'TerminalExpression' class <remarks>
/// Ten checks for X, XL, L and XC </remarks>
/// </summary>

public class TenExpression : Expression
{
    public override string One() { return "X"; }
    public override string Four() { return "XL"; }
    public override string Five() { return "L"; }
    public override string Nine() { return "XC"; }
    public override int Multiplier() { return 10; }
}


/// <summary>
/// A 'TerminalExpression' class <remarks>
/// One checks for I, II, III, IV, V, VI, VI, VII,
VIII, IX </remarks>
/// </summary>

public class OneExpression : Expression
{
    public override string One() { return "I"; }
    public override string Four() { return "IV"; }
    public override string Five() { return "V"; }
    public override string Nine() { return "IX"; }
    public override int Multiplier() { return 1; }
}
}
```

ITERATOR PATTERN

The Iterator Pattern is a Behavioral Design Pattern that allows us to explore the items of collections without exposing the element's in-depth features. It allows you to access the elements of a complicated data structure sequentially without having to repeat them.

Iterator Pattern is used "to retrieve the elements of an aggregate object progressively without disclosing its underlying implementation," according to GangOfFour.

The Problem without Employing the Iterator Pattern

Consider designing an application for tiny children that accepts any legitimate alphabet as input and returns all alphabets up to that. When this program is just used a few times, it is OK to execute the For loop and While loop repeatedly, but as the frequency of running rises, this procedure becomes rather wasteful. As a result, we must devise a method to prevent these loops. This issue may grow more severe when we deal with complicated non-linear data structures like Trees and Graphs, where traversing is not as straightforward as it is in an array.

Iterator Pattern for Solution

The solution to the aforementioned issue will be discussed in this section. Iterators are always useful for Python users when traversing any kind of data structure, whether linear or non-linear. We have two alternatives for implementing iterators in Python: we may utilize the built-in iterators to yield useful results, or we can manually define iterators using Generators. The iterators in the following code were specifically constructed using generators.

The following code is an example of an Iterator Pattern that was intentionally built.

```python
""" helper method for the iterator"""


def alphabets_upto(letter):
    """Counts by the word numbers, up to a maximum of
five"""
    for c in range(65, ord(letter)+1):
        yield chr(c)


"""main-method"""
if __name__ == "__main__":

    alphabets_upto_K = alphabets_upto('K')
    alphabets_upto_M = alphabets_upto('M')

    for alpha in alphabets_upto_K:
        print(alpha, end=" ")

    print()

    for alpha in alphabets_upto_M:
        print(alpha, end=" ")
```

The following code demonstrates the use of an in-built Iterator Pattern.

```
"""utility-function"""
def inBuilt_Iterator1():

    alphabets = [chr(i) for c in range(55, 92)]

    """using the in-built iterator"""
    for alpha in alphabets:
        print(alpha, end = " ")
    print()

"""utility-function"""
def inBuilt_Iterator2():

    alphabets = [chr(i) for c in range(93, 133)]

    """using the in-built iterator"""
    for alpha in alphabets:
        print(alpha, end = " ")
    print()

"""main-method"""
if __name__ == "__main__" :

    """call inbuiltIterators"""
    inBuilt_Iterator1()
    inBuilt_Iterator2()
```

Advantages

- **Single Responsibility Principle:** The Iterator Pattern makes it very simple to divide large algorithms into different classes.

- Passing new iterators and collections into the client code does not damage the code and can be simply implemented into it.

- **Easy to Use Interface:** It makes the interface very simple to use and also permits changes in collection traversal.

Disadvantages

- **Unnecessary Wasting Resources:** Using the Iterator Pattern is not always a good practice since it might be overuse of resources in a small application where advanced things are not necessary.

- **Increases Complexity:** As previously stated, employing the Iterator Pattern complicates basic applications.

- **Reduces Efficiency:** In terms of efficiency, accessing elements directly is much superior to accessing elements through the iterator.

Applicability

- When we wish to access the elements at a lower level and are not concerned with the underlying implementation of the elements, the Iterator Pattern is always chosen.

- **Traversing Unknown Data Structures:** Because the code offers a pair of generic interfaces for both collections and iterators, the Iterator Pattern may be simply used to traverse many sorts of data structures like Trees, Graphs, Stacks, Queues, and so on.

Implementation of Iterator Pattern in Java

- **Step 1:** Create Iterartor interface.

```
public interface Iterator {
    public boolean hasNext();
    public Object next();
}
```

- **Step 2:** Create Container interface.

```
public interface Container {
    public Iterator getIterator();
}// End of Iterator interface.
```

- **Step 3:** Create CollectionofNames class that will implement the Container interface.
  File: CollectionofNames.java

```
public class CollectionofNames implements Container {
    public String name[]={"Ashwani Rajput", "Sonu
Pswal","Tishi Kaur","Raman Mehra","Heena Garg"};
```

```
    @Override
        public Iterator getIterator() {
            return new CollectionofNamesIterate() ;
        }
        private class CollectionofNamesIterate
implements Iterator{
            int x;
            @Override
            public boolean hasNext() {
                if (x<name.length){
                    return true;
                }
                return false;
            }
            @Override
            public Object next() {
                if(this.hasNext()){
                    return name[x++];
                }
                return null;
            }
        }
    }
}
```

- **Step 4:** Create IteratorPatternDemo class.
  File: IteratorPatternDemo.java

```
public class IteratorPatternDemo {
    public static void main(String[] args) {
        CollectionofNames cmpnyRepository = new
CollectionofNames();

        for(Iterator iter = cmpnyRepository.
getIterator(); iter.hasNext();){
            String name = (String)iter.next();
            System.out.println("Name is : " + name);
        }
    }
}
```

Iterator Pattern in C#

The Iterator Design Pattern enables sequential access to the constituents of an aggregate object without disclosing its underlying representation.

C# Structural Code

This structural code exhibits the Iterator Pattern, which allows us to traverse (iterate) across a collection of objects without revealing the collection's underlying structure.

```csharp
using System;
using System.Collections.Generic;

namespace Iterator.Structural
{
    /// <summary> Iterator Design Pattern
    /// </summary>

    public class Program
    {
        public static void Main(string[] args)
        {
            ConcreteAggregate x = new ConcreteAggregate();
            x[0] = "Item A";
            x[1] = "Item B";
            x[2] = "Item C";
            x[3] = "Item D";

            // Create Iterator and provide aggregate

            Iterator i = x.CreateIterator();

            Console.WriteLine("Iterating over collection:");

            object item = i.First();

            while (item != null)
            {
                Console.WriteLine(item);
                item = i.Next();
            }

            // Wait for the user

            Console.ReadKey();
        }
    }

    /// <summary> The 'Aggregate' abstract class
    /// </summary>
```

```
public abstract class Aggregate
{
    public abstract Iterator CreateIterator();
}

/// <summary> The 'ConcreteAggregate' class
/// </summary>

public class ConcreteAggregate : Aggregate
{
    List<object> items = new List<object>();

    public override Iterator CreateIterator()
    {
        return new ConcreteIterator(this);
    }

    // Get the item count

    public int Count
    {
        get { return items.Count; }
    }

    // Indexer

    public object this[int index]
    {
        get { return items[index]; }
        set { items.Insert(index, value); }
    }
}

/// <summary> The 'Iterator' abstract class
/// </summary>

public abstract class Iterator
{
    public abstract object First();
    public abstract object Next();
    public abstract bool IsDone();
    public abstract object CurrentItem();
}

/// <summary> The 'ConcreteIterator' class
/// </summary>

public class ConcreteIterator : Iterator
{
```

```
        ConcreteAggregate aggregate;
        int current = 0;

        // Constructor

        public ConcreteIterator(ConcreteAggregate
aggregate)
        {
            this.aggregate = aggregate;
        }

        // Gets the first iteration item

        public override object First()
        {
            return aggregate[0];
        }

        // Gets the next iteration item

        public override object Next()
        {
            object ret = null;
            if (current < aggregate.Count - 1)
            {
                ret = aggregate[++current];
            }

            return ret;
        }

        // Gets the current iteration item

        public override object CurrentItem()
        {
            return aggregate[current];
        }

        // Gets the whether iterations are complete

        public override bool IsDone()
        {
            return current >= aggregate.Count;
        }
    }
}
```

Real-World C# Code

This real-world code displays the Iterator Pattern, which is used to iterate over a collection of things while skipping a set amount of items each time.

```csharp
using System;
using System.Collections.Generic;

namespace Iterator.RealWorld
{
    /// <summary> Iterator Design Pattern
    /// </summary>

    public class Program
    {
        public static void Main(string[] args)
        {
            // Build collection

            Collection collection = new Collection();
            collection[0] = new Item("Item 0");
            collection[1] = new Item("Item 1");
            collection[2] = new Item("Item 2");
            collection[3] = new Item("Item 3");
            collection[4] = new Item("Item 4");
            collection[5] = new Item("Item 5");
            collection[6] = new Item("Item 6");
            collection[7] = new Item("Item 7");
            collection[8] = new Item("Item 8");

            // Create the iterator

            Iterator iterator = collection.CreateIterator();

            // Skip the every other item

            iterator.Step = 2;

            Console.WriteLine("Iterating over collection:");

            for (Item item = iterator.First();
                !iterator.IsDone; item = iterator.Next())
            {
                Console.WriteLine(item.Name);
            }

            // Wait for the user
```

```csharp
            Console.ReadKey();
        }
    }
    /// <summary> A collection item
    /// </summary>

    public class Item
    {
        string name;

        // Constructor

        public Item(string name)
        {
            this.name = name;
        }

        public string Name
        {
            get { return name; }
        }
    }

    /// <summary> The 'Aggregate' interface
    /// </summary>

    public interface IAbstractCollection
    {
        Iterator CreateIterator();
    }

    /// <summary> The 'ConcreteAggregate' class
    /// </summary>

    public class Collection : IAbstractCollection
    {
        List<Item> items = new List<Item>();

        public Iterator CreateIterator()
        {
            return new Iterator(this);
        }

        // Gets item count

        public int Count
        {
            get { return items.Count; }
        }
```

```csharp
    // Indexer

    public Item this[int index]
    {
        get { return items[index]; }
        set { items.Add(value); }
    }
}


/// <summary> The 'Iterator' interface
/// </summary>

public interface IAbstractIterator
{
    Item First();
    Item Next();
    bool IsDone { get; }
    Item CurrentItem { get; }
}


/// <summary> The 'ConcreteIterator' class
/// </summary>

public class Iterator : IAbstractIterator
{
    Collection collection;
    int current = 0;
    int step = 1;

    // Constructor

    public Iterator(Collection collection)
    {
        this.collection = collection;
    }

    // Gets the first item

    public Item First()
    {
        current = 0;
        return collection[current] as Item;
    }

    // Gets the next item

    public Item Next()
    {
```

```
        current += step;
        if (!IsDone)
                return collection[current] as Item;
        else
                return null;
    }

    // Gets or sets the stepsize

    public int Step
    {
        get { return step; }
        set { step = value; }
    }

    // Gets the current iterator item

    public Item CurrentItem
    {
        get { return collection[current] as Item; }
    }

    // Gets whether the iteration is complete

    public bool IsDone
    {
        get { return current >= collection.Count; }
    }
  }
}
```

MEDIATOR PATTERN

The Mediator Pattern is a Behavioral Design Pattern that allows us to reduce the objects' unordered dependencies. Objects in a mediator environment use mediator object to communicate with one another. It decreases coupling by removing dependencies between communication items. The mediator acts as a conduit between objects and might have its logic to facilitate communication.

Components of Design

The mediator defines the interface for communication between coworker objects.

- **Concrete Mediator:** This object implements the mediator interface and organizes communication among colleagues.

- **Colleague:** It defines the communication interface with other colleagues.

- **Concrete Colleague:** It uses its mediator to interact with colleagues and implements the colleague interface.

The Problem without Employing the Mediator Pattern

Consider enrolling in one of the premier courses provided by PeeksforPeeks, such as DSA, SDE, or STL. Initially, there were relatively few students interested in enrolling in these classes. Initially, the developer may establish distinct objects and classes to link students and courses. Still, as the courses gain popularity among students, it becomes difficult for developers to manage such a large number of subclasses and associated objects.

Solution Using the Mediator Pattern

Consider how a professional developer might utilize the Mediator Design Pattern to handle such a circumstance. We may construct a distinct mediator class called Course and a User Class from which we can generate different Course class objects. In the main function, we will construct a distinct object for each student, and within the User class, we will build the object for the Course class, preventing unordered code.

```python
class Course(object):
    """Mediator class."""

    def displayCourse(self, user, course_name):
        print("[{}'s course ]: {}".format(user, course_name))


class User(object):
    '''A class whose instances want to interact with the
each other.'''

    def __init__(self, name):
        self.name = name
        self.course = Course()

    def sendCourse(self, course_name):
        self.course.displayCourse(self, course_name)

    def __str__(self):
        return self.name
```

```
"""main-method"""

if __name__ == "__main__":

    sayank = User('Sayank')     # user-object
    nakshya = User('Nakshya')   # user-object
    mrishna = User('Mrishna')   # user-object


    sayank.sendCourse("Data-Structures and Algorithms")
    nakshya.sendCourse("Software-Development Engineer")
    mrishna.sendCourse("Standard-Template Library")
```

Advantages

- **Single Responsibility Principle:** The Mediator Pattern allows for the extraction of communications between diverse components into a single location that is simpler to manage.

- The open/closed principle states that it is simple to add new mediators without disrupting the current client code.

- **Allows Inheritance:** Because of the Inheritance, we may reuse the different components of the mediators.

- **Few Subclasses:** The mediator restricts the Subclassing since the mediator localizes the behavior that would otherwise be disrupted among the several objects.

Disadvantages

- Because the Mediator Pattern sacrifices interaction complexity for mediator complexity, it entirely centralizes control.

- A Mediator may be transformed into a God Object (an object that knows too much or does too much).

- **Increased Complexity:** If we place too much logic within the mediator object, its structure may become too complicated.

Applicability

- **Reduce the Number of Subclassifications:** When you notice you've built a lot of superfluous subclasses, it's best to utilize the Mediator Pattern to prevent these extraneous subclasses.

- **Air Traffic Controller:** The airport control center serves as a mediator for communication between various planes, which is a perfect example of a Mediator Pattern.

Implementation of Mediator Pattern in Java

- **Step 1:** Create ApnaChatRoom interface.

```
//This is an interface.
public interface ApnaChatRoom {

    public void showMsg(String msg, Participant p1);

}// End of ApnaChatRoom interface.
```

- **Step 2:** Create an ApnaChatRoomIml class that implements the ApnaChatRoom interface and also uses the Participant interface to count the number of people conversing.

```
//This is a class.
import java.text.DateFormat;
import java.text.SimpleDateFormat;
import java.util.Date;

public class ApnaChatRoomImpl implements ApnaChatRoom{
    //get the current date time
    DateFormat dateFormat = new SimpleDateFormat("E
dd-MM-yyyy hh:mm a");
    Date date = new Date();
    @Override
    public void showMsg(String msg, Participant p1) {

        System.out.println(p1.getName()+"'gets
message: "+msg);
        System.out.println("\t\t\t\t"+"["+dateFormat.
format(date).toString()+"]");
    }
}// End of ApnaChatRoomImpl class.
```

- **Step 3:** Create Participant abstract class.

```
//This is abstract class.
public abstract class Participant {
    public abstract void sendMsg(String msg);
    public abstract void setname(String name);
    public abstract String getName();
}// End of Participant abstract class.
```

- **Step 4:** Create a User1 class that extends the abstract Participant class and implements the ApnaChatRoom interface.

```
//This is class.

public class User1 extends Participant {

    private String name;
    private ApnaChatRoom chat;

    @Override
    public void sendMsg(String msg) {
    chat.showMsg(msg,this);

    }

    @Override
    public void setname(String name) {
        this.name=name;
    }

    @Override
    public String getName() {
        return name;
    }

    public User1(ApnaChatRoom chat){
        this.chat=chat;
    }

}// End of User1 class.
```

- **Step 5:** Create a User2 class that extends the abstract Participant class and implements the ApnaChatRoom interface.

```
//This is class.

public class User2 extends Participant {

    private String name;
    private ApnaChatRoom chat;

    @Override
    public void sendMsg(String msg) {
    this.chat.showMsg(msg,this);

    }

    @Override
    public void setname(String name) {
        this.name=name;
    }

    @Override
    public String getName() {
        return name;
    }

    public User2(ApnaChatRoom chat){
        this.chat=chat;
    }


}
// End of User2 class.
```

- **Step 6:** Create a MediatorPatternDemo class that will utilize chat participants.

```
//This is class.

public class MediatorPatternDemo {

    public static void main(String args[])
    {
```

```
        ApnaChatRoom chat = new ApnaChatRoomImpl();

        User1 u1=new User1(chat);
        u1.setname("Swani Rai");
        u1.sendMsg("Hello Swani! how are you
    doing?");


        User2 u2=new User2(chat);
        u2.setname("Sonu Rajpal");
        u2.sendMsg("I'm Fine ! U tell?");
    }

}// End of MediatorPatternDemo class.
```

Mediator Pattern in C#

The Mediator Design Pattern describes an entity that captures how a group of items communicate with one another. The mediator encourages loose coupling by preventing objects from directly referring to each other, allowing us to alter their interaction freely.

C# Structural Code

This structured code exemplifies the Mediator Pattern, which enables loosely connected communication between various objects and object kinds. The mediator serves as a central hub through which all interactions must pass.

```
using System;

namespace Mediator.Structural
{
    /// <summary> Mediator Design Pattern
    /// </summary>

    public class Program
    {
        public static void Main(string[] args)
        {
            ConcreteMediator mt = new ConcreteMediator();

            ConcreteColleague1 ct1 = new
    ConcreteColleague1(m);
```

```
            ConcreteColleague2 ct2 = new
ConcreteColleague2(m);

        mt.Colleague1 = ct1;
        mt.Colleague2 = ct2;

        ct1.Send("How are you doing?");
        ct2.Send("Fine, thankyou");

        // Wait for the user

        Console.ReadKey();
    }
}

/// <summary> The 'Mediator' abstract class
/// </summary>

public abstract class Mediator
{
    public abstract void Send(string message,
        Colleague colleague);
}

/// <summary> The 'ConcreteMediator' class
/// </summary>

public class ConcreteMediator : Mediator
{
    ConcreteColleague1 colleague1;
    ConcreteColleague2 colleague2;

    public ConcreteColleague1 Colleague1
    {
        set { colleague1 = value; }
    }

    public ConcreteColleague2 Colleague2
    {
        set { colleague2 = value; }
    }

    public override void Send(string message, Colleague
colleague)
    {
        if (colleague == colleague1)
        {
            colleague2.Notify(message);
        }
```

```csharp
        else
        {
            colleague1.Notify(message);
        }
    }
}

/// <summary> The 'Colleague' abstract class
/// </summary>

public abstract class Colleague
{
    protected Mediator mediator;

    // Constructor

    public Colleague(Mediator mediator)
    {
        this.mediator = mediator;
    }
}

/// <summary> A 'ConcreteColleague' class
/// </summary>

public class ConcreteColleague1 : Colleague
{
    // Constructor

    public ConcreteColleague1(Mediator mediator)
        : base(mediator)
    {
    }

    public void Send(string message)
    {
        mediator.Send(message, this);
    }

    public void Notify(string message)
    {
        Console.WriteLine("Colleague1 gets the message: "
            + message);
    }
}

/// <summary> A 'ConcreteColleague' class
/// </summary>
```

```
public class ConcreteColleague2 : Colleague
{
    // Constructor

    public ConcreteColleague2(Mediator mediator)
        : base(mediator)
    {
    }

    public void Send(string message)
    {
        mediator.Send(message, this);
    }

    public void Notify(string message)
    {
        Console.WriteLine("Colleague2 gets the
message: "
            + message);
    }
}
}
```

Real-World C# Code

This real-world code exemplifies the Mediator Pattern, which facilitates loosely connected communication between multiple Chatroom Participants. The Chatroom serves as the major focus for all conversations. The Chatroom now only supports one-to-one conversation; however, changing to one-to-many would be simple.

```
using System;
using System.Collections.Generic;

namespace Mediator.RealWorld
{
    /// <summary> Mediator Design Pattern
    /// </summary>

    public class Program
    {
        public static void Main(string[] args)
        {
            // Create the chatroom
```

```
            Chatroom chatroom = new Chatroom();

            // Create the participants and register them

            Participant George = new Beatle("Korge");
            Participant Paul = new Beatle("Naun");
            Participant Ringo = new Beatle("Lingo");
            Participant John = new Beatle("Rohan");
            Participant Yoko = new NonBeatle("Loko");

            chatroom.Register(Korge);
            chatroom.Register(Naun);
            chatroom.Register(Lingo);
            chatroom.Register(Rohan);
            chatroom.Register(Loko);

            // Chatting participants

            Yoko.Send("John", "Hello Rohan!");
            Paul.Send("Ringo", "All we need is love");
            Ringo.Send("George", "Sweet Lord");
            Paul.Send("John", "Money Can't buy me love");
            John.Send("Yoko", "My sweet Sugar");

            // Wait for the user

            Console.ReadKey();
        }
    }

    /// <summary> The 'Mediator' abstract class
    /// </summary>

    public abstract class AbstractChatroom
    {
        public abstract void Register(Participant
    participant);
        public abstract void Send(
            string from, string to, string message);
    }

    /// <summary> The 'ConcreteMediator' class
    /// </summary>

    public class Chatroom : AbstractChatroom
    {
        private Dictionary<string, Participant>
    participants = new Dictionary<string, Participant>();
```

```
    public override void Register(Participant participant)
    {
        if (!participants.ContainsValue(participant))
        {
            participants[participant.Name] =
participant;
        }

        participant.Chatroom = this;
    }

    public override void Send(string from, string to,
string message)
    {
        Participant participant = participants[to];

        if (participant != null)
        {
            participant.Receive(from, message);
        }
    }
}

/// <summary> The 'AbstractColleague' class
/// </summary>

public class Participant
{
    Chatroom chatroom;
    string name;

    // Constructor

    public Participant(string name)
    {
        this.name = name;
    }

    // Gets the participant name

    public string Name
    {
        get { return name; }
    }

    // Gets the chatroom

    public Chatroom Chatroom
```

```csharp
    {
        set { chatroom = value; }
        get { return chatroom; }
    }

    // Sends a message to the given participant

    public void Send(string to, string message)
    {
        chatroom.Send(name, to, message);
    }

    // Receives message from the given participant

    public virtual void Receive(
        string from, string message)
    {
        Console.WriteLine("{0} to {1}: '{2}'",
            from, Name, message);
    }
}

/// <summary> A 'ConcreteColleague' class
/// </summary>

public class Beatle : Participant
{
    // Constructor

    public Beatle(string name)
        : base(name)
    {
    }

    public override void Receive(string from, string
message)
    {
        Console.Write("To a Beatle: ");
        base.Receive(from, message);
    }
}

/// <summary> A 'ConcreteColleague' class
/// </summary>

public class NonBeatle : Participant
{
    // Constructor
```

```
        public NonBeatle(string name)
            : base(name)
        {
        }

        public override void Receive(string from, string
message)
        {
            Console.Write("To non-Beatle: ");
            base.Receive(from, message);
        }
    }
}
```

MEMENTO PATTERN

The Memento Pattern is a Behavioral Design Pattern that allows us to return an item to its earlier state. It enables us to save and restore the previous version of the object without disclosing the specifics of particular implementations. It strives not to break the code's encapsulation and enables us to capture and externalize an object's internal state.

The Problem without Employing the Memento Pattern

Assume we are a student who wants to flourish in the world of competitive programming, but you are having difficulty finding a decent Code Editor for programming. None of the existing code editors meet our expectations, so we attempt to create one for ourselves. UNDO and REDO are two of the most critical capabilities in any Code Editor, and we'll need them both. As novice developers, we just took the straightforward way of saving all accomplished activities. Of sure, this method will work, but it will be inefficient.

Memento Pattern Solution

Let's talk about how to solve the previously mentioned difficulty. The whole issue can be simply fixed by not altering the code's encapsulation. The issue emerges when certain items attempt to execute additional duties that are not allocated to them, so invading the private space of other objects. The Memento Pattern depicts the process of producing state snapshots for the true owner of that state, the originator object. As a result, rather than other objects attempting to duplicate the editor's state from the "outside," the editor class may take a snapshot since it has complete access to its state.

According to the pattern, we should save a replica of the object's state in a special object called Memento. The content of the Memento objects should be available only to the object that created it.

```python
"""Memento class for saving data"""

class Memento:

    """Constructor-function"""
    def __init__(self, file, content):

        """put all our file content here"""

        self.file = file
        self.content = content

"""It's a File Writing Utility"""

class FileWriterUtility:

    """Constructor-Function"""

    def __init__(self, file):

        """store the input file data"""
        self.file = file
        self.content = ""

    """Write data into the file"""

    def write(self, string):
        self.content += string

    """save data into the Memento"""

    def save(self):
        return Memento(self.file, self.content)

    """UNDO-feature provided"""

    def undo(self, memento):
        self.file = memento.file
        self.content = memento.content

"""CareTaker for the FileWriter"""

class FileWriterCaretaker:

    """saves-data"""
```

```
    def save(self, writer):
        self.obj = writer.save()

    """undo the content"""

    def undo(self, writer):
        writer.undo(self.obj)


if __name__ == '__main__':

    """create caretaker object"""
    caretaker = FileWriterCaretaker()

    """create writer object"""
    writer = FileWriterUtility("PFP.txt")

    """write data into file using the writer object"""
    writer.write("First vision of PeeksforPeeks\n")
    print(writer.content + "\n\n")

    """save-file"""
    caretaker.save(writer)

    """again write using the writer """
    writer.write("Second vision of PeeksforPeeks\n")

    print(writer.content + "\n\n")

    """undo-file"""
    caretaker.undo(writer)

    print(writer.content + "\n\n")
```

Advantages

- **Encourages Encapsulation:** The Memento Pattern may assist in creating the state of the object without violating the client's code's encapsulation.

- **Simplifies Code:** We may use a caretaker to assist us in simplifying the code by preserving the history of the originator's code.

- **General Memento's Implementation:** It is preferable to utilize Serialization to obtain a more generic Memento Pattern implementation rather than Memento Pattern where each object must have its own Memento class implementation.

Disadvantages

- **Huge Memory Consumption:** If the Originator's object is extremely large, the Memento object size will be large, using a lot of memory, which is clearly not the most efficient method to complete the task.

- **Problem with Dynamic Languages:** Because dynamic languages, such as Ruby, Python, and PHP, are dynamically typed, they cannot ensure that the memento object will not touch.

- **Difficult Deletion:** Deleting the memento object is difficult since the caretaker must trace the originator's lifespan to get the outcome.

Applicability

- **UNDO and REDO:** For the convenience of the client, most software products, such as Paint, coding IDEs, text editors, and many more, have UNDO and REDO functions.

- **Encapsulation:** We may utilize Memento's approach to avoid encapsulation breakdown in the client's code, which could be caused by direct access to the object's internal implementation.

Memento

- Stores the originating object's internal state. The state can have an unlimited number of state variables.

- The Memento must have two interfaces: one to the outside world and one to the caretaker. This interface must not enable any actions or access to the memento's internal state to preserve encapsulation. The other interface is Originator, which allows the Originator to access any state variables required to restore the prior state.

Originator

- Generates a memento object that captures Originator's internal state.

- Use the memento object to return it to its original condition.

Caretaker

- In charge of maintaining the remembrance.

- The memento is visible to the caretaker, and the caretaker must not use it.

Memento Pattern Implementation in Java

- **Step 1:** Create an Originator class that will use a Memento object to recover its earlier state.

```
//This is class.

public class Originator {

    private String state;

    public void setState(String state){
        this.state = state;
    }

    public String getState(){
        return state;
    }

    public Memento saveStateToMemento(){
        return new Memento(state);
    }

    public void getStateFromMemento(Memento Memento){
        state = Memento.getState();
    }
}// End of Originator class.
```

- **Step 2:** Create a Memento class to store the Originator object's internal state.

```
//This is class.

public class Memento {

    private String state;

    public Memento(String state) {
        this.state=state;
    }
    public String getState() {
        return state;
    }

}// End of Memento class.
```

- **Step 3:** Make a Caretaker class that will be in charge of preserving the Memento.

```java
//This is class.

import java.util.ArrayList;
import java.util.List;


public class Caretaker {

    private List mementoList = new ArrayList();

        public void add(Memento state){
            mementoList.add(state);
        }

        public Memento get(int index){
            return mementoList.get(index);
        }

}// End of Caretaker class.
```

- **Step 4:** Create MementoPatternDemo class.

```java
//This is class.

public class MementoPatternDemo {

    public static void main(String[] args) {

        Originator originator = new Originator();

        Caretaker careTaker = new Caretaker();

        originator.setState("State#1");
        careTaker.add(originator.
saveStateToMemento());
        originator.setState("State#2");
        careTaker.add(originator.saveStateToMemento());
        originator.setState("State#3");
        careTaker.add(originator.saveStateToMemento());
        originator.setState("State#4");
```

```
              System.out.println("Current State: "
+ originator.getState());
              originator.getStateFromMemento(careTaker.
get(0));
              System.out.println("First saved State:
" + originator.getState());
              originator.getStateFromMemento(careTaker.
get(1));
              System.out.println("Second saved State:
" + originator.getState());
              originator.getStateFromMemento(careTaker.
get(2));
              System.out.println("Third saved State is:
" + originator.getState());
           }

}
// End of MementoPatternDemo class.
```

Memento Pattern in C#

The Memento Design Pattern captures and externalizes an object's internal state without breaching encapsulation so that the object may be restored to this state later.

C# Structural Code

This structured code exemplifies the Memento Pattern, which temporarily saves and restores the internal state of another object.

```
using System;

namespace Memento.Structural
{
    /// <summary> Memento Design Pattern
    /// </summary>

    public class Program
    {
        public static void Main(string[] args)
        {
            Originator or = new Originator();
            or.State = "On";

            // Store the internal state
```

```csharp
            Caretaker cr = new Caretaker();
            cr.Memento = or.CreateMemento();

            // Continue the changing originator

            or.State = "Off";

            // Restore the saved state

            or.SetMemento(cr.Memento);

            // Wait for the user

            Console.ReadKey();
        }
    }

    /// <summary> The 'Originator' class
    /// </summary>

    public class Originator
    {
        string state;

        public string State
        {
            get { return state; }
            set
            {
                state = value;
                Console.WriteLine("State = " + state);
            }
        }

        // Creates the memento

        public Memento CreateMemento()
        {
            return (new Memento(state));
        }

        // Restores the original state

        public void SetMemento(Memento memento)
        {
            Console.WriteLine("Restoring state.");
            State = memento.State;
        }
    }
```

```
/// <summary> The 'Memento' class
/// </summary>

public class Memento
{
    string state;

    // Constructor

    public Memento(string state)
    {
        this.state = state;
    }

    public string State
    {
        get { return state; }
    }
}

/// <summary> The 'Caretaker' class
/// </summary>

public class Caretaker
{
    Memento memento;

    public Memento Memento
    {
        set { memento = value; }
        get { return memento; }
    }
}
}
```

Real-World C# Code

This real-world code exhibits the Memento Pattern, which saves and then restores the internal state of the SalesProspect.

```
using System;

namespace Memento.RealWorld
{
    /// <summary> Memento Design Pattern
    /// </summary>
```

```csharp
public class Program
{
    public static void Main(string[] args)
    {
        SalesProspect sp = new SalesProspect();
        sp.Name = "Niel ban Alen";
        sp.Phone = "(312) 246-0980";
        sp.Budget = 29000.0;

        // Store the internal state

        ProspectMemory mt = new ProspectMemory();
        mt.Memento = sp.SaveMemento();

        // Continue the changing originator

        sp.Name = "Jeo Nelch";
        sp.Phone = "(210) 309-7111";
        sp.Budget = 1500000.0;

        // Restore the saved state

        sp.RestoreMemento(m.Memento);

        // Wait for the user

        Console.ReadKey();
    }
}

/// <summary> The 'Originator' class
/// </summary>

public class SalesProspect
{
    string name;
    string phone;
    double budget;

    // Gets or sets the name

    public string Name
    {
        get { return name; }
        set
        {
            name = value;
            Console.WriteLine("Name:    " + name);
```

```
        }
    }

    // Gets or sets the phone

    public string Phone
    {
        get { return phone; }
        set
        {
            phone = value;
            Console.WriteLine("Phone:   " + phone);
        }
    }

    // Gets or sets the budget

    public double Budget
    {
        get { return budget; }
        set
        {
            budget = value;
            Console.WriteLine("Budget: " + budget);
        }
    }

    // Stores-memento

    public Memento SaveMemento()
    {
        Console.WriteLine("\nSaving state --\n");
        return new Memento(name, phone, budget);
    }

    // Restores-memento

    public void RestoreMemento(Memento memento)
    {
        Console.WriteLine("\nRestoring state --\n");
        Name = memento.Name;
        Phone = memento.Phone;
        Budget = memento.Budget;
    }
}

/// <summary> The 'Memento' class
/// </summary>
```

```csharp
public class Memento
{
    string name;
    string phone;
    double budget;

    // Constructor
    public Memento(string name, string phone, double
budget)
    {
        this.name = name;
        this.phone = phone;
        this.budget = budget;
    }

    public string Name
    {
        get { return name; }
        set { name = value; }
    }

    public string Phone
    {
        get { return phone; }
        set { phone = value; }
    }

    public double Budget
    {
        get { return budget; }
        set { budget = value; }
    }
}

/// <summary> The 'Caretaker' class
/// </summary>

public class ProspectMemory
{
    Memento memento;

    public Memento Memento
    {
        set { memento = value; }
        get { return memento; }
    }
}
}
```

STATE PATTERN

The State Pattern is a Behavioral Design Pattern that enables an object to adjust its behavior when its internal state changes. It aids in the implementation of the State Pattern interface as a derived class. If we need to modify an object's behavior depending on its state, we may create a state variable in the Object and use an if-else condition block to do various actions based on the state. It is known as the object-oriented state machine. It implements the state transitions by calling methods from the superclass of the pattern.

The Problem without Employing the State Pattern

The State Pattern represents the Finite State Machine.

At any one time, the program may include a limited number of states. Each stage is distinct in terms of behavior and other characteristics. Even the software may transition from one state to another at any time. A program may transition from one state to another if and only if the necessary transition is defined in the rules. When we add a big number of states, it will undoubtedly become problematic. It will become tough to maintain the code since every little change in transition logic may result in a change in state conditionals in each method.

Solution Based on the State Pattern

Let's have a look at the answer to the above-mentioned problem using Radio as an example. The radio has two states in this country: AM and FM. We may switch between these two states by using the switch. The state approach advises that we construct a new class for each of an object's potential states and isolate all state-specific activities into these classes. Rather than implementing all actions on its own, the initial object named context keeps a reference to one of the state objects that reflects its current state and assigns all state-related tasks to that object.

```
"""State class: Base State class"""
class State:

    """Base state. This is to share the functionality"""

    def scan(self):

        """Scan the dial to next station"""
        self.pos += 1
```

```
            """check for the last station"""
            if self.pos == len(self.stations):
                self.pos = 0
            print("Visiting... Station is {} {}".format(self.
stations[self.pos], self.name))


"""Separate Class for the AM state of the radio"""
class AmState(State):

    """constructor for the AM state class"""
    def __init__(self, radio):

        self.radio = radio
        self.stations = ["1250", "1380", "1510"]
        self.pos = 0
        self.name = "AM"

    """method for the toggling the state"""
    def toggle_amfm(self):
        print("Switching to FM")
        self.radio.state = self.radio.fmstate


"""Separate class for the FM state"""
class FmState(State):

    """Constriuctor for FM state"""
    def __init__(self, radio):
        self.radio = radio
        self.stations = ["82.3", "88.1", "103.9"]
        self.pos = 0
        self.name = "FM"

    """method for the toggling the state"""
    def toggle_amfm(self):
        print("Switching to AM")
        self.radio.state = self.radio.amstate


"""Dedicated class Radio"""
class Radio:

    """A radio. It has scan button, and AM / FM toggle
switch."""

    def __init__(self):

        """We have AM state and FM state"""
        self.fmstate = FmState(self)
        self.amstate = AmState(self)
        self.state = self.fmstate
```

```
    """method to toggle the switch"""
    def toggle_amfm(self):
        self.state.toggle_amfm()


    """method to scan """
    def scan(self):
        self.state.scan()

""" main-method """
if __name__ == "__main__":

    """ create radio object"""
    radio = Radio()
    actions = [radio.scan] * 3 + [radio.toggle_amfm] +
[radio.scan] * 3
    actions *= 2

    for action in actions:
        action()
```

Advantages

- **Open/Closed Principle:** We can simply add new states without affecting the content of the client's current states.

- **Single Responsibility Principle:** It aids in structuring the code of certain states into distinct classes, making the code more accessible to other developers.

- It also enhances cohesion since state-specific activities are aggregated into ConcreteState classes, which are stored in a single location in the code.

Disadvantages

- **Making the System Complex:** If a system just has a few states, using the State Pattern is not a smart solution since you will wind up adding unnecessary code.

- **Changing States at Run-Time:** The State Pattern is used when we need to alter the state at run-time by inputting various subclasses. This is also a drawback since we have distinct separate State classes with some logic, but the number of classes rises.

- **Subclass Dependencies:** Each state-derived class is related to its sibling, which establishes dependencies between subclasses directly or indirectly.

Implementation of State Pattern in Java

- **Step 1:** Make a Connection interface that will connect to the Controller class.

```java
//This is an interface.

public interface Connection {

    public void open();
    public void close();
    public void log();
    public void update();
}// End of the Connection interface.
```

- **Step 2:** Make an Accounting class that complies with the Connection interface.

```java
//This is class.
public class Accounting implements Connection {
    @Override
    public void open() {
        System.out.println("open database for the
accounting");
    }
    @Override
    public void close() {
        System.out.println("close database");
    }

    @Override
    public void log() {
        System.out.println("log-activities");
    }

    @Override
    public void update() {
        System.out.println("Accounting has update");
    }
}// End of Accounting class.
```

- **Step 3:** Develop a Sales class that implements the Connection interface.

```java
//This is class.
public class Sales implements Connection {

    @Override
    public void open() {
        System.out.println("open database for the
sales");
    }
    @Override
    public void close() {
        System.out.println("close database");
    }

    @Override
    public void log() {
        System.out.println("log-activities");
    }

    @Override
    public void update() {
        System.out.println("Sales has update");
    }

}// End of Sales class.
```

- **Step 4:** Develop a Sales class that implements the Connection interface.

```java
//This is class.

public class Sales implements Connection {

    @Override
    public void open() {
        System.out.println("open database for the
sales");
    }
    @Override
    public void close() {
        System.out.println("close database");
    }
```

```
    @Override
    public void log() {
        System.out.println("log-activities");
    }
    @Override
    public void update() {
        System.out.println("Sales has update");
    }
}// End of Sales class.
```

- **Step 5:** Make a Management class that complies with the Connection interface.

```
//This is class.

public class Management implements Connection {

    @Override
    public void open() {
        System.out.println("open database for the
Management");
    }
    @Override
    public void close() {
        System.out.println("close database");
    }

    @Override
    public void log() {
        System.out.println("log-activities");
    }

    @Override
    public void update() {
        System.out.println("Management has update");
    }

}
// End of Management class.
```

- **Step 6:** Create a Controller class that will connect to various sorts of connections using the Connection interface.

```java
//This is class.

public class Controller {

    public static Accounting acct;
    public static Sales sales;
    public static Management management;

    private static Connection con;

    Controller() {
        acct = new Accounting();
        sales = new Sales();
        management = new Management();
    }

    public void setAccountingConnection() {
        con = acct;
    }
    public void setSalesConnection() {
        con  = sales;
    }
    public void setManagementConnection() {
        con  = management;
    }
    public void open() {
        con .open();
    }
    public void close() {
        con .close();
    }
    public void log() {
        con .log();
    }
    public void update() {
        con .update();
    }

}// End of Controller class.
```

- **Step 7:** Make a class called StatePatternDemo.

```
//This is class.


public class StatePatternDemo {

    Controller controller;
    StatePatternDemo(String con) {
        controller = new Controller();
        //following trigger should made by the user
        if(con.equalsIgnoreCase("management"))
            controller.setManagementConnection();
        if(con.equalsIgnoreCase("sales"))
            controller.setSalesConnection();
        if(con.equalsIgnoreCase("accounting"))
                controller.setAccountingConnection();
        controller.open();
        controller.log();
        controller.close();
        controller.update();
    }


    public static void main(String args[]) {

        new StatePatternDemo(args[0]);

    }

}// End of StatePatternDemo class.
```

State Pattern in C#

When an object's internal state changes, the State Design Pattern allows it to adapt its behavior. The item seems to change class.

C# Structural Code

This structured code exemplifies the State Pattern, which enables an Account to act differently based on its balance. State objects termed RedState, SilverState, and GoldState are responsible for the differences in behavior. These states indicate checking accounts, new accounts, and accounts in good standing.

```
using System;

namespace State.Structural
{
    /// <summary> State Design Pattern
    /// </summary>

    public class Program
    {
        public static void Main(string[] args)
        {
            // Setup context in state

            var context = new Context(new
ConcreteStateA());

            // Issue requests, which toggles the state

            context.Request();
            context.Request();
            context.Request();
            context.Request();

            // Wait for the user

            Console.ReadKey();
        }
    }

    /// <summary> The 'State' abstract class
    /// </summary>

    public abstract class State
    {
        public abstract void Handle(Context context);
    }

    /// <summary> A 'ConcreteState' class
    /// </summary>

    public class ConcreteStateA : State
    {
        public override void Handle(Context context)
        {
            context.State = new ConcreteStateB();
        }
    }
```

```csharp
/// <summary> A 'ConcreteState' class
/// </summary>

public class ConcreteStateB : State
{
    public override void Handle(Context context)
    {
        context.State = new ConcreteStateA();
    }
}

/// <summary> The 'Context' class
/// </summary>

public class Context
{
    State state;

    // Constructor

    public Context(State state)
    {
        this.State = state;
    }

    // Gets or sets state

    public State State
    {
        get { return state; }
        set
        {
            state = value;
            Console.WriteLine("State: " + state.
GetType().Name);
        }
    }

    public void Request()
    {
        state.Handle(this);
    }
}
}
```

Real-World C# Code

This real-world code exemplifies the State Pattern, which enables an Account to act differently based on its balance. State objects termed RedState, SilverState, and GoldState are responsible for the differences in behavior. These states indicate checking accounts, new accounts, and accounts in good standing.

```csharp
using System;

namespace State.RealWorld
{
    /// <summary> State Design Pattern
    /// </summary>

    public class Program
    {
        public static void Main(string[] args)
        {
            // Open new account

            Account account = new Account
("Rim Johnsp");

            // Apply the financial transactions

            account.Deposit(600.0);
            account.Deposit(400.0);
            account.Deposit(650.0);
            account.PayInterest();
            account.Withdraw(3000.00);
            account.Withdraw(1400.00);

            // Wait for the user

            Console.ReadKey();
        }
    }

    /// <summary> The 'State' abstract class
    /// </summary>

    public abstract class State
    {
        protected Account account;
        protected double balance;

        protected double interest;
        protected double lowerLimit;
        protected double upperLimit;

        // Properties
```

```
    public Account Account
    {
        get { return account; }
        set { account = value; }
    }

    public double Balance
    {
        get { return balance; }
        set { balance = value; }
    }

    public abstract void Deposit(double amount);
    public abstract void Withdraw(double amount);
    public abstract void PayInterest();
}

/// <summary> 'ConcreteState' class
/// <remarks> Red indicates that account is overdrawn
/// </remarks> </summary>

public class RedState : State
{
    private double serviceFee;

    // Constructor

    public RedState(State state)
    {
        this.balance = state.Balance;
        this.account = state.Account;
        Initialize();
    }

    private void Initialize()
    {
        // Should come from datasource

        interest = 0.0;
        lowerLimit = -120.0;
        upperLimit = 0.0;
        serviceFee = 14.00;
    }

    public override void Deposit(double amount)
    {
        balance += amount;
        StateChangeCheck();
    }
```

```
        public override void Withdraw(double amount)
        {
            amount = amount - serviceFee;
            Console.WriteLine("No funds is available for
withdrawal!");
        }

        public override void PayInterest()
        {
            // No-interest is paid
        }

        private void StateChangeCheck()
        {
            if (balance > upperLimit)
            {
                account.State = new SilverState(this);
            }
        }
    }

    /// <summary> A 'ConcreteState' class
    /// <remarks>
    /// Silver indicates a non-interest bearing state </
remarks>
    /// </summary>

    public class SilverState : State
    {
        // Overloaded-constructors

        public SilverState(State state) :
            this(state.Balance, state.Account)
        {
        }

        public SilverState(double balance, Account account)
        {
            this.balance = balance;
            this.account = account;
            Initialize();
        }

        private void Initialize()
        {
            // Should come from datasource
            interest = 0.0;
            lowerLimit = 0.0;
            upperLimit = 1000.0;
        }
```

```csharp
    public override void Deposit(double amount)
    {
        balance += amount;
        StateChangeCheck();
    }

    public override void Withdraw(double amount)
    {
        balance -= amount;
        StateChangeCheck();
    }

    public override void PayInterest()
    {
        balance += interest * balance;
        StateChangeCheck();
    }

    private void StateChangeCheck()
    {
        if (balance < lowerLimit)
        {
            account.State = new RedState(this);
        }
        else if (balance > upperLimit)
        {
            account.State = new GoldState(this);
        }
    }
}

/// <summary> A 'ConcreteState' class
/// <remarks> Gold indicates an interest bearing state
/// </remarks> </summary>

public class GoldState : State
{
    // Overloaded-constructors
    public GoldState(State state)
        : this(state.Balance, state.Account)
    {
    }

    public GoldState(double balance, Account account)
    {
        this.balance = balance;
        this.account = account;
        Initialize();
    }
```

```
    private void Initialize()
    {
        // Should come from database
        interest = 0.06;
        lowerLimit = 1400.0;
        upperLimit = 15000000.0;
    }

    public override void Deposit(double amount)
    {
        balance += amount;
        StateChangeCheck();
    }

    public override void Withdraw(double amount)
    {
        balance -= amount;
        StateChangeCheck();
    }

    public override void PayInterest()
    {
        balance += interest * balance;
        StateChangeCheck();
    }

    private void StateChangeCheck()
    {
        if (balance < 0.0)
        {
            account.State = new RedState(this);
        }
        else if (balance < lowerLimit)
        {
            account.State = new SilverState(this);
        }
    }
}

/// <summary> The 'Context' class
/// </summary>

public class Account
{
    private State state;
    private string owner;

    // Constructor
```

```csharp
        public Account(string owner)
        {
            // New accounts are 'Silver' by default
            this.owner = owner;
            this.state = new SilverState(0.0, this);
        }

        public double Balance
        {
            get { return state.Balance; }
        }

        public State State
        {
            get { return state; }
            set { state = value; }
        }

        public void Deposit(double amount)
        {
            state.Deposit(amount);
            Console.WriteLine("Deposited {0:C} -- ", amount);
            Console.WriteLine(" Balance = {0:C}", this.
Balance);
            Console.WriteLine(" Status  = {0}",
                this.State.GetType().Name);
            Console.WriteLine("");
        }

        public void Withdraw(double amount)
        {
            state.Withdraw(amount);
            Console.WriteLine("Withdrew {0:C} -- ", amount);
            Console.WriteLine(" Balance = {0:C}", this.
Balance);
            Console.WriteLine(" Status  = {0}\n",
                this.State.GetType().Name);
        }

        public void PayInterest()
        {
            state.PayInterest();
            Console.WriteLine("Interest Paid -- ");
            Console.WriteLine(" Balance = {0:C}", this.
Balance);
            Console.WriteLine(" Status  = {0}\n",
                this.State.GetType().Name);
        }
    }
}
```

VISITOR PATTERN

The Visitor Pattern is a Behavioral Design Pattern that enables us to decouple the algorithm from the object structure on which it works. It allows us to dynamically add new features to an existing class hierarchy without modifying it. All of the behavioral patterns have proven to be the most effective ways to manage object communication. It is also utilized when we need to conduct an operation on a set of related items.

A Visitor Pattern is made up of two parts:

- The visitor implements a method called Visit(), which is utilized and invoked for each member of the data structure.

- Accept() methods on visitable classes accept visitors.

Components of Design

- **Client:** The Client class is the consumer of the Visitor Design Pattern classes. It may get access to the data structure objects and direct them to accept a visitor for future processing.

- **Visitor:** An abstract class that is used to specify all visitable classes' visit operations.

- **Concrete Visitor:** Each Visitor will be in charge of several operations. All Visit Patterns described in the abstract visitor must be implemented for each kind of visitor.

- This class declares that it accepts operations. It also serves as the entrance point for visitors to visit an item.

- **Visitable Concrete:** These classes implement the visitable class and describe the accepted operation. The accept operation is used to send the visitor object to this object.

The Problem without Employing the Visitor Pattern

Assume we are in charge of PeeksforPeeks' software management. They have begun specific courses, such as DSA, SDE, and STL, that are unquestionably valuable for students preparing for product-based firms. However, how will we manage all of the Courses, Instructors, Students, Classes, and IDs in your database? If we take a straightforward approach to dealing with such a problem, we will almost certainly end up in shambles.

Solution Based on the Visitor Pattern

Let's have a look at the answer to the previously discussed problem. Instead of mixing it with the current classes, the Visitor technique advises introducing a new behavior in a distinct class named Visitor. We will send the original object as arguments to the visitor's function, allowing the method to access all relevant information.

```
""" The Courses hierarchy can't change to add new
    functionality dynamically. Abstract Crop class for the
 Concrete Courses_At_PFP classes: methods defined in
this class
 will inherit by all the Concrete Courses_At_PFP
classes."""

class Courses_At_PFP:

    def accept(self, visitor):
        visitor.visit(self)

    def teaching(self, visitor):
        print(self, "Taught by ", visitor)

    def studying(self, visitor):
        print(self, "studied by ", visitor)


    def __str__(self):
        return self.__class__.__name__


"""Concrete Courses_At_PFP class: Classes being visited."""
class SDE(Courses_At_PFP): pass

class STL(Courses_At_PFP): pass

class DSA(Courses_At_PFP): pass

""" Abstract Visitor class for the Concrete Visitor
classes:
 the method defined in this class will inherit by all
the Concrete Visitor classes."""
class Visitor:

    def __str__(self):
        return self.__class__.__name__
```

```
""" Concrete Visitors: Classes visiting the Concrete Course
objects.
 These classes have visit() method which is called by
 accept() method of Concrete Course_At_PFP classes."""
class Instructor(Visitor):
    def visit(self, crop):
        crop.teaching(self)


class Student(Visitor):
    def visit(self, crop):
        crop.studying(self)


"""creating objects for the concrete classes"""
sde = SDE()
stl = STL()
dsa = DSA()

"""Creating-Visitors"""
instructor = Instructor()
student = Student()

"""Visitors visiting the courses"""
sde.accept(instructor)
sde.accept(student)

stl.accept(instructor)
stl.accept(student)

dsa.accept(instructor)
dsa.accept(student)
```

Advantages

- **Open/Closed Principle:** It is simple to provide new functionality in a class that can deal with objects from various classes without modifying these classes.

- The principle of single responsibility states that several variants of the same activity may put into the same class.

- **Entity Addition:** Adding a new entity in the Visitor Pattern is simple since we simply need to alter the visitor class and the existing item will not be affected.

- **Updating Logic:** If the operation logic is altered, we just need to replace the visitor implementation rather than all of the item classes.

Disadvantages

- **Several Updates:** We must notify each and every visitor anytime a class is added or withdrawn from the main hierarchy.

- **Extensibility:** If there are too many visitor classes, it becomes quite difficult to expand the whole interface of the class.

- **Inadequate Access:** Visitors may not always have access to the private fields of certain classes with which they are meant to work.

Applicability

- **Recursive Structures:** Visitor Pattern works well with recursive structures such as directory trees and XML structures. The Visitor object may visit each node in the recursive structure.

- **Performing Operations:** We may use the Visitor Pattern to execute operations on all components of a complicated object, such as a Tree.

Implementation of Visitor Pattern in Java

We'll build a ComputerPart interface that defines accept operation. Concrete classes that implement the ComputerPart interface include the keyboard, mouse, monitor, and computer. We will design another interface, ComputerPartVisitor, which will specify the operations of the visitor class. The computer employs a certain visitor to do the appropriate activity.

- **Step 1:** Define an interface to represent element.
  Filename: ComputerPart.java

```
public interface ComputerPart {
    public void accept(ComputerPartVisitor
computerPartVisitor);
}
```

- **Step 2:** Create concrete classes extending the above class.
  Filename: Keyboard.java

```java
public class Keyboard implements ComputerPart {

    @Override
    public void accept(ComputerPartVisitor
computerPartVisitor) {
        computerPartVisitor.visit(this);
    }
}
```

Filename: Monitor.java

```java
public class Monitor implements ComputerPart {

    @Override
    public void accept(ComputerPartVisitor
computerPartVisitor) {
        computerPartVisitor.visit(this);
    }
}
```

Filename: Mouse.java

```java
public class Mouse implements ComputerPart {

    @Override
    public void accept(ComputerPartVisitor
computerPartVisitor) {
        computerPartVisitor.visit(this);
    }
}
```

Filename: Computer.java

```java
public class Computer implements ComputerPart {

    ComputerPart[] parts;
```

```
public Computer(){
    parts = new ComputerPart[] {new Mouse(), new
Keyboard(), new Monitor()};
}

@Override
public void accept(ComputerPartVisitor
computerPartVisitor) {
    for (int x = 0; x < parts.length; x++) {
        parts[x].accept(computerPartVisitor);
    }
    computerPartVisitor.visit(this);
}
}
```

- **Step 3:** Define an interface to represent visitor.
  Filename: ComputerPartVisitor.java

```
public interface ComputerPartVisitor {
    public void visit(Computer computer);
    public void visit(Mouse mouse);
    public void visit(Keyboard keyboard);
    public void visit(Monitor monitor);
}
```

- **Step 4:** Create concrete visitor implementing the above class.
  Filename: ComputerPartDisplayVisitor.java

```
public class ComputerPartDisplayVisitor implements
ComputerPartVisitor {

    @Override
    public void visit(Computer computer) {
        System.out.println("Displaying Computer.");
    }

    @Override
    public void visit(Mouse mouse) {
        System.out.println("Displaying Mouse.");
    }
```

```
    @Override
    public void visit(Keyboard keyboard) {
        System.out.println("Displaying Keyboard.");
    }

    @Override
    public void visit(Monitor monitor) {
        System.out.println("Displaying Monitor.");
    }
}
```

- **Step 5:** Use the ComputerPartDisplayVisitor to display parts of Computer.

    Filename: VisitorPatternDemo.java

```
public class VisitorPatternDemo {
    public static void main(String[] args) {

        ComputerPart computer = new Computer();
        computer.accept(new
ComputerPartDisplayVisitor());
    }
}
```

Visitor Pattern in C#

The Visitor Design Pattern depicts an operation on the elements of an object structure. This pattern allows us to specify a new operation while keeping the classes of the components on which it works the same.

C# Structural Code

This structural code exemplifies the Visitor Pattern, in which an object traverses an object structure and executes the same operation on each node. Different visitor objects define distinct operations.

```
using System;
using System.Collections.Generic;

namespace Visitor.Structural
{
```

```
/// <summary> Visitor Design Pattern
/// </summary>

public class Program
{
    public static void Main(string[] args)
    {
        // Setup structure

        ObjectStructure or = new ObjectStructure();
        or.Attach(new ConcreteElementA());
        or.Attach(new ConcreteElementB());

        // Create the visitor objects

        ConcreteVisitor1 v1 = new ConcreteVisitor1();
        ConcreteVisitor2 v2 = new ConcreteVisitor2();

        // Structure accepting visitors

        or.Accept(v1);
        or.Accept(v2);

        // Wait for the user

        Console.ReadKey();
    }
}

/// <summary> The 'Visitor' abstract class
/// </summary>

public abstract class Visitor
{
    public abstract void VisitConcreteElementA(
        ConcreteElementA concreteElementA);
    public abstract void VisitConcreteElementB(
        ConcreteElementB concreteElementB);
}

/// <summary> A 'ConcreteVisitor' class
/// </summary>

public class ConcreteVisitor1 : Visitor
{
    public override void VisitConcreteElementA(
        ConcreteElementA concreteElementA)
    {
```

```
            Console.WriteLine("{0} visited by {1}",
                concreteElementA.GetType().Name, this.
GetType().Name);
        }

        public override void VisitConcreteElementB(
            ConcreteElementB concreteElementB)
        {
            Console.WriteLine("{0} visited by {1}",
                concreteElementB.GetType().Name, this.
GetType().Name);
        }
    }

    /// <summary> A 'ConcreteVisitor' class
    /// </summary>

    public class ConcreteVisitor2 : Visitor
    {
        public override void VisitConcreteElementA(
            ConcreteElementA concreteElementA)
        {
            Console.WriteLine("{0} visited by {1}",
                concreteElementA.GetType().Name, this.
GetType().Name);
        }

        public override void VisitConcreteElementB(
            ConcreteElementB concreteElementB)
        {
            Console.WriteLine("{0} visited by {1}",
                concreteElementB.GetType().Name, this.
GetType().Name);
        }
    }

    /// <summary> The 'Element' abstract class
    /// </summary>

    public abstract class Element
    {
        public abstract void Accept(Visitor visitor);
    }

    /// <summary> A 'ConcreteElement' class
    /// </summary>

    public class ConcreteElementA : Element
```

```csharp
{
    public override void Accept(Visitor visitor)
    {
        visitor.VisitConcreteElementA(this);
    }

    public void OperationA()
    {
    }
}

/// <summary> A 'ConcreteElement' class
/// </summary>

public class ConcreteElementB : Element
{
    public override void Accept(Visitor visitor)
    {
        visitor.VisitConcreteElementB(this);
    }

    public void OperationB()
    {
    }
}

/// <summary> The 'ObjectStructure' class
/// </summary>

public class ObjectStructure
{
    List<Element> elements = new List<Element>();

    public void Attach(Element element)
    {
        elements.Add(element);
    }

    public void Detach(Element element)
    {
        elements.Remove(element);
    }

    public void Accept(Visitor visitor)
    {
        foreach (Element element in elements)
        {
            element.Accept(visitor);
        }
    }
}
}
```

Real-World C# Code

The Visitor Pattern is demonstrated in this real-world code, in which two objects scan a list of Employees and execute an identical operation on each Employee. The two visitor objects specify two distinct operations: one that changes vacation days and the other that calculates revenue.

```csharp
using System;
using System.Collections.Generic;

namespace Visitor.RealWorld
{
    /// <summary> Visitor Design Pattern
    /// </summary>

    public class Program
    {
        public static void Main(string[] args)
        {
            // Setup employee-collection

            Employees employee = new Employees();
            employee.Attach(new Clerk());
            employee.Attach(new Director());
            employee.Attach(new President());

            // Employees 'visited'

            employee.Accept(new IncomeVisitor());
            employee.Accept(new VacationVisitor());

            // Wait for the user

            Console.ReadKey();
        }
    }

    /// <summary> The 'Visitor' interface
    /// </summary>

    public interface IVisitor
    {
        void Visit(Element element);
    }

    /// <summary> A 'ConcreteVisitor' class
    /// </summary>
```

```csharp
public class IncomeVisitor : IVisitor
{
    public void Visit(Element element)
    {
        Employee employee = element as Employee;

        // Provide the 10% pay raise

        employee.Income *= 1.10;

        Console.WriteLine("{0} {1}'s new
income: {2:C}",
                employee.GetType().Name, employee.Name,
                employee.Income);
    }
}

/// <summary> A 'ConcreteVisitor' class
/// </summary>

public class VacationVisitor : IVisitor
{
    public void Visit(Element element)
    {
        Employee employee = element as Employee;

        // Provide 3 extra vacation days

        employee.VacationDays += 3;

        Console.WriteLine("{0} {1}'s new vacation days:
{2}",
                employee.GetType().Name, employee.Name,
                employee.VacationDays);
    }
}

/// <summary> The 'Element' abstract class
/// </summary>

public abstract class Element
{
    public abstract void Accept(IVisitor visitor);
}

/// <summary> The 'ConcreteElement' class
/// </summary>
```

```csharp
public class Employee : Element
{
    private string name;
    private double income;
    private int vacationDays;

    // Constructor

    public Employee(string name, double income,
        int vacationDays)
    {
        this.name = name;
        this.income = income;
        this.vacationDays = vacationDays;
    }

    public string Name
    {
        get { return name; }
        set { name = value; }
    }

    public double Income
    {
        get { return income; }
        set { income = value; }
    }

    public int VacationDays
    {
        get { return vacationDays; }
        set { vacationDays = value; }
    }

    public override void Accept(IVisitor visitor)
    {
        visitor.Visit(this);
    }
}

/// <summary> The 'ObjectStructure' class
/// </summary>

public class Employees
{
    private List<Employee> employees = new
List<Employee>();
```

```csharp
    public void Attach(Employee employee)
    {
        employees.Add(employee);
    }

    public void Detach(Employee employee)
    {
        employees.Remove(employee);
    }

    public void Accept(IVisitor visitor)
    {
        foreach (Employee employee in employees)
        {
            employee.Accept(visitor);
        }
        Console.WriteLine();
    }
}

// Three-employee types

public class Clerk : Employee
{
    // Constructor

    public Clerk()
        : base("Kevin", 26000.0, 14)
    {
    }
}

public class Director : Employee
{
    // Constructor
    public Director()
        : base("Elly", 39000.0, 16)
    {
    }
}

public class President : Employee
{
    // Constructor
    public President()
        : base("Eric", 49000.0, 21)
    {
    }
}
}
```

Bibliography

Alle, M. (2021, May 3). *Singleton Design Pattern In C#*. Singleton Design Pattern In C#; www.c-sharpcorner.com. https://www.c-sharpcorner.com/UploadFile/8911c4/singleton-design-pattern-in-C-Sharp/

Baeldung. (2019, September 11). *Composite Design Pattern in Java*. Composite Design Pattern in Java. https://www.baeldung.com/java-composite-pattern#:~:text=The%20composite%20pattern%20is%20meant,a%20whole%20hierarchy%20of%20objects

Baeldung. (2019, November 10). *Proxy, Decorator, Adapter and Bridge Patterns*. Proxy, Decorator, Adapter and Bridge Patterns. https://www.baeldung.com/java-structural-design-patterns#:~:text=Adapter%20pattern%20is%20used%20after,before%20the%20components%20are%20designed

Baeldung. (2022, June 7). *The Adapter Pattern in Java*. The Adapter Pattern in Java. https://www.baeldung.com/java-adapter-pattern

Balasubramaniam, Vivek. (2022, June 24). *Prototype Pattern in Java*. Prototype Pattern in Java. https://www.baeldung.com/java-pattern-prototype

Bradley, S. (2021, October 20). *Visitor Pattern*. Medium; medium.com. https://medium.com/design-patterns-in-python/visitor-pattern-b9227759d6be

Bradley, S. (2022, April 18). *Observer Pattern*. Medium; medium.com. https://medium.com/design-patterns-in-python/observer-pattern-c58820ad3c9f

Bradley, S. (n.d.). *Composite – Design Patterns in Python*. Composite – Design Patterns in Python; sbcode.net. Retrieved July 9, 2022, from https://sbcode.net/python/composite/

Bradley, S. (n.d.). *State – Design Patterns in Python*. State – Design Patterns in Python; sbcode.net. Retrieved July 9, 2022, from https://sbcode.net/python/state/

C# Adapter Design Pattern – Dofactory. (n.d.). C# Adapter Design Pattern – Dofactory; www.dofactory.com. Retrieved July 9, 2022, from https://www.dofactory.com/net/adapter-design-pattern

C# Prototype Design Pattern – Dofactory. (n.d.). C# Prototype Design Pattern – Dofactory; www.dofactory.com. Retrieved July 9, 2022, from https://www.dofactory.com/net/prototype-design-pattern

C# State Design Pattern – Dofactory. (n.d.). C# State Design Pattern – Dofactory; www.dofactory.com. Retrieved July 9, 2022, from https://www.dofactory.com/net/state-design-pattern

Chauhan, S. (2001, July 8). *Bridge Design Pattern – C#*. Bridge Design Pattern – C#; www.dotnettricks.com. https://www.dotnettricks.com/learn/designpatterns/bridge-design-pattern-dotnet

Chauhan. S. (2001, July 8). *Factory Method Design Pattern – C#*. Factory Method Design Pattern – C#; www.dotnettricks.com. https://www.dotnettricks.com/learn/designpatterns/factory-method-design-pattern-dotnet

Creational Design Patterns – Javatpoint. (n.d.). Www.Javatpoint.Com; www.javatpoint.com. Retrieved July 9, 2022, from https://www.javatpoint.com/creational-design-patterns

Design Pattern – Overview. (n.d.). Design Pattern – Overview; www.tutorialspoint.com. Retrieved July 9, 2022, from https://www.tutorialspoint.com/design_pattern/design_pattern_overview.htm

Design Pattern – Singleton Pattern. (n.d.). Design Pattern – Singleton Pattern; www.tutorialspoint.com. Retrieved July 9, 2022, from https://www.tutorialspoint.com/design_pattern/singleton_pattern.htm

Design Patterns – Bridge Pattern. (n.d.). Design Patterns – Bridge Pattern; www.tutorialspoint.com. Retrieved July 9, 2022, from https://www.tutorialspoint.com/design_pattern/bridge_pattern.htm

Design Patterns – Facade Pattern. (n.d.). Design Patterns – Facade Pattern; www.tutorialspoint.com. Retrieved July 9, 2022, from https://www.tutorialspoint.com/design_pattern/facade_pattern.htm

Design Patterns – Iterator Pattern. (n.d.). Design Patterns – Iterator Pattern; www.tutorialspoint.com. Retrieved July 9, 2022, from https://www.tutorialspoint.com/design_pattern/iterator_pattern.htm#:~:text=Iterator%20pattern%20is%20very%20commonly,falls%20under%20behavioral%20pattern%20category

Design Patterns – Visitor Pattern. (n.d.). Design Patterns – Visitor Pattern; www.tutorialspoint.com. Retrieved July 9, 2022, from https://www.tutorialspoint.com/design_pattern/visitor_pattern.htm

Design Patterns and Refactoring. (n.d.). Adapter Design Pattern; sourcemaking.com. Retrieved July 9, 2022, from https://sourcemaking.com/design_patterns/adapter

Design Patterns and Refactoring. (n.d.). Behavioral Patterns; sourcemaking.com. Retrieved July 9, 2022, from https://sourcemaking.com/design_patterns/behavioral_patterns

Design Patterns and Refactoring. (n.d.). Composite Design Pattern in Python; sourcemaking.com. Retrieved July 9, 2022, from https://sourcemaking.com/design_patterns/composite/python/1

Design Patterns and Refactoring. (n.d.). Creational Patterns; sourcemaking.com. Retrieved July 9, 2022, from https://sourcemaking.com/design_patterns/creational_patterns

Design Patterns and Refactoring. (n.d.). Design Patterns; sourcemaking.com. Retrieved July 9, 2022, from https://sourcemaking.com/design_patterns

Design Patterns and Refactoring. (n.d.). Facade Design Pattern; sourcemaking.com. Retrieved July 9, 2022, from https://sourcemaking.com/design_patterns/facade

Design Patterns and Refactoring. (n.d.). Iterator Design Pattern in Python; sourcemaking.com. Retrieved July 9, 2022, from https://sourcemaking. com/design_patterns/iterator/python/1

Design Patterns and Refactoring. (n.d.). Singleton Design Pattern; sourcemaking.com. Retrieved July 9, 2022, from https://sourcemaking.com/ design_patterns/singleton

Design Patterns and Refactoring. (n.d.). Template Method Design Pattern in Python; sourcemaking.com. Retrieved July 9, 2022, from https://sourcemaking.com/design_patterns/template_method/python/1

Design Patterns in Java – Javatpoint. (n.d.). www.javatpoint.Com; www.javatpoint.com. Retrieved July 9, 2022, from https://www.javatpoint.com/design-patterns-in-java#:~:text=But%20remember%20one%2Dthing%2C%20design,more%20flexible%2C%20reusable%20and%20maintainable

Design Patterns Tutorial => Bridge pattern implementation in java. (n.d.). Design Patterns Tutorial => Bridge Pattern Implementation in Java; riptutorial. com. Retrieved July 9, 2022, from https://riptutorial.com/design-patterns/example/14007/bridge-pattern-implementation-in-java

Design Patterns Tutorial => Chain of Responsibility example (Php). (n.d.). Design Patterns Tutorial => Chain of Responsibility Example (Php); riptutorial. com. Retrieved July 9, 2022, from https://riptutorial.com/design-patterns/example/21215/chain-of-responsibility-example--php-

Design Patterns Tutorial => Command pattern example in Java. (n.d.). Design Patterns Tutorial => Command Pattern Example in Java; riptutorial. com. Retrieved July 9, 2022, from https://riptutorial.com/design-patterns/example/8933/command-pattern-example-in-java

Design Patterns Tutorial => Decorator pattern. (n.d.). Design Patterns Tutorial => Decorator Pattern; riptutorial.com. Retrieved July 9, 2022, from https:// riptutorial.com/design-patterns/topic/1720/decorator-pattern

Design Patterns Tutorial => Flyweight Factory (C#). (n.d.). Design Patterns Tutorial => Flyweight Factory (C#); riptutorial.com. Retrieved July 9, 2022, from https://riptutorial.com/design-patterns/example/14128/flyweight-factory--csharp-

Design Patterns Tutorial => Flyweight Factory (C#). (n.d.). Design Patterns Tutorial => Flyweight Factory (C#); riptutorial.com. Retrieved July 9, 2022, from https://riptutorial.com/design-patterns/example/14128/flyweight-factory--csharp-

Design Patterns Tutorial => Flyweight Factory (C#). (n.d.). Design Patterns Tutorial => Flyweight Factory (C#); riptutorial.com. Retrieved July 9, 2022, from https:// riptutorial.com/design-patterns/example/14128/flyweight-factory--csharp-

Design Patterns Tutorial => Getting started with Design Patterns. (n.d.). Design Patterns Tutorial => Getting Started with Design Patterns; riptutorial.com. Retrieved July 9, 2022, from https://riptutorial.com/design-patterns

Design Patterns Tutorial => Lazy Singleton practical example in java. (n.d.). Design Patterns Tutorial => Lazy Singleton Practical Example in Java; riptutorial. com. Retrieved July 9, 2022, from https://riptutorial.com/design-patterns/example/20847/lazy-singleton-practical-example-in-java

Design Patterns Tutorial => Mediator pattern example in java. (n.d.). Design Patterns Tutorial => Mediator Pattern Example in Java; riptutorial.com. Retrieved July 9, 2022, from https://riptutorial.com/design-patterns/example/21456/mediator-pattern-example-in-java

Design Patterns Tutorial => Observer/Java. (n.d.). Design Patterns Tutorial => Observer/Java; riptutorial.com. Retrieved July 9, 2022, from https://riptutorial.com/design-patterns/example/10889/observer---java

Design Patterns Tutorial => Repository Pattern. (n.d.). Design Patterns Tutorial => Repository Pattern; riptutorial.com. Retrieved July 9, 2022, from https://riptutorial.com/design-patterns/topic/6254/repository-pattern

Design Patterns Tutorial => The Iterator Pattern. (n.d.). Design Patterns Tutorial => The Iterator Pattern; riptutorial.com. Retrieved July 9, 2022, from https://riptutorial.com/design-patterns/example/6420/the-iterator-pattern

Design Patterns. (n.d.). Design Patterns; refactoring.guru. Retrieved July 9, 2022, from https://refactoring.guru/design-patterns

Design Patterns: Adapter in C#. (n.d.). Design Patterns: Adapter in C#; refactoring.guru. Retrieved July 9, 2022, from https://refactoring.guru/design-patterns/adapter/csharp/example#:~:text=Adapter%20is%20a%20structural%20design,recognizable%20by%20the%20second%20object

Design Patterns: Bridge in Java. (n.d.). Design Patterns: Bridge in Java; refactoring.guru. Retrieved July 9, 2022, from https://refactoring.guru/design-patterns/bridge/java/example#:~:text=Bridge%20is%20a%20structural%20design,the%20second%20hierarchy%20(Implementation)

Design Patterns: Factory Method in C#. (n.d.). Design Patterns: Factory Method in C#; refactoring.guru. Retrieved July 9, 2022, from https://refactoring.guru/design-patterns/factory-method/csharp/example#:~:text=Factory%20method%20is%20a%20creational,constructor%20call%20(%20new%20operator)

Design Patterns: Flyweight in Python. (n.d.). Design Patterns: Flyweight in Python; refactoring.guru. Retrieved July 9, 2022, from https://refactoring.guru/design-patterns/flyweight/python/example#:~:text=Flyweight%20is%20a%20structural%20design,object%20state%20between%20multiple%20objects

Design Patterns: Memento in Java. (n.d.). Design Patterns: Memento in Java; refactoring.guru. Retrieved July 9, 2022, from https://refactoring.guru/design-patterns/memento/java/example#:~:text=Memento%20is%20a%20behavioral%20design,data%20kept%20inside%20the%20snapshots

Design Patterns: Observer in Python. (n.d.). Design Patterns: Observer in Python; refactoring.guru. Retrieved July 9, 2022, from https://refactoring.guru/design-patterns/observer/python/example#:~:text=Observer%20is%20a%20behavioral%20design,that%20implements%20a%20subscriber%20interface

Design Patterns: Prototype in Java. (n.d.). Design Patterns: Prototype in Java; refactoring.guru. Retrieved July 9, 2022, from https://refactoring.guru/design-patterns/prototype/java/example#:~:text=Prototype%20is%20a%20creational%20design,their%20concrete%20classes%20are%20unknown

Design Patterns: State in Python. (n.d.). Design Patterns: State in Python; refactoring.guru. Retrieved July 9, 2022, from https://refactoring.guru/design-patterns/state/python/example#:~:text=State%20is%20a%20behavioral%20 design,of%20acting%20on%20its%20own

Design Patterns: Visitor in C#. (n.d.). Design Patterns: Visitor in C#; refactoring. guru. Retrieved July 9, 2022, from https://refactoring.guru/design-patterns/ visitor/csharp/example#:~:text=Visitor%20is%20a%20behavioral%20 design,article%20Visitor%20and%20Double%20Dispatch

designpatterns. (n.d.). Designpatterns; cs.lmu.edu. Retrieved July 9, 2022, from https://cs.lmu.edu/~ray/notes/designpatterns/

devs5003. (2021, June 13). *Creational Design Patterns In Java | Making Java Easy To Learn.* Making Java Easy to Learn; javatechonline.com. https:// javatechonline.com/creational-design-patterns-in-java/

Elisabeth Robson, E. F. (2016, October 12). *5 reasons to finally learn design patterns – O'Reilly.* 5 Reasons to Finally Learn Design Patterns; www.oreilly.com. https:// www.oreilly.com/content/5-reasons-to-finally-learn-design-patterns/

Factory Design Pattern in Java – JournalDev. (2013, May 22). JournalDev; www. journaldev.com. https://www.journaldev.com/1392/factory-design-pattern-in-java

Flyweight Method – Python Design Patterns – GeeksforGeeks. (2020, February 9). GeeksforGeeks; www.geeksforgeeks.org. https://www.geeksforgeeks.org/ flyweight-method-python-design-patterns/

Goals of Design Patterns (OO, Patterns, UML and Refactoring forum at Coderanch). (n.d.). Goals of Design Patterns (OO, Patterns, UML and Refactoring Forum at Coderanch); coderanch.com. Retrieved July 9, 2022, from https:// coderanch.com/t/99290/engineering/Goals-Design-Patterns

Gupta, L. (2014, May 9). *Builder Design Pattern – HowToDoInJava.* HowToDoInJava; howtodoinjava.com. https://howtodoinjava.com/design-patterns/creational/builder-pattern-in-java/

Gupta, L. (2015, October 19). *Composite Design Pattern – HowToDoInJava.* HowToDoInJava; howtodoinjava.com. https://howtodoinjava.com/design-patterns/structural/composite-design-pattern/

Gupta, L. (2018, December 13). *Flyweight Design Pattern – Flyweight Pattern in Java- HowToDoInJava.* HowToDoInJava; howtodoinjava.com. https:// howtodoinjava.com/design-patterns/structural/flyweight-design-pattern/

Gupta, L. (2018, December 13). *Flyweight Design Pattern – Flyweight Pattern in Java- HowToDoInJava.* HowToDoInJava; howtodoinjava.com. https:// howtodoinjava.com/design-patterns/structural/flyweight-design-pattern/

Gupta, L. (2018, December 17). *Iterator Design Pattern – Iterator Pattern in Java – HowToDoInJava.* HowToDoInJava; howtodoinjava.com. https://howtodoin-java.com/design-patterns/behavioral/iterator-design-pattern/

Gupta, L. (2019, January 23). *State Design Pattern – State Pattern in Java – HowToDoInJava.* HowToDoInJava; howtodoinjava.com. https://howtodoin-java.com/design-patterns/behavioral/state-design-pattern/

Gupta, L. (2019, March 6). *Design Patterns in Java.* HowToDoInJava; howtodoinjava .com. https://howtodoinjava.com/gang-of-four-java-design-patterns/

Hurtado, J. (2021, June 2). *Template Method Design Pattern in Python*. Stack Abuse; stackabuse.com. https://stackabuse.com/template-method-design-pattern-in-python/

Implementing the Singleton Pattern in C#. (n.d.). Implementing the Singleton Pattern in C#; csharpindepth.com. Retrieved July 9, 2022, from https://csharpindepth.com/articles/singleton

Iterator Design Pattern in Java – JournalDev. (2013, July 26). JournalDev; www.journaldev.com. https://www.journaldev.com/1716/iterator-design-pattern-java

Jarmuż, B. (2022, February 8). *Visitor Design Pattern in C# – Code Maze*. Code Maze; code-maze.com. https://code-maze.com/csharp-visitor-design-pattern/

Java Singleton Design Pattern Example Best Practices – JournalDev. (2013, March 3). JournalDev; www.journaldev.com. https://www.journaldev.com/1377/java-singleton-design-pattern-best-practices-examples

javinpaul. (2022, January 27). *11 Essential Skills to become Software Developer in 2022 | by javinpaul | Javarevisited | Medium*. Medium; medium.com. https://medium.com/javarevisited/11-essential-skills-to-become-software-developer-in-2020-c617e293e90e

Jones, M. (2016, June 13). *Observer Pattern in C#*. Exception Not Found; exceptionnotfound.net. https://exceptionnotfound.net/observer-pattern-in-csharp/

Jones, M. (2016, June 9). *Template Method Pattern in C#*. Exception Not Found; exceptionnotfound.net. https://exceptionnotfound.net/template-method-pattern-in-csharp/

Kanjilal, J. (2017, June 5). *How to implement the template method Design Pattern in C# | InfoWorld*. InfoWorld; www.infoworld.com. https://www.infoworld.com/article/3199484/how-to-implement-the-template-method-design-pattern-in-c.html

Kiran, R. (2019, July 11). *Important Java Design Patterns You Need to Know About | Edureka*. Edureka; www.edureka.co. https://www.edureka.co/blog/java-design-patterns/

Kumar, S. (2016, May 3). *Adapter Pattern – GeeksforGeeks*. GeeksforGeeks; www.geeksforgeeks.org. https://www.geeksforgeeks.org/adapter-pattern/

M, N. (2020, December 26). *Composite Design Pattern Using Python*. Composite Design Pattern Using Python; www.c-sharpcorner.com. https://www.c-sharpcorner.com/article/composite-design-pattern-using-python/

Maheshwari, B. (2021, February 20). *Adapter Pattern—What It Is and How to Use It?* Medium; medium.com. https://medium.com/swlh/adapter-pattern-what-it-is-and-how-to-use-it-83e35a02e7f9#:~:text=The%20adapter%20pattern%20convert%20the,another%20interface%20the%20clients%20expect

Mallik, U. (2020, April 24). *The Bridge Design Pattern with Python*. Stack Abuse; stackabuse.com. https://stackabuse.com/the-bridge-design-pattern-in-python/

Memento Method – Python Design Patterns – GeeksforGeeks. (2020, February 18). GeeksforGeeks; www.geeksforgeeks.org. https://www.geeksforgeeks.org/memento-method-python-design-patterns/

Omprakash. (n.d.). *Bridge Design Pattern with Python.* Bridge Design Pattern with Python; pythonwife.com. Retrieved July 9, 2022, from https://pythonwife.com/bridge-design-pattern-with-python/

Omprakash. (n.d.). *Iterator Design Pattern with Python.* Iterator Design Pattern with Python; pythonwife.com. Retrieved July 9, 2022, from https://pythonwife.com/iterator-design-pattern-with-python/

oodesign. (n.d.). *Singleton Pattern | Object Oriented Design.* Singleton Pattern | Object Oriented Design; www.oodesign.com. Retrieved July 9, 2022, from https://www.oodesign.com/singleton-pattern

Pankaj. (2013, March 3). *Java Singleton Design Pattern Example Best Practices – JournalDev.* JournalDev; www.journaldev.com. https://www.journaldev.com/1377/java-singleton-design-pattern-best-practices-examples

Pankaj. (2013, May 22). *Factory Design Pattern in Java – JournalDev.* JournalDev; www.journaldev.com. https://www.journaldev.com/1392/factory-design-pattern-in-java

Pankaj. (2013, June 20). *Builder Design Pattern in Java – JournalDev.* JournalDev; www.journaldev.com. https://www.journaldev.com/1425/builder-design-pattern-in-java

Paul, J. (2019, March 31). *Observer Design Pattern in C#.* Observer Design Pattern in C#; www.c-sharpcorner.com. https://www.c-sharpcorner.com/uploadfile/40e97e/observer-design-pattern-in-C-Sharp/

Prototype Method – Python Design Patterns – GeeksforGeeks. (2020, January 30). GeeksforGeeks; www.geeksforgeeks.org. https://www.geeksforgeeks.org/prototype-method-python-design-patterns/#:~:text=Prototype%20Method%20is%20a%20Creational,concrete%20implementation%20of%20their%20classes

Python Design Patterns – State. (n.d.). Python Design Patterns – State; www.tutorialspoint.com. Retrieved July 9, 2022, from https://www.tutorialspoint.com/python_design_patterns/python_design_patterns_state.htm

Rahman, S. (2019, July 24). *The 3 Types of Design Patterns All Developers Should Know (with code examples of each).* freeCodeCamp.Org; www.freecodecamp.org. https://www.freecodecamp.org/news/the-basic-design-patterns-all-developers-need-to-know/

Saxena, B. (2020, October 12). *Iterator Design Pattern In Java – DZone Java.* Dzone.Com; dzone.com. https://dzone.com/articles/iterator-design-pattern-in-java

Singh, J. (2013, December 25). *Memento Design Pattern Using C#.* www.c-sharpcorner.com. https://www.c-sharpcorner.com/UploadFile/b1df45/memento-design-pattern-using-C-Sharp/

Singla, L. (2022, January 5). *What's a Software Design Pattern? (+7 Most Popular Patterns).* Insights – Web and Mobile Development Services and Solutions; www.netsolutions.com. https://www.netsolutions.com/insights/software-design-pattern/

Singleton Class in C#. (n.d.). Singleton Class in C#; www.tutorialspoint.com. Retrieved July 9, 2022, from https://www.tutorialspoint.com/Singleton-Class-in-Chash

Singleton Pattern – Software Design Patterns: Best Practices for Software Developers. (n.d.). Educative: Interactive Courses for Software Developers; www.educative.io. Retrieved July 9, 2022, from https://www.educative.io/courses/software-design-patterns-best-practices/B8nMkqBWONo

Singleton. (n.d.). Singleton; refactoring.guru. Retrieved July 9, 2022, from https://refactoring.guru/design-patterns/singleton

Singleton. (n.d.). Singleton; refactoring.guru. Retrieved July 9, 2022, from https://refactoring.guru/design-patterns/singleton

Software Design Patterns – GeeksforGeeks. (2018, August 31). GeeksforGeeks; www.geeksforgeeks.org. https://www.geeksforgeeks.org/software-design-patterns/

Software Design Patterns: A Guide. (2017, March 7). Airbrake; airbrake.io. https://airbrake.io/blog/design-patterns/software-design-patterns-guide#:~:text=Working%20with%20design%20patterns%20during,that%20might%20arise%20during%20development

Son, B. (2019, July 15). *Understanding Software Design Patterns | Opensource. com.* Understanding Software Design Patterns | Opensource.Com; opensource.com. https://opensource.com/article/19/7/understanding-software-design-patterns

Spasojevic, M. (2019, February 18). *C# Design Patterns – Factory Method – Code Maze.* Code Maze; code-maze.com. https://code-maze.com/factory-method/

State Design Pattern in Java – JournalDev. (2013, July 29). JournalDev; www.journaldev.com. https://www.journaldev.com/1751/state-design-pattern-java

Szczukocki, Denis. (2019, September 11). State Design Pattern in Java. State Design Pattern in Java. https://www.baeldung.com/java-state-design-pattern

Tarek, A. (2022, February 7). *Prototype Design Pattern In .NET C#.* Medium; levelup.gitconnected.com. https://levelup.gitconnected.com/prototype-design-pattern-in-net-c-67db46c3d28f?gi=5f58569b2632

Tauqir. (2020, December 16). *Composite Design Pattern in C#.* ExecuteCommands; executecommands.com. https://executecommands.com/composite-design-pattern-csharp-simple-example/

Tauqir. (2020, December 27). *Bridge Design Pattern in C#.* ExecuteCommands; executecommands.com. https://executecommands.com/bridge-design-pattern-in-csharp-simple-example/

Team, I. E. (2022, June 28). *12 Software Developer Skills To Learn (With Examples) | Indeed.com.* Indeed Career Guide; www.indeed.com. https://www.indeed.com/career-advice/career-development/software-developer-skills

Team, T. E. (2019, September 16). *The 7 Most Important Software Design Patterns | by The Educative Team | Dev Learning Daily.* Medium; learningdaily.dev. https://learningdaily.dev/the-7-most-important-software-design-patterns-d60e546afb0e

The Bridge Pattern in Java. (2022, June 24). The Bridge Pattern in Java. https://www.baeldung.com/java-bridge-pattern

The Iterator Pattern. (n.d.). The Iterator Pattern; python-patterns.guide. Retrieved July 9, 2022, from https://python-patterns.guide/gang-of-four/iterator/

Tittle is missing. (n.d.).; subscription.packtpub.com. Retrieved July 9, 2022, from https://subscription.packtpub.com/book/application-development/9781782173656/1/ch01lvl1sec14/advantages-of-design-patterns

Tutorials, D. N. (2020, August 9). *State Design Pattern in C# with Examples – Dot Net Tutorials.* Dot Net Tutorials; dotnettutorials.net. https://dotnettutorials.net/lesson/state-design-pattern/

Tutorials, D. N. (2020, September 1). *Bridge Design Pattern Real-Time Example in C# – Dot Net Tutorials.* Dot Net Tutorials; dotnettutorials.net. https://dotnettutorials.net/lesson/bridge-design-pattern-real-time-example/

Tutorials, D. N. (2020, September 1). *Memento Design Pattern in C# with Examples – Dot Net Tutorials.* Dot Net Tutorials; dotnettutorials.net. https://dotnettutorials.net/lesson/memento-design-pattern/

Tutorials, D. N. (2021, April 1). *Iterator Design Pattern in C# with Realtime Example – Dot Net Tutorials.* Dot Net Tutorials; dotnettutorials.net. https://dotnettutorials.net/lesson/iterator-design-pattern/

Tutorials, D. N. (2021, April 30). *Observer Design Pattern in C# with Examples – Dot Net Tutorials.* Dot Net Tutorials; dotnettutorials.net. https://dotnettutorials.net/lesson/observer-design-pattern/

Tutorials, D. N. (2021, August 20). *Composite Design Pattern in C# with Examples – Dot Net Tutorials.* Dot Net Tutorials; dotnettutorials.net. https://dotnettutorials.net/lesson/composite-design-pattern/

Visitor – Python 3 Patterns, Recipes and Idioms. (n.d.). Visitor – Python 3 Patterns, Recipes and Idioms; python-3-patterns-idioms-test.readthedocs.io. Retrieved July 9, 2022, from https://python-3-patterns-idioms-test.readthedocs.io/en/latest/Visitor.html

Visitor design pattern – GeeksforGeeks. (2017, August 6). GeeksforGeeks; www.geeksforgeeks.org. https://www.geeksforgeeks.org/visitor-design-pattern/

Visitor Design Pattern in Java – JournalDev. (2013, July 31). JournalDev; www.journaldev.com. https://www.journaldev.com/1769/visitor-design-pattern-java

Visitor Method – Python Design Patterns – GeeksforGeeks. (2020, February 19). GeeksforGeeks; www.geeksforgeeks.org. https://www.geeksforgeeks.org/visitor-method-python-design-patterns/#:~:text=Visitor%20Method%20is%20a%20Behavioral,hierarchy%20dynamically%20without%20changing%20it

Visitor Pattern In C#. (2015, November 14). www.c-sharpcorner.com. https://www.c-sharpcorner.com/UploadFile/efa3cf/visitor-pattern-in-C-Sharp/

Index

Printed in the United States
by Baker & Taylor Publisher Services